Learn C# with Visual Studio 2022

Comprehensive guide to C# fundamentals,
Core .NET concepts, advanced features, and
building with Visual Studio 2022

Marcelo Guerra Hahn

bpb

www.bpbonline.com

First Edition 2025

Copyright © BPB Publications, India

ISBN: 978-93-65896-503

To View Complete
BPB Publications Catalogue
Scan the QR Code:

Dedicated to

My students, past and present

About the Author

Marcelo Guerra Hahn is an associate professor at **Lake Washington Institute of Technology (LWTech)**. At LWTech, he has developed and taught various courses, including quality assurance methodologies, algorithms and data structures, C++ programming, C# programming, data analytics, cloud computing, big data application development, IT project, and job search and interviewing. Since 2017, he has also been a guest lecturer at the University of Washington.

His professional background includes significant engineering leadership roles, such as director of engineering at SoundCommerce, senior manager and manager at Tableau Software, and various roles, including senior software engineering manager at Microsoft Corporation, where he worked on technologies like C++, Azure AD, and the C# Compiler.

Academically, Marcelo Guerra Hahn holds multiple master of science degrees in areas such as computer science, applied mathematics, statistics, and data analytics, as well as other master's degrees and a certificate in applied machine learning.

He is the author of two other books, and his contributions include a patent related to two-way communication of events between a mobile device and remote client and publications on web data warehouses, web service compositions, and automatic scoring and feedback systems for programming assignments.

About the Reviewers

❖ **Yassin Lokhat** embarked on his programming journey in 2008 at the age of 15, discovering the vast world of C programming. His dedication and talent quickly became evident, and in 2010, he was qualified to represent Madagascar at the **International Olympiad in Informatics (IOI)**. Driven by a passion for technology, Yassin pursued higher education at the Polytechnic High Institute of Madagascar.

Throughout his five years of rigorous study, he learned and used C# and desktop development, graduating with honors in electronics, computer systems, and artificial intelligence. With his distinguished diploma, Yassin ventured to Mauritius to further his professional career, where he honed his skills and expertise, becoming a senior software engineer. After these productive years, he returned to Madagascar, taking on the leadership of the Malagasy team within his project. Currently, Yassin serves as the senior software engineer - technical lead for the Astek Group, where he continues to drive innovation and excellence in the field of development. His journey is a testament to his unwavering commitment to growth and his passion for technology.

❖ **Ockert J. Du Preez** is a passionate coder who is always willing to learn. Having been in the training and coding industry, he has a wealth of experience. He has written hundreds of developer articles over the years detailing his programming quests and adventures. These can be found on CodeGuru, Developer.com, and Database Journal.

He knows a broad spectrum of development languages, including C++, C#, VB.NET, JavaScript, T-SQL, MySQL, PostgreSQL, and HTML. He has written the following books and was a Microsoft Most Valuable Professional for .NET (2008–2017):

Visual Studio 2019 In-Depth

JavaScript for Gurus

Cross-Platform Modern Apps with VS Code

High Performance Enterprise Apps using C# 10 and .NET 6

Visual Studio 2022 In-Depths

Acknowledgement

Creating this book has been a journey shaped by many influences. My deepest gratitude is to my students, past and present, whose engagement in C# programming and object-oriented concepts inspired and proposed this work.

Microsoft, the creator of C# and the .NET platform, deserves special recognition. My experience on the C# Compiler team offered unique insights reflected throughout the book.

Thank you to the vibrant C# community for continuously enhancing this platform.

Finally, sincere thanks to the reviewers whose valuable feedback helped refine the manuscript.

Preface

Welcome to the world of C# programming. C# is a modern, versatile, robust, and adaptable programming language in today's rapidly evolving software development landscape. Developed by Microsoft, it is renowned for its object-oriented design, contemporary features, and ease of use. It is built on top of the .NET platform, which provides platform independence and a robust ecosystem for creating a wide range of applications.

This book explores the versatile C# and .NET ecosystem, covering syntax basics, control structures, methods, OOP concepts like classes, objects, interfaces, and polymorphism. It delves into collections, delegates, events, exception handling, file I/O, asynchronous, reflection, dynamic programming, and application frameworks like Windows Forms, WPF, ASP.NET Core, and Blazor. It introduces the C# programming language, aiming to provide a foundational understanding of its principles and practical applications. Whether you are new to programming or looking to deepen your knowledge of C#, this text is designed to equip you with the essential skills to tackle real-world programming challenges.

We begin by exploring the basics of C#, including its history, adaptability, essential features, and fundamental components, such as syntax rules, variables and data types, operators, and the basic structure of a C# program. You will learn to set up your development environment using Visual Studio 2022, a powerful and user-friendly code editor.

A significant focus is placed on **object-oriented programming (OOP)** in C#, which is integral to the language. We will delve into core OOP concepts, including defining and understanding classes and objects, encapsulation, inheritance, and polymorphism through interfaces and abstract classes. The book also covers essential programming constructs like control structures for directing program flow and methods for creating modular and reusable code.

Moving beyond the fundamentals, you will explore crucial topics for managing data and complex application logic. This includes working with collections and generics, essential tools for efficient data handling and manipulation. We will also cover delegates and events, key to building flexible and dynamic applications, and robust exception handling and debugging techniques for creating stable and reliable programs.

Further chapters introduce how C# handles file and stream I/O, enabling persistent data storage, and the principles of asynchronous programming for building responsive applications. You will also gain insights into advanced features like reflection and attributes, which allow for dynamic inspection and manipulation of code at runtime.

Finally, the book introduces major application development frameworks within the C# and .NET ecosystem. You will explore building desktop applications using Windows Forms and **Windows Presentation Foundation (WPF)**, as well as modern web applications and interactive UIs using ASP.NET Core and Blazor. These frameworks demonstrate the versatility of C# as a gateway to various platforms such as desktop, web, and mobile applications.

Drawing upon years of experience as an associate professor teaching C# programming and object-oriented concepts and as a senior software engineering manager at microsoft, where I worked on the C# Compiler [Resume], this book aims to blend academic rigor with practical industry insights.

We are excited for you to embark on this journey. By mastering the concepts presented here, you will be well-equipped to develop efficient, scalable, and maintainable C# applications.

Let us begin.

Chapter 1: Introduction to the C# Programming Language - This chapter provides a foundational understanding of C#, a modern and versatile programming language developed by Microsoft. It begins with an overview of C#, including its history, adaptability, and essential features. The chapter guides you through setting up Visual Studio 2022 for C# programming, covering installation, customization, and interface acquaintance. You will learn the basics of C# programming, including fundamental components like syntax rules, variables, data types, and operators. The chapter also introduces the basics of object-oriented programming in C# and touches upon advanced concepts like delegates, events, generics, Lambda expressions, and LINQ. By the end of this chapter, you will understand C#, its evolution, benefits, and how to write your first C# program using Visual Studio 2022. This foundational knowledge is essential for anyone aspiring to become proficient in modern software development, serving as a gateway to various platforms such as desktop, web, and mobile applications.

Chapter 2: C# Basics - This chapter delves into the fundamental aspects of C# programming. It covers basic syntax rules, emphasizing case sensitivity, using semicolons to end statements, and curly brackets for code sections. You will learn the basic structure of a C# program, recognizing essential components and the significance of the Main function as the entry point. The chapter explains how to use comments effectively to improve code readability. A key focus is declaring and initializing variables and data types, highlighting C#'s strong typing system for early error identification. Finally, you will learn to perform basic operations using C# operators. By the end of this chapter, you will be able to understand and apply fundamental C# syntax, recognize program components, work with variables and data types, and perform basic operations, which is crucial for writing clear and maintainable code.

Chapter 3: Introduction to Control Structures - This chapter introduces control structures as essential components in programming that direct program execution. It covers understanding and using conditional statements like if, else if, and switch to allow programs to take different execution routes based on conditions. You will explore looping structures for while, do-while, and for each for automating repetitive processes and handling data efficiently. The chapter also discusses interrupting looping structures using branching statements like break and continue. It also introduces exception handling in C# for gracefully managing runtime errors. By the end of this chapter, you will effectively use control structures to manage program flow, write efficient, readable, and maintainable code, and handle exceptions.

Chapter 4: Introduction to Methods in C# - This chapter delves into the core concepts of methods in C#, which are fundamental building blocks for creating clean, efficient, and maintainable code by encapsulating functionality into reusable, modular pieces. It explores what methods are and how they are defined. You will learn about method parameters, including value, reference, output, and parameter arrays, and understand their different uses. The chapter covers method overloading, enabling multiple methods with the same name but different parameter lists. It also discusses the scope and lifetime of variables within methods. Finally, you will learn best practices for writing methods such as ensuring single responsibility, conciseness, meaningful naming conventions, documentation, and debugging and testing strategies like using breakpoints, stepping through code, inspecting variables, and writing unit tests. By the end of this chapter, you will have a comprehensive understanding of how to create, use, and maintain methods to develop efficient, scalable, and maintainable C# applications.

Chapter 5: Classes and Objects in C# - This chapter explores classes and objects, which form the backbone of OOP in C#, allowing developers to model real-world entities and abstract concepts. You will learn to define classes, which act as blueprints, and create objects, which are instances of those classes. The chapter covers managing properties, methods, constructors, and access modifiers like public and private for encapsulation. You will also explore static members, nested, and partial classes for organizing and sharing code. By the end of this chapter, you will understand core OOP concepts implemented through classes and objects, apply these skills to build practical applications, and have a strong foundation in C# OOP for developing scalable and maintainable software.

Chapter 6: C# Interfaces and Polymorphism - This chapter introduces interfaces and polymorphism as crucial features for creating flexible, reusable, and maintainable code in C#. You will learn that interfaces act as contracts, defining methods and properties without implementation, ensuring consistency across classes. You will explore implementing interfaces in a class. The chapter covers understanding polymorphism, which enables objects of different classes to be treated uniformly based on a common superclass or interface. You will learn to differentiate between compile-time and run-time polymorphism. Additionally, it discusses abstract classes and methods and how to use them alongside interfaces for flexible design. By the end of this chapter, you will understand the purpose and structure of interfaces, implement them, leverage polymorphism to write adaptable code, and apply these concepts to design robust software systems.

Chapter 7: C# Collections and Generics - This chapter focuses on collections, generics, and LINQ as essential tools for efficiently managing and manipulating data in C#. You will understand collections like lists, dictionaries, queues, and stacks for storing and organizing groups of objects, learning when and how to use each. The chapter explains generics, which allow creating reusable, type-safe classes, methods, and collections that work with any data type without sacrificing performance. You will also learn to concisely leverage LINQ to query, filter, sort, group, and join data across various sources. By the end of this chapter, you will effectively use collections and generics to handle complex data structures and manipulate collections efficiently using LINQ, writing more efficient, scalable, and maintainable code.

Chapter 8: C# Delegates and Events - This chapter covers delegates and events, which are crucial for understanding C#'s event-driven architecture. You will learn about delegate basics, understanding them as type-safe function pointers that allow methods to be passed as parameters and invoked dynamically, enhancing flexibility. The chapter explores multicast delegates, anonymous methods, and Lambda expressions. You will understand event basics, how they build on delegates to provide a structured way for objects to communicate, and how to implement and manage them. By the end of this chapter, you will be equipped to use delegates and events effectively, utilize anonymous methods and Lambda expressions in event handling, and differentiate between delegates and events to build interactive, event-driven C# applications.

Chapter 9: C# Exception Handling and Debugging - This chapter addresses managing unexpected code behavior using exception handling and debugging to create stable and reliable applications in C#. You will understand that an exception is an event disrupting normal program flow and how C# uses exception objects to represent error conditions. It covers basic exception handling using the try-catch block to manage errors and multiple exceptions, and the finally block for cleanup actions. You will also learn to create custom exceptions to depict application-specific conditions. The chapter introduces debugging, involving running an application under controlled conditions to identify and resolve issues. By the end of this chapter, you will implement basic and custom exception handling, apply best practices, and use debugging tools like breakpoints and step-through code execution to build resilient and error-handling-capable applications.

Chapter 10: C# File and Stream Input/Output - This chapter explores I/O operations, fundamental components for managing data beyond a program's lifespan. You will understand the basic concepts of file and stream I/O using the System.IO namespace. The chapter covers file handling in C#, including creating, reading, writing, and deleting files using classes like File and FileInfo, and working with directories using Directory and DirectoryInfo. You will learn to read from and write to text and binary files using StreamReader, StreamWriter, and FileStream. Furthermore, it explores streams in C# as abstract representations of data sequences, introducing types like BufferedStream, MemoryStream, and NetworkStream to optimize performance. By the end of this chapter, you will have a solid understanding of integrating file and stream operations into your C# projects, enhancing their functionality and reliability.

Chapter 11: C# Asynchronous Programming - This chapter focuses on asynchronous programming in C# to handle time-consuming tasks without blocking the main thread, ensuring responsiveness and efficiency. You will learn how the async and await keywords enable writing asynchronous code that looks similar to synchronous code. The chapter discusses when and why asynchronous programming is preferred for improved performance and scalability. It covers strategies for combining multiple async methods, whether sequentially or concurrently. You will learn to manage task cancellations using CancellationToken and set timeouts for long-running operations. Finally, it explores exception handling in asynchronous programming using try-catch blocks and the Task—exception property to build resilient applications. By the end of this chapter, you will effectively use asynchronous programming to create scalable, high-performance applications.

Chapter 12: C# Reflection and Attributes - This chapter explores reflection and attributes in C#, which enhance applications' flexibility and dynamic capabilities. You will understand reflection, which allows inspecting a program's structure during runtime and dynamically accessing and manipulating types, methods, and properties using the system. Reflection namespace. The chapter covers reflection and assemblies. You will explore working with attributes, which provide a way to associate metadata with your code. Finally, you will gain skills to retrieve and process attributes dynamically using reflection. By the end of this chapter, you will have a thorough understanding of C# reflection and attributes, enabling dynamic interaction with objects, dynamic method invocation, instance creation, and creating more flexible and maintainable applications.

Chapter 13: C# Dynamic Programming - This chapter delves into C# programming primarily through the dynamic type, which brings flexibility and adaptability. You will understand how dynamic typing differs from traditional static typing by bypassing compile-time type checking and resolving types at runtime. The chapter explores practical applications like interoperability with COM objects and integration with dynamic languages. You will gain insight into concepts such as the DLR. It covers Dynamic LINQ queries. By the end of this chapter, you will understand the fundamentals of dynamic programming, use the dynamic type effectively while implementing error handling, and learn best practices for building adaptable and maintainable applications.

Chapter 14: Windows Forms and Windows Presentation Foundation - This chapter covers Windows Forms and Windows Presentation Foundation, two key frameworks for building desktop applications in C#. You will understand Windows Forms as a GUI toolkit for creating traditional Windows-style interfaces with familiar controls and rapid prototyping. You will learn to develop basic Windows Forms applications with essential controls and event handling. The chapter introduces WPF as a more advanced framework, exploring the role of XAML for declarative UI design, and learning to implement data binding and layout management. By the end of this chapter, you will understand the fundamental concepts of both frameworks, develop basic Windows Forms applications, explore WPF features, and identify the key differences to choose the appropriate framework for your project needs.

Chapter 15: ASP.NET Core and Blazor - This chapter introduces ASP.NET Core and Blazor, powerful tools in the C# ecosystem for building modern web applications. You will learn about ASP.NET Core as an open-source, cross-platform framework for creating web applications, APIs, and real-time applications, covering critical concepts like the middleware pipeline, MVC architecture, and routing. The chapter then explores Blazor, a web framework enabling interactive web applications using C# for client-side development, covering Blazor components and data binding. By the end of this chapter, you will have a solid understanding of these frameworks, set up environments, create basic applications, implement key ASP.NET Core features, and develop interactive web applications using Blazor components, leveraging C# for both server and client-side development.

Code Bundle and Coloured Images

Please follow the link to download the
Code Bundle and the *Coloured Images* of the book:

https://rebrand.ly/ny5v7sl

The code bundle for the book is also hosted on GitHub at
https://github.com/bpbpublications/Learn-CSharp-with-Visual-Studio-2022.
In case there's an update to the code, it will be updated on the existing GitHub repository.

We have code bundles from our rich catalogue of books and videos available at
https://github.com/bpbpublications. Check them out!

Errata

We take immense pride in our work at BPB Publications and follow best practices to ensure the accuracy of our content to provide with an indulging reading experience to our subscribers. Our readers are our mirrors, and we use their inputs to reflect and improve upon human errors, if any, that may have occurred during the publishing processes involved. To let us maintain the quality and help us reach out to any readers who might be having difficulties due to any unforeseen errors, please write to us at :

errata@bpbonline.com

Your support, suggestions and feedbacks are highly appreciated by the BPB Publications' Family.

Did you know that BPB offers eBook versions of every book published, with PDF and ePub files available? You can upgrade to the eBook version at www.bpbonline. com and as a print book customer, you are entitled to a discount on the eBook copy. Get in touch with us at :

business@bpbonline.com for more details.

At **www.bpbonline.com**, you can also read a collection of free technical articles, sign up for a range of free newsletters, and receive exclusive discounts and offers on BPB books and eBooks.

Piracy

If you come across any illegal copies of our works in any form on the internet, we would be grateful if you would provide us with the location address or website name. Please contact us at **business@bpbonline.com** with a link to the material.

If you are interested in becoming an author

If there is a topic that you have expertise in, and you are interested in either writing or contributing to a book, please visit **www.bpbonline.com**. We have worked with thousands of developers and tech professionals, just like you, to help them share their insights with the global tech community. You can make a general application, apply for a specific hot topic that we are recruiting an author for, or submit your own idea.

Reviews

Please leave a review. Once you have read and used this book, why not leave a review on the site that you purchased it from? Potential readers can then see and use your unbiased opinion to make purchase decisions. We at BPB can understand what you think about our products, and our authors can see your feedback on their book. Thank you!

For more information about BPB, please visit **www.bpbonline.com**.

Join our book's Discord space

Join the book's Discord Workspace for Latest updates, Offers, Tech happenings around the world, New Release and Sessions with the Authors:

https://discord.bpbonline.com

Table of Contents

Chapter 1

Introduction to the C# Programming Language

Introduction

In the first chapter, we will dive into the basics of C# and learn how it integrates with Visual Studio 2022. We will start with an overview of C#, briefly covering its history, adaptability, and essential features for use in the current market. The next step will be to set up Visual Studio 2022 for C# programming. We will guide you through the entire installation process. After that comes the customization and getting acquainted with the IDE's user interface. We will handle the setup process before working on our first C# program.

Structure

This chapter covers the following topics:

- Introduction to C#
- Basics of C# programming
- C-Class language family
- Visual Studio 2022

Objectives

In this chapter, you will learn about C#, a modern and versatile programming language that can be used to create various types of applications. You will explore the features and benefits of C# as a language and how it has evolved over the years to incorporate new paradigms and technologies. You will also learn the basics of object-oriented programming in C# and how to use advanced C# concepts such as delegates, events, generics, lambda expressions, and LINQ. Finally, you will write your first C# program using Visual Studio 2022, a powerful and user-friendly code editor with many tools and features to help you write and debug your code.

Introduction to C#

C# (pronounced "C sharp") is a high-level, general-purpose programming language created by Microsoft. It is a robust and adaptable programming language renowned for its object-oriented design, contemporary features, and ease of use. It is built on top of the .NET framework, which provides platform independence, enabling programmers to create code only once and execute it on several different systems. C# promotes code safety and scalability across a wide range of applications, including desktop software, web development, game programming, and enterprise-level applications, thanks to its static type system and integration. Some of its salient characteristics are object-oriented programming, type safety, contemporary language structures, and smooth integration with frameworks like the gaming engine Unity and the web development tools in ASP. NET Core. If you are developing desktop apps, web services, business software, or games, C# has the capabilities and tools required to meet your development objectives.

History and evolution of C#

A team of engineers led by Microsoft's architect *Anders Hejlsberg* developed the C# programming language in 2000. It became an international standard in 2002, being registered with ECMA. After ECMA, ISO, and IEC accepted C#'s international standards status in 2003. Microsoft released C# together with the.NET Framework and Visual Studio. Microsoft did not have any open-source products then, so Mono's open-source project was launched in 2004, offering a cross-platform compiler and runtime environment for the C# programming language. Ten years later, Microsoft introduced the free, open-source, cross-platform Visual Studio Code code editor, Roslyn compiler, and unified .NET platform software framework, all of which supported C#. The language's most current stable version, as of 2025, is C# 13.0, which was made available in November 2024 with .NET 9.0.

Basics of C# programming

This section will examine the fundamental components that make up C# programming. Let us take a look at them:

- **Operators and expressions**: The basic units of C# expressions are operators, which allow programmers to work with data in bitwise, logical, and arithmetic ways. To efficiently handle numeric and Boolean data, C# provides a wide range of operators for addition, subtraction, and comparison.

- **Syntax**: C# syntax takes a while to understand as it uses characters not commonly used in ordinary writing. C# is an object-oriented language with data at the program's center, with classes, objects, and methods reflecting data structures and their functions.

- **Control flow**: The execution flow of a C# program is managed using control flow statements, which give programmers the ability to make selections, cycle through data, and handle exceptions dynamically. C# has a range of control flow structures to support different programming scenarios, from if-else statements for conditional branching to switch statements for multi-branching logic. Developers can design code that intelligently reacts to changing conditions and user inputs skillfully using control flow statements.

- **Variables and data types**: In C#, data types define the sorts of data stored in variables and the operations performed on them. C# has many built-in data types to satisfy various programming needs, such as strings (text), whole numbers (integers), arrays, and floating-point numbers. Furthermore, by allowing the creation of custom data types using classes and structures, C# enables developers to express complicated entities and connections accurately.

Object-orientation in C#

As stated earlier, C# was initially designed as an object-oriented programming language. Programmers can quickly define data structures (and types) in **object-oriented programming** (**OOP**). Objects are formed from classes. Consider classes as blueprints and objects as the things you construct from them. Data encapsulation, inheritance, polymorphism, and interfaces are supported in C#. In Java, primitive types (int, float, and double) cannot be objects. However, C# provides structures that allow these to become objects—creating, maintaining, and reusing code when data is grouped as this is simpler. It also reduces error-proneness and facilitates code correction. Some characteristics of C# include the following:

- **Inheritance and polymorphism**: A fundamental component of OOP is inheritance, which lets classes inherit attributes and functions from other classes, encouraging code reuse and supporting a hierarchical structure. Developers may design versatile and extendable class hierarchies in C# by leveraging interfaces to establish numerous base classes or single inheritance to inherit from a single base class. Conversely, polymorphism allows objects to display distinct behaviors according to their underlying.

  These types allow for runtime flexibility and dynamic method dispatch. Through the use of inheritance and polymorphism, developers may build codebases that are resilient and flexible enough to change as needed.

- **Interfaces and abstract classes**: In C#, interfaces and abstract classes are useful tools for creating agreements and standardizing class behavior. To enable polymorphic behavior and promote code compatibility, an interface creates a contract outlining a set of methods and attributes a class must implement. Conversely, abstract classes give derived classes a path to follow, enabling programmers to specify shared behavior and guarantee uniformity between related classes. Developers may create adaptable and extensible systems that can handle various requirements and future improvements by utilizing interfaces and abstract classes in their design process.

- **Classes and objects**: Classes and objects, the basic building blocks of OOP in C#, simulate real-world objects and behaviors. An object's state and behavior are encapsulated in a class, which is a blueprint that defines its methods and attributes. In contrast, objects are just instances of classes that stand in for distinct entities with their special characteristics and behaviors. Developers can assist in better program logic structure, code reuse, and modularization by generating classes and instantiating objects.

- **Encapsulation**: OOP's core concepts of encapsulation encourage modularity, information hiding, and code maintainability. Encapsulation is the process of grouping procedures and data within a class, protecting the internal state of an object from outside interference, and guaranteeing data integrity. Conversely, abstraction entails hiding implementation details, revealing critical aspects to the outside world, and describing complicated systems using simpler models. Developers may design self-contained, reusable components that are simple to understand and manage by abstracting behavior and encapsulating data.

Advanced C# concepts

Advanced language features, including lambda expressions, delegates, events, generics, extension methods, and attributes, are available in C#. We will briefly discuss a few:

- **Generics**: C# generics offer a robust approach for building reusable components compatible with any data. Using generics, developers may construct type-safe code without compromising efficiency or flexibility. Custom data structures, algorithms, and collections (like List<T>) are common use cases for generics.

- **Delegates and events**: In C#, delegates and events effectively create loosely connected components and implement callback functionality. By acting as function pointers, delegates enable the dynamic invocation and passing of methods as parameters. Events offer a practical means of putting the observer pattern into practice by allowing objects to subscribe to and get alerts about actions or changes.

- **Lambda expressions**: In C#, anonymous functions may be defined with a clear and expressive syntax thanks to lambda expressions. They are beneficial for constructing inline functions, such as predicates for collections filtering or defining asynchronously executed actions. For LINQ queries, code readability may be increased, and the boilerplate may be reduced.

- **Asynchronous programming with async/await**: A key component of contemporary C# development is asynchronous programming with async/await, which makes programs responsive and scalable. By enabling developers to create asynchronous code synchronously using async/await, they may escape callback hell and reason about asynchronous processes more efficiently. Developers may create responsive user interfaces, optimize resource usage, and effectively manage CPU and I/O-bound processes by utilizing async/await.

Error handling and debugging in C#

Debugging and error handling are crucial components of C# program development. Keeping mistakes and defects under control makes your apps more reliable and speeds up development. This section will cover a variety of methods and best practices for managing errors and debugging C# code:

- **Debugging techniques**: The practice of finding and fixing errors in software code is known as debugging. To help with this process, developers working in C# have access to various practical debugging tools and methodologies. The primary IDE for C# development, Visual Studio, has tools like watch windows, step-through debugging, and breakpoints that let programmers examine the state of their application and follow its execution path. Developers may increase productivity and code quality by effectively identifying and resolving problems in their code by learning debugging techniques.

- **Exception handling**: In C# programs, exception handling addresses runtime failures. Try-catch blocks allow developers to handle errors gracefully and avoid unplanned crashes. Furthermore, C# has features like exception filters and finally blocks, enabling fine-grained exception management and resource cleaning. For software systems to be robust and dependable, robust exception-handling techniques must be implemented.

- **Logging and tracing**: In production contexts, logging and tracing are essential tools for tracking program activity and troubleshooting problems. To log events, failures, and performance data in C#, developers can utilize frameworks like log4net and Serilog. Furthermore, distributed tracing and structured logging are supported natively by .NET Core and .NET 5+, giving developers further visibility into microservices architectures and distributed systems. Software engineers may create more stable and dependable software by proactively identifying and resolving issues using logging and tracing.

Working with collections and Language Integrated Query

A fundamental component of C# programming is working with collections and **Language Integrated Query** (**LINQ**), which allows programmers to manage and query data effectively. This part will examine several data structures and C#'s LINQ capabilities. Let us take a look at them:

- **Dictionaries and sets**: In C#, they are specific data structures with distinct keys and their corresponding values. While sets guarantee uniqueness by keeping only different components, dictionaries offer quick lookup speeds by storing key-value pairs in a hash table. Dictionary and set functions provide practical ways to add, remove, and query components; hence, they are the best options for operations like caching, indexing, and deleting duplicates.

- **LINQ**: With the help of C#'s strong LINQ capability, developers may query and alter data using a standard syntax. With LINQ, developers can construct queries directly in C# code, eliminating the need for laborious manual collection manipulation and iteration. Developers use LINQ to enhance the readability and clarity of code by enabling the simple expression of complicated data operations like filtering, sorting, grouping, and joining.

- **Arrays and lists**: The two primary data structures in C# for storing collections of items are arrays and lists. Lists can increase or shrink dynamically, while arrays have a fixed size and store entries of the same type sequentially. Arrays and lists are flexible options for storing and altering data in C# because they offer practical ways to access, change, and iterate over their elements.

- **Querying data with LINQ**: For accessing and processing data from various data sources, including arrays, databases, collections, and XML, LINQ offers an extensive range of operators and methods. Because LINQ queries are modular, programmers may construct sophisticated inquiries by combining many processes. Furthermore, LINQ allows for postponed execution, facilitating effective query optimization and execution. Developers may build expressive, effective, and maintainable code for jobs involving data manipulation and analysis by becoming proficient with LINQ.

C-Class language family

C# is not that new. It has been around for over 20 years. When you consider the lineage of programming languages, you can see that C# is a very reliable and well-maintained language that software development companies and professionals can rely on. Interoperability is a fundamental characteristic of C#, which supports other C-family language features, allowing you to combine them. Given that programming languages such as C, C++, and Java are part of the C family, a C# programmer can likely understand C, C++, and Java code.

One language for structured programming

C# is a structured programming language in addition to being type-safe, object-oriented, and both. As the name would suggest, this implies that C# programs are written in a logical, organized fashion, divided into manageable modules called functions and procedures. This code organization makes the code easier to read, comprehend, maintain, debug, and execute.

Learning C# programming has several benefits, including familiarity with its documentation and support. C# is developed and maintained by Microsoft, which also regularly releases new language versions with enhanced features. Because of this support and the language's continuous growth, C# is here to stay and will be used by businesses for a long time. This translates to job stability and a user base for your development of C# programs and apps. C# has undergone thorough testing and patching due to its extended lifespan, contributing to its exceptional security. Due to its history, it has also accumulated a large amount of documentation, with many books, tutorials, and how-to guides accessible worldwide. In addition, Microsoft maintains its knowledge base, which offers both written and video lessons. Finally, C# has a sizable user community because of its history. This means that many programmers are familiar with the language and can assist you in learning it or troubleshooting your code if you encounter any issues.

Memory management

It may be difficult for developers to manage memory in languages like C as they have to remember to take into consideration garbage collection, which is the process of working memory resources and memory cleanup. An application's performance may be impacted by improper memory resource allocation, resulting in sluggish software, errors, and crashes. This load is relieved from the developer by C#, which has an integrated garbage collector, or GC. The garbage collector in C# monitors unused objects and automatically releases memory when it's no longer needed.

Cross-platform

The cross-platform nature of the C# programming language is another benefit. Alternatively, you may write applications in C# and have them operate on any platform or operating system, such as Windows, Android, Apple, iOS, or cloud computing.

Visual Studio 2022

Microsoft created Visual Studio, an **integrated development environment** (IDE). It is employed in developing computer programs, such as mobile applications, online services, websites, and web apps. Visual Studio 2022 uses the Microsoft software development platforms **Windows Presentation Foundation** (**WPF**), Windows Store, Windows API, Windows Forms, and Microsoft Silverlight. Additionally, It uses various technologies, such as MAUI and Xamarin, to create feature-rich client applications. Both native and managed code can be produced in Visual Studio 2022.

Furthermore, a code editor for Visual Studio supports code refactoring, and IntelliSense, a code completion tool, is an integrated debugger that functions as a machine-level and source-level debugger. Some other built-in tools are a code profiler, a designer for creating GUI apps, a web designer, a class designer, and a database schema designer. It is compatible with plug-ins that extend its functionality in nearly every direction. For example, you can add new Toolsets for domain-specific languages, such as editors and visual designers, or tools for other stages of the software development lifecycle, such as Team Explorer from the Azure DevOps client. It can also support source control systems, such as Subversion and Git.

New features and enhancements

Microsoft originally published Visual Studio in 1997. It was the first time that several of its programming tools were bundled together. Two versions of Visual Studio 97 were available: Visual Studio Professional and Visual Studio Enterprise. Ever since then, Microsoft has been improving its capabilities in Visual Studio. Those capabilities now include the following:

- **Debugging**: Debugging is one of the building blocks of the software development process. It comes in the initial stages of the development cycle. Visual Studio 2022 has improved the debugging experience of programmers to help speed up finding and resolving issues. The first improvement is the addition of new debugging tools. The tools allow programmers to find and fix the problems in their code, including memory inefficiency, performance issues, and others. The tools include performance diagnostics, new advanced breakpoints, and enhanced debugging support for threaded applications.

- **Support for the latest frameworks and languages**: Visual Studio 2022 has the tools and technologies that enable programmers to work efficiently. Visual Studio 2022 supports the new versions of programming languages and technologies. The supported languages are C# F# and Visual Basic, which support many frameworks, including the .NET framework.

- **Enhanced code navigation and editing experience**: In Visual Studio 2022, developers can enjoy enhanced code navigation and editing capabilities. The IDE provides code navigation tools like *Peek Definition, Find All References*, and *Go To Definition* to help developers better understand and navigate codebases efficiently. Coding is seamless and features like IntelliSense provide intelligent code suggestions and completions.

- **Built-in Git integration**: Visual Studio 2022 boasts a comprehensive integration of Git, which gives developers powerful version management from within the IDE. By streamlining the development workflow and promoting teamwork, developers can quickly clone repositories, manage branches, commit changes, and carry out other Git activities without leaving the Visual Studio environment.

- **Integration with cloud services**: By integrating with cloud services, VS 2022 enables developers to harness the power of the cloud directly within the IDE. Creating, launching, and overseeing native applications has become more convenient for developers. They can effortlessly utilize cloud resources and collaborate on projects hosted in the cloud thanks to the integrated assistance for platforms like Azure. Cloud services are best suited for organizational use or collaboration between groups of developers.

- **Improved performance and responsiveness**: Significant performance and responsiveness enhancements in VS 2022 let developers work more productively, especially when working on large and complex systems. The IDE is tuned to perform better overall during code editing and debugging operations, faster during startup times, and rapid code compilation.

- **Accessibility improvements**: Developers with impairments may now utilize the IDE more efficiently, thanks to improvements made to accessibility capabilities in VS 2022. Smoother screen reader support, smoother keyboard navigation, and better color contrast choices are just a few of the IDE's features that ensure all developers can utilize Visual Studio efficiently and comfortably.

Downloading and installing Visual Studio 2022

You can download the latest versions of Visual Studio 2022 from the official Microsoft website: **https://visualstudio.microsoft.com/vs/**

There are three different variants for Visual Studio 2022, each designed for individual users and organizational utilization. A thorough description is discussed as follows:

- Community 2022
- Professional 2022
- Enterprise 2022

Visual Studio community is free to use and is intended for individual developers, open-source projects, and scholarly study. It has most of the functionality included in the other versions, including collaborative tools, debugging, testing, and support for several programming languages and platforms. However, only single users and small teams with a maximum of five people can use it for non-commercial purposes.

More significant development teams, businesses, and enterprise-level applications are the intended audience for the Professional and Enterprise versions of Visual Studio 2022, with more sophisticated features and capabilities. These packages provide extra features, including performance profiling, cloud integration, enhanced testing and debugging tools, and support for bigger development teams. The Professional and Enterprise versions of Visual Studio demand a subscription fee or a perpetual license for usage in business settings.

In conclusion, Visual Studio Community is a free version of the program geared toward independent developers, open-source projects, and scholarly research. On the other hand, other Visual Studio editions are more sophisticated regarding features, capabilities, and licensing terms and are intended for larger development teams, organizations, and enterprise-level applications.

Setting up Visual Studio 2022

After downloading the software from the preceding link, you will get the installer file below in your download folder. Open the installer and begin the setup process:

Figure 1.1: Visual Studio installation file

After opening the installer, you might see this pop-up. Click on **Continue**, and it will automatically download the Visual Studio 2022 IDE on your computer, as shown:

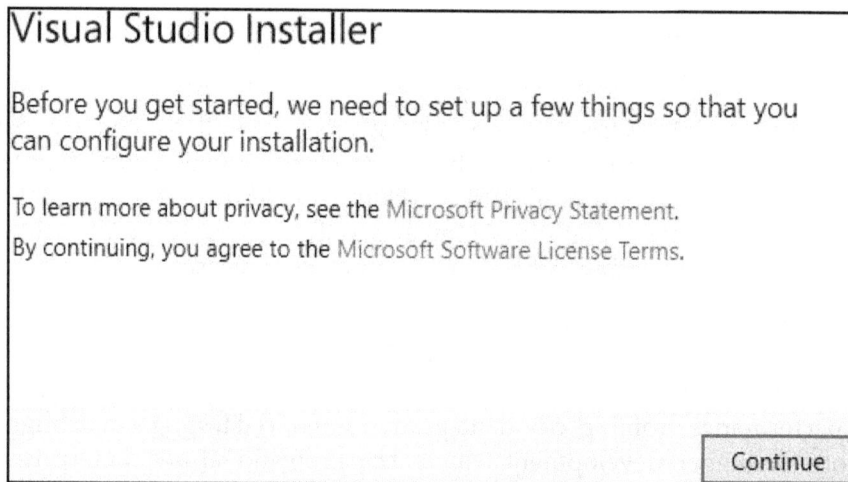

Figure 1.2: Visual Studio installer window

Wait for a while until the download has been finished. The following figure shows the installation video:

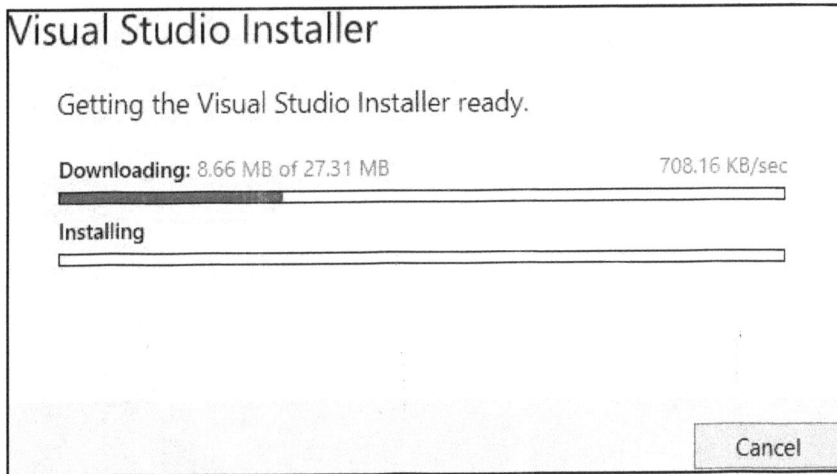

Figure 1.3: *Visual Studio Installation Progress Window*

Configuring Visual Studio for C# development

When the download process finishes, you will see the following window. You should select the .NET desktop development package for C# development because it contains many SDK files required for future C# projects:

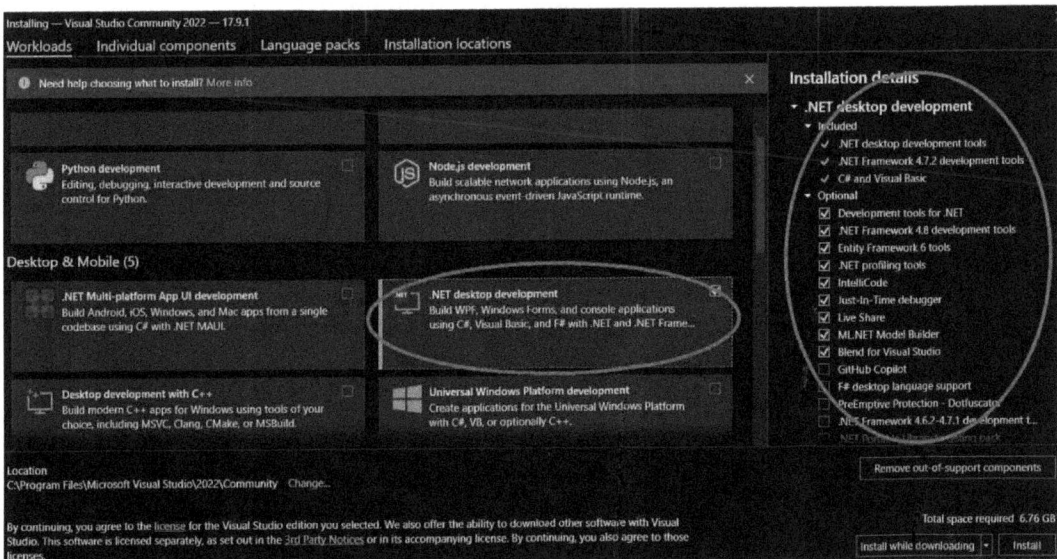

Figure 1.4: *Visual Studio Workload installation window*

After selecting the .NET desktop development package, hit install on the bottom right and wait for the downloads to be completed, as shown in the following figure:

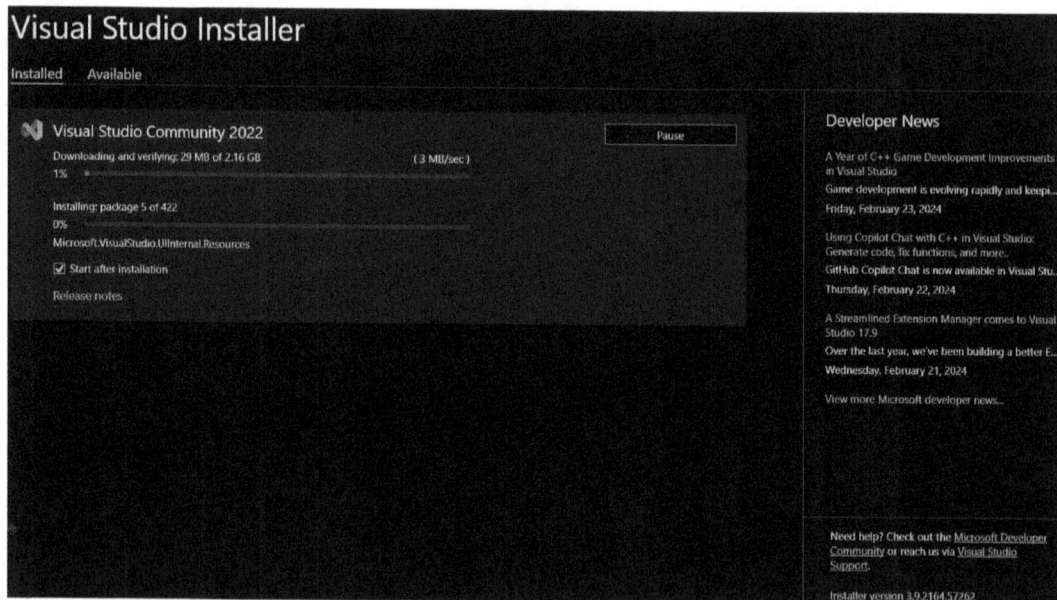

Figure 1.5: Visual Studio Workload installation progress

After the download process is complete, you will see the interface below. You can choose any customization option of your choice, or let the factory settings and click **Start Visual Studio**. (you can always customize your interface within the IDE settings), as shown:

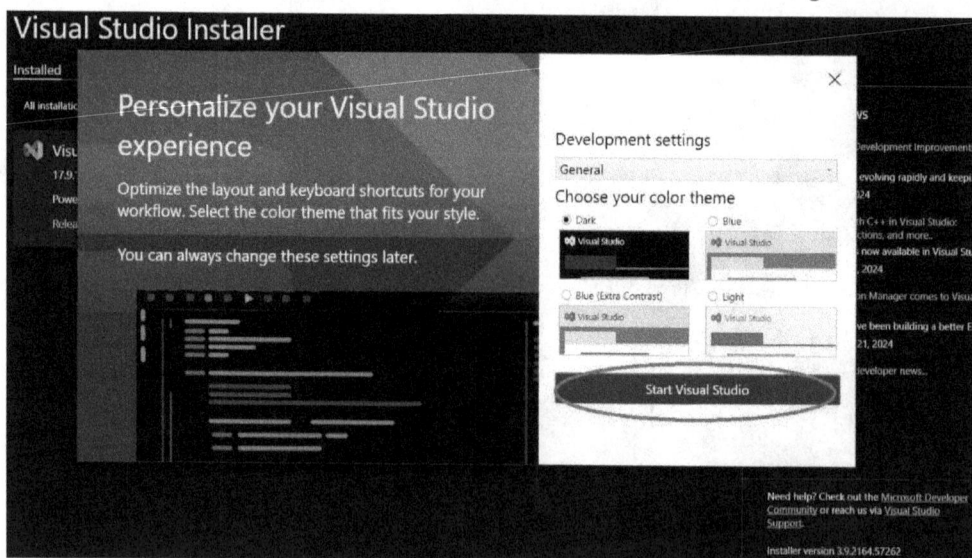

Figure 1.6: Visual Studio Start window

The next step is to set your IDE for C# development. After you start Visual Studio, you will see the interface below with multiple options:

- **Clone a repository**: Cloning a repository allows you to obtain a copy of a codebase placed on a version control system like Azure DevOps or GitHub. Allowing you collaboration, version control, and access to the scripts for individual development, we will not use that option because we are just setting up our IDE for new growth.

- **Open a project or solution**: It refers to accessing and loading an existing application project or solution file (`.sln`) into the IDE for development, editing, debugging, and other tasks.

- **Open a local folder**: It allows you to work with files and resources stored in a specific directory on your local machine directly within the IDE without necessarily being tied to a formal project or solution file (`.sln`).

- **Create a new project**: Because we are just starting with Visual Studio 2022, we will go for a new project and set up the IDE environment for our C# scripts:

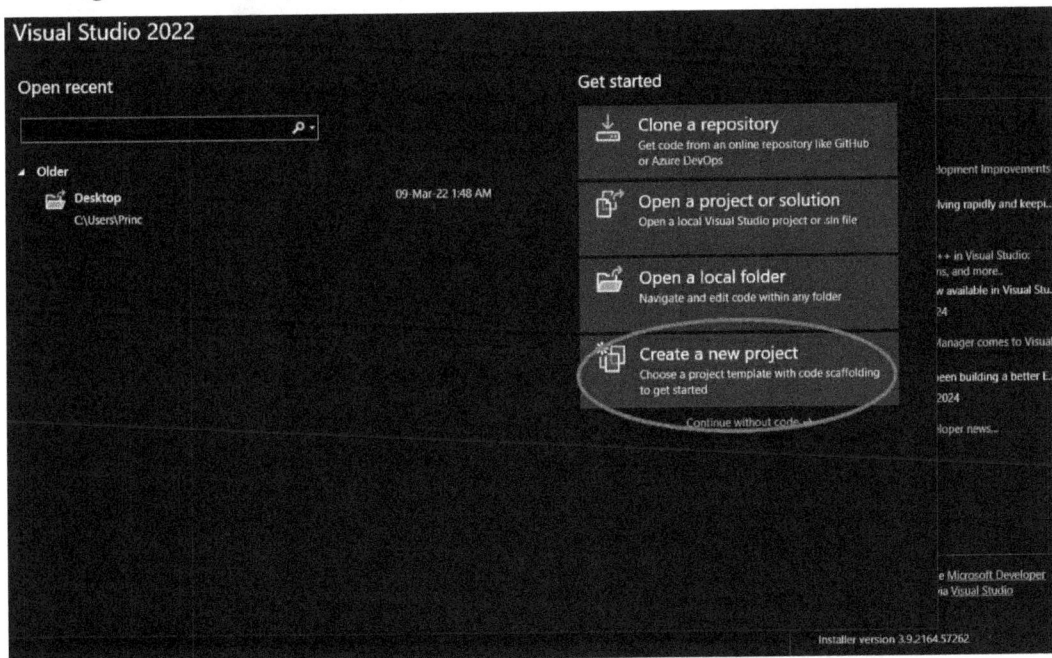

Figure 1.7: Create project interface

Creating a new C# project in Visual Studio

You will have multiple options when you create a new project in Visual Studio 2022, as shown below. For the sake of this course, we will select a **Console App** because a Console Application does not have a graphical user interface and is very easy to comprehend for beginners. Follow these steps:

1. Select **Console App** and hit **Next**:

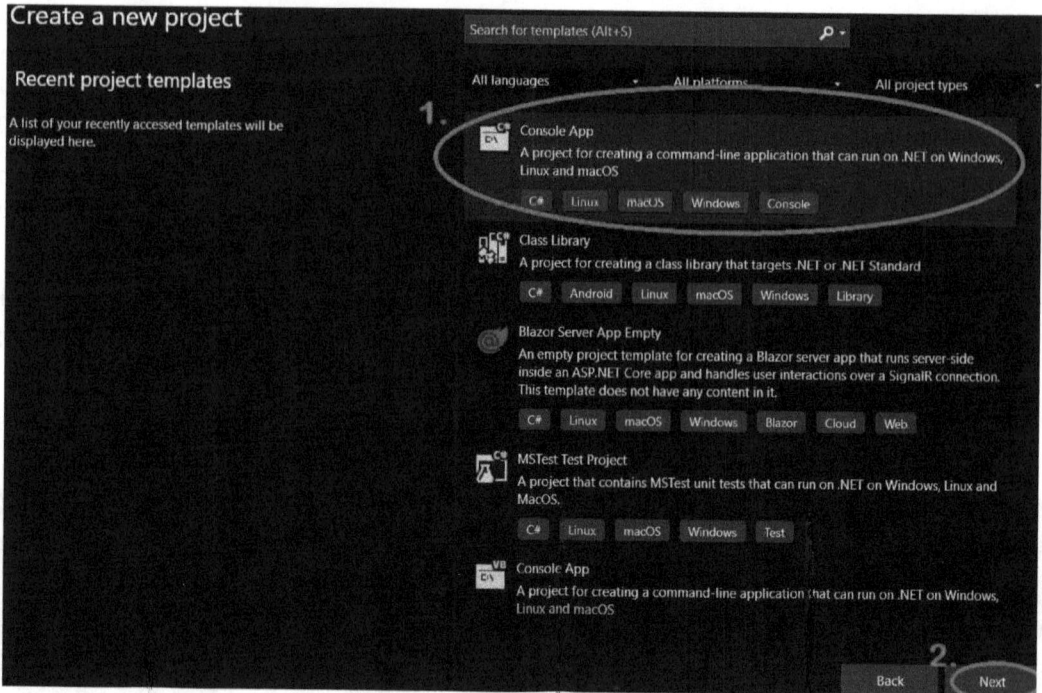

Figure 1.8: Project type selection window

a. Name your project **"HelloWorld"**.

b. Specify a folder in your computer to save your project files. (In Visual Studio, a Solution can have one or more projects. In this case, we will only have one Project and one Solution).

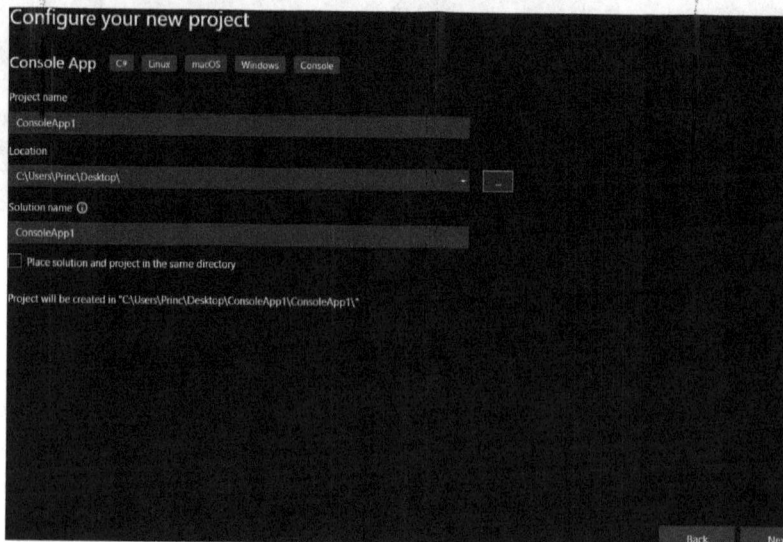

Figure 1.9: Visual Studio project configuration window

c. The following screen should appear:

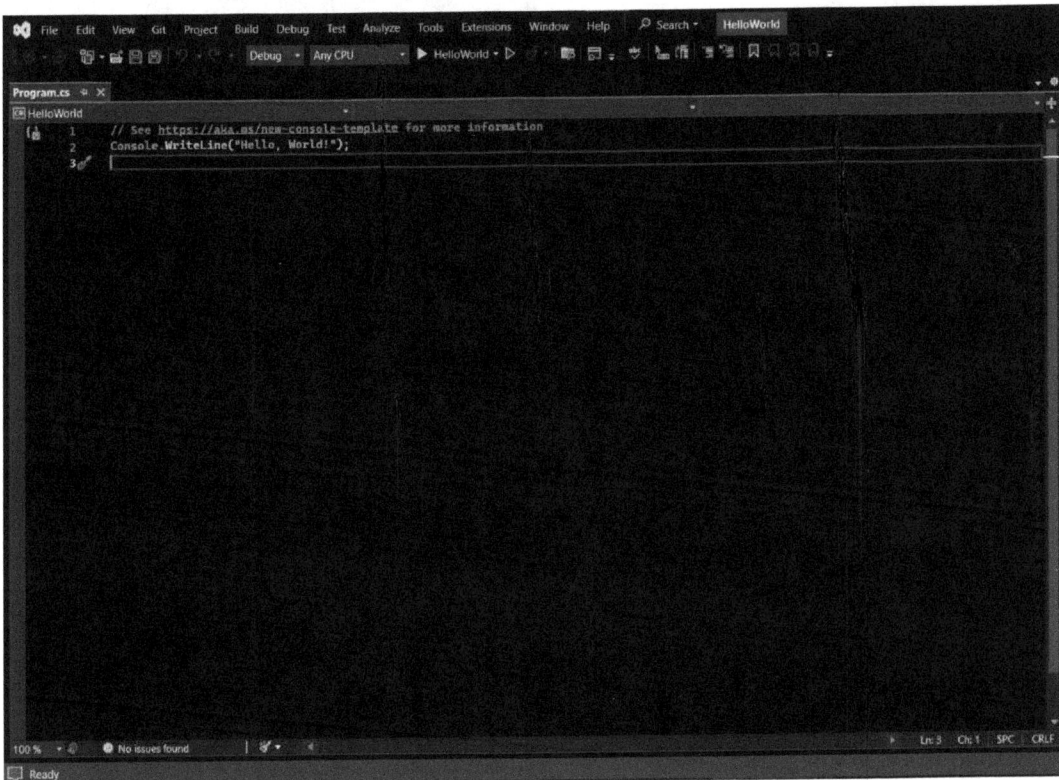

Figure 1.10: *Visual Studio programming environment*

This screen includes many options and features. We will gradually understand each functionality and section of the IDE to understand the environment better. On the right-hand side, you can see the solution explorer panel. Right now, we have a solution that has only one project. But for now, we will only focus on our *Hello World* program.

When you create a Console app on Visual Studio 2022, the IDE automatically writes the line of code that consists of the Hello World program. You can change the text to whatever you desire, which will output the text on the console screen. Let us run the program without debugging by clicking on the top center green play button icon to run our program, as shown:

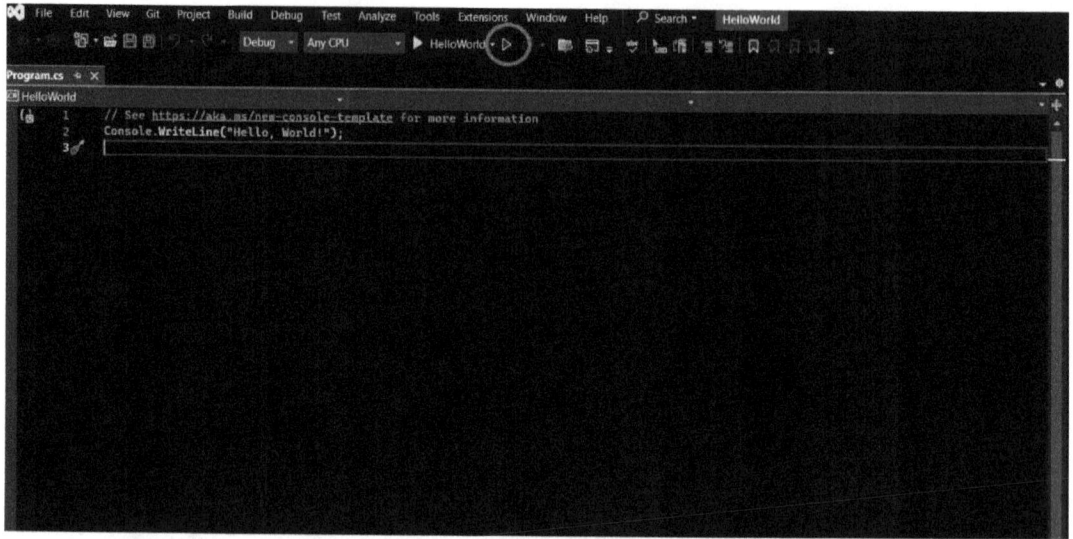

Figure 1.11: Running a program in Visual Studio

The code is as follows:

```
Console.WriteLine("Hello, World!");
```

Note: The line (// See https://aka.ms/new-console-template for more information) above the code is just a comment, starting with "//". It does not compile with the code and is used to understand the script better. It is commonly used in large applications.

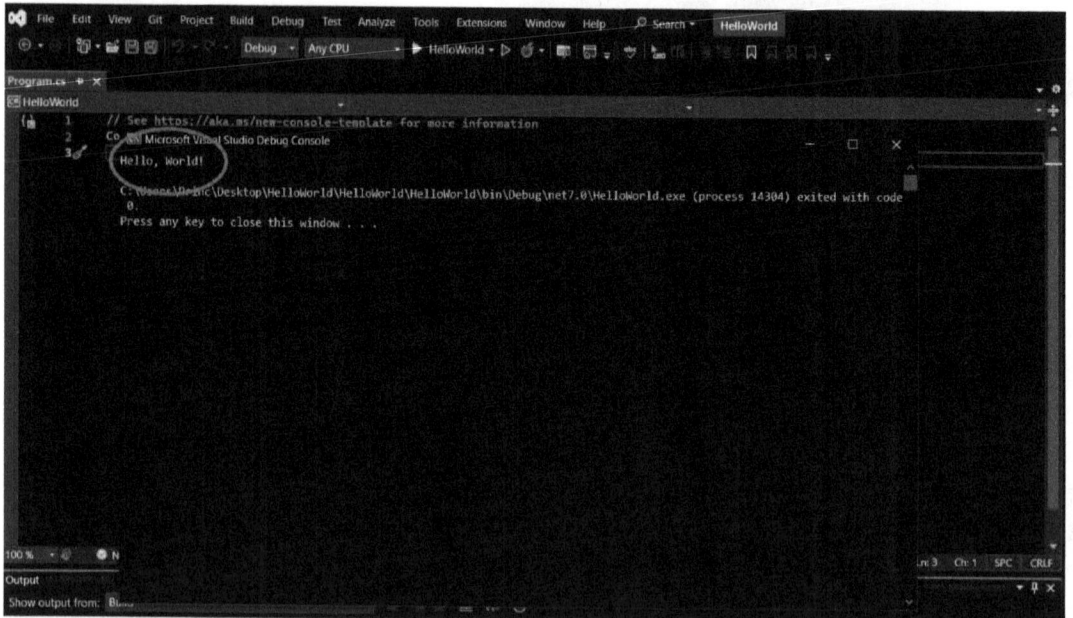

Figure 1.12: Execution output in Visual Studio

In the following code: **"Console.WriteLine("Hello, World!");"** **Console"** is a class in the system that can write data to the console or read data from the command line. It has various methods, and the **"."** is used to access the method **"WriteLine"**. The **"WriteLine"** method accepts the text that we want to display as a parameter, so we added the string **"Hello World"** in parenthesis. We then end the line with **";"** as most lines of code in C# end with a semicolon.

We will learn more about code structure and other constructs in future lessons.

Conclusion

In conclusion, this chapter has provided a foundational understanding of C#, a powerful programming language developed by Microsoft. We have explored its history, features, and importance in the software development landscape. Understanding the fundamentals of C# is essential for anyone aspiring to become proficient in modern software development, as it serves as a gateway to various platforms such as desktop, web, and mobile applications. As we delve deeper into subsequent chapters. We will build upon this introductory knowledge to explore C#'s syntax, concepts, and practical applications, equipping you with the skills to tackle real-world programming challenges.

Multiple choice questions

1. **Who developed C# as a programming language?**

    a. Google

    b. Apple

    c. Microsoft

    d. IBM

2. **What is the name of the platform that allows C# to run on different operating systems?**

    a. .NET Framework

    b. Java Virtual Machine

    c. Python Interpreter

    d. Node.js

3. **What are some of the features of C# that make it a powerful and versatile language?**

    a. Object-oriented, generic, and functional

    b. Static, dynamic, and scripting

    c.   Imperative, declarative, and concurrent

    d.   All of the above

4.   **What are some of the platforms that C# can be used to develop applications for?**

    a.   Desktop

    b.   Web

    c.   Mobile

    d.   All of the above

Answers

1.   (c) Microsoft

2.   (a) .NET Framework

3.   (a) Object-oriented, generic, and functional

4.   (d) All of the above

Join our book's Discord space

Join the book's Discord Workspace for Latest updates, Offers, Tech happenings around the world, New Release and Sessions with the Authors:

https://discord.bpbonline.com

CHAPTER 2
C# Basics

Introduction

This chapter introduces C#, an object-oriented programming language developed by Microsoft as part of the .NET platform. Known for its modern and clear syntax, C# combines robustness with simplicity, making it suitable for a wide range of applications. This chapter covers the fundamental aspects of C# programming, including the structure of C# programs, the use of namespaces, classes, and methods. It explains how C# employs strong typing to ensure every variable has a declared type at compile time, which helps in identifying errors early. Additionally, the chapter discusses basic programming components such as variables, data types, operators, control structures (like if-else statements and loops), and exception-based error management.

Structure

This chapter covers the following topics:

- Basic syntax rules
- Basic structure of a C# program
- Comments in C#
- Variables and data types

- Basic data types in C#
- Operations in C#

Objectives

By the end of this chapter, you should be able to understand and apply basic syntax rules in C# and recognize the essential components of a C# program and their roles. You will learn to utilize comments effectively to improve code readability and declare and initialize variables correctly.

You will also be able to identify and use various data types in C# and perform basic operations using C# operators.

Basic syntax rules

Developers need to understand the key ideas behind the C# syntax to develop concise and error-free code. Some of those ideas include case sensitivity, which states that names are considered equal only if they have the same capitalization. Another key idea is that C# statements end in a semicolon (**;**), and code sections are surrounded by curly brackets (**{}**). Comments are added using **'//'** for single-line or **'/* */'** for multi-line. Comments should make the code more understandable. Although not enforced by the compiler, appropriate indentation and spacing are suggested for improved readability.

When developing a C# program, the point of entry, the first thing that is executed when starting the program, is the main function. That function should be included in a class. C# requires everything; variables, objects; to be associated with a particular type, stressing on its robust typing system. Adopting these grammar standards will guarantee that the C# code is well-organized, easy to understand, and well maintained.

Case sensitivity

In C#, case sensitivity is critical in helping define keywords and names of variables and functions. In a case-sensitive language, the capitalization of each letter needs to match. For example, **myVariable** and **MyVariable** would be considered separate names. This feature is intended to keep everything uniform throughout the program. While it may be annoying at the beginning, it is an essential aspect of keeping your C# code clean and maintainable. Here is an example of the effect of case sensitivity on variable names:

```
int number = 8; int Number = 2;
Console.WriteLine("Subtraction: " + (number - Number));
```

This C# program demonstrates the case sensitivity of variable names in C#. Here is a line-by-line explanation of the code:

- **Using system**: This line includes the system namespace in the program, which contains fundamental classes and base classes that define commonly-used value and reference data types, events and event handlers, interfaces, attributes, and processing exceptions.

- **Namespace case sensitivity**: This line declares a namespace named **CaseSensitivity.** Namespaces provide a way to group related classes.

- **Class variable case**: This line declares a class named **VariableCase**. In C#, every program has at least one class.

- **Static void main (String args[])**: This line declares the **Mainmethod**, which is the entry point for the program. The **static** keyword means that the method belongs to the class. Whereas the **void** keyword means that the method does not return a value.

- **int number = 8**: This line declares an integer variable named **number** and assigns it the value **8**.

- **int Number = 2**: This line declares an integer variable named **Number** and assigns it the value **2**. Note that **number** and **Number** are two different variables because C# is case-sensitive.

- **Console write line ("Subtraction: "+ (number - Number))**: This line prints the string **"Subtraction: "** followed by the result of number - **Number** to the console. In this case, it will print **"Subtraction: 6"** because **8** minus **2** equals **6**.

Keywords

Keywords are reserved words with a pre-defined meaning within the C# language. Keywords cannot be used as names for variables, functions, classes, etc. Keywords are integral to the language's structure and syntax. Keywords include int, class, using, void, etc. Here is an example of keywords in C#:

```
int number = 8;
string text = "I am the string text";
Console.WriteLine("Number: " + number);
Console.WriteLine("String: " + text);
```

Here is an explanation of the program from the perspective of the keywords being used:

- **using:** The using keyword is used to include namespaces in the program. In this case, the **System** namespace contains fundamental and base classes that define commonly used value and reference data types, events and event handlers, interfaces, attributes, and processing exceptions.

- **namespace:** The namespace keyword is used to declare a namespace named **ExampleofKeywords**. Namespaces in C# are used to organize and provide a level of separation of codes. They can contain classes, structs, interfaces, enums, and delegates.

- **class**: The **class** keyword is used to declare a class named example. In C#, a class is like a blueprint of the data and methods.

- **static**: The **static** keyword declares that a member belongs to the type rather than an instance of the type. Here, it is used to declare that the **Main** method belongs to the **Example** class.

- **void**: The **void** keyword represents the absence of a type. Here, it indicates that the **Main** method does not return a value.

- **string**: The **string** keyword is used to declare a sequence of characters. Here, it is used to declare a string variable text.

- **int**: The **int** keyword is used to declare an integer (a whole number). Here, it is used to declare an integer variable number.

- **Console.WriteLine**: Console is a class of the **System** namespace. **WriteLine** is a method of the **Console** class, and it is used to output (print) text. In this case, it is used to print numbers and text values.

Basic structure of a C# program

Many components work together in a C# application to complete specified tasks. At its core, the code is organized into classes, each with data elements and functions that determine how it operates. The main method is the entrance of a C# code. This is where the running of the program begins. There are multiple ways to declare a **Main** method. However, it is commonly specified as **'static void Main (String args[])'**. The **static** term specifies that the function is part of the type, not a class member. The **void** word denotes that the function does not produce anything. The **'String args[]'** option lets the application receive command-line parameters. The **'Main'** function is important since it is the primary function after a C# program begins, coordinating the initial processing sequence and frequently establishing its operating environment. Following is an example of a **'Main'** used to print **"Hello World"**:

```
using System;
namespace SimpleText
{
    class Components
    {
        static void Main(string[] args)
        {
            Console.WriteLine("Hello World");
        }
    }
}
```

Comments in C#

Comments are non-executable statements used to provide explanations or annotations in the code. Comments are not considered during compilation; however, they are an important source of information for programmers to understand the intent of the code. Comments improve clarity and maintenance by describing the behavior of code sections, which is especially beneficial when revisiting the code after a long period or when other developers need to understand that code. A properly commented program is more straightforward to comprehend, debug, and expand. Hence, using comments is an ideal technique for constructing software:

- Inline or single-line comments begin with // and extend to the end of the line. They are used for brief explanations or annotations directly above or beside the code they describe. Single-line comments are ideal for noting quick insights, clarifications, or TODOs. An example of a single-line comment is as follows:

```
// This is a single-line comment
```

An example of an inline comment looks like this:

```
int number = 5; // This comment explains the variable declaration
```

- Multiple-line comments are enclosed by /* */. They can cover numerous lines, which makes them ideal for longer descriptions like detailing the rationale underlying complicated procedures or presenting details on an entire piece of code. Here is an example of a multi-line comment:

```
/* This is a
multi-line comment */
int number = 5;
```

XML comments start with /// and can be used to generate documentation from the code. These comments follow a specific XML format and are typically placed above classes, methods, properties, and other members to describe their purpose and usage. Software such as Microsoft Visual Studio can employ XML annotations to create reference documents that briefly describe the source. Here is an example:

```
/// <summary>
/// This function displays a text message.
/// </summary>
public void DisplayText()
{
    Console.WriteLine("Hello World");
}
```

XML comments provide a way to document code directly within the source file, offering structured and detailed explanations for methods, properties, and classes. The **<summary>** tag gives a brief overview of the purpose of a method or class, while the **<param>** tag describes each parameter, including its name and role. The **`<returns>`** tag specifies the value returned by a method, if applicable, and the **`<remarks>`** tag provides additional context or notes about the code. To demonstrate usage, the **`<example>`** tag includes example code snippets. The **`<exception>`** tag documents potential exceptions that the method might throw, helping users understand edge cases. Lastly, the **`<value>`** tag describes properties, detailing what they represent or hold. Together, these tags create clear and comprehensive documentation, aiding developers in understanding and using the code effectively while supporting external documentation generation.

Variables and data types

Variables in C# hold data that may be retrieved and updated during the program. Because C# is a strongly typed language, each variable must be defined with a data type, determining what data type it stores. The most common data types are:

- **`int`**: is a whole number (no decimals)
- **`double`**: is a number with decimals
- **`char`**: a single character
- **`string`**: is a series of characters
- **`bool`**: true or false

Aside from these basic types, C# includes more complex types such as Array, List, and other classes. Examples of variable declarations are as follows:

```
string name = "Frank"; // This is a string variable with the "Frank" value
assigned
int numb                                              er = 37; //
This is an integer variable with the number 37 assigned
```

The names of the variables can be a mix of letters, numbers, and underscores with the condition that they must start with a letter or an underscore. They must not begin with a number and cannot include other characters or white spaces. Here is an example of possible variable names:

```
// Valid variable name starting with an underscore
int _counter;


// Valid variable name using camel case
double totalAmount;


// Valid variable name containing letters, digits, and underscores
string userName123;
```

Declaring and initializing variables

When working with variables in C#, there are two key steps: declaration and initialization. Variable declaration is the step where the variable gets its type and name. Initialization gives the variable its first value. These two steps can be done in one line or separate lines. The format used for defining a variable in C# involves the type accompanied by the identifier. For example:

```
int studentid;
```

In this code segment, '**int**' is the data type, indicating that '**studentid**' will store integer values. The variable '**studentid**' is now defined, and the program understands how to allocate memory storage for an integer. Defining variables without assigning value is beneficial when the value is not yet determined but will be supplied further during the code. Once the variable is declared, it can be initialized as shown here:

```
studentid = 3;
```

The variable '**studentid**' is assigned the value '**3**' in this code. This can also be done in one step with the following code:

```
int studentid = 3;
```

Here are examples of variable declarations:

```
// Declare an integer variable named 'number'
int number;
// Declare a string variable named 'text'
string text;
// Declare a double-precision floating point variable named 'decimalNumber'
double decimalNumber;
// Declare a character variable named 'letter'
char letter;
// Declare a boolean variable named 'isTrue'
bool isTrue;
```

Here are some examples of variable declarations and initializations:

```
// Declares an integer variable named 'number' and assigns it the value 10
int number = 10;

// Declares a string variable named 'text' and assigns it the value "Hello, World!"
string text = "Hello, World!";

// Declares a double-precision floating point variable named 'decimalNumber'
```

```
and assigns it the value 3.14
double decimalNumber = 3.14;
// Declares a character variable named 'letter' and assigns it the value
'A'
char letter = 'A';
// Declares a boolean variable named 'isTrue' and assigns it the value true
bool isTrue = true;
```

Basic data types in C#

C# includes numerous fundamental data types that may be stored values. Learning these data types is important because they lay the groundwork for program data storage and processing. These types are incorporated into both C# and the .NET platform, providing a variety of ways to store numbers, letters, and logical values. Choosing the correct data type for a variable promotes optimal storage utilization and precise data handling, essential for creating durable and successful applications.

Integer types

Integer types include int, long, short, and byte. Each of these stores a particular kind of number, as shown here:

- **int:** The most used integral type represents a **32-bit** signed integer. The range of this data type is from **-2147483648** to **+2147483647**.

- **long:** Represents a **64-bit** signed integer suitable for large numbers, ranging from **-9,223,372,036,854,775,808** to **9,223,372,036,854,775,807.**

- **short:** A **16-bit** signed integer with a range from **-32,768** to **32,767**. It is useful when memory conservation is important and the value range is sufficient.

- **byte:** An **8-bit** unsigned integer ranging from **0** to **255**. It is often used for binary data or when working with raw bytes.

- **uint**: A 32-bit unsigned integer, suitable for non-negative numbers, with a range from 0 to **4,294,967,295**. It is useful when working with large positive numbers and ensuring no negative values are involved.

Floating point types

Floating point types include floats and doubles and are used to store decimal numbers. These types work as follows:

- **float:** Represents a **32-bit** floating-point number. It is suited for scenarios requiring significant memory reductions while maintaining a fair degree of correctness, and it can handle around **7 decimal** places of accuracy.

- **double**: Represents a **64-bit** floating-point number and is the default choice for representing real numbers. It is highly accurate, with around **15-16 decimals** in place, which makes it suitable for a wide range of scientific and technological calculations.

Boolean type

The **'bool'** type represents a Boolean value (true or false). It is commonly used for conditional logic, controlling the flow of programs through if statements, loops, and logical operations. For example:

```
bool andResult = 1 < 2 && 3 < 4;
```

This line of code declares a Boolean variable named and result and assigns it the result of the logical **AND** operation **1 < 2 && 3 < 4**:

- **1 < 2**: This comparison operation checks if 1 is less than 2. This is true, so this operation returns true.

- **3 < 4**: This comparison operation checks if 3 is less than 4. This is also true, so this operation returns true.

- **&&:** This is the logical **AND** operator. It takes two Boolean operands and returns true if both are true or false.

So, **1 < 2 && 3 < 4** returns true because **1 < 2** and **3 < 4** are true. Therefore, and the result is assigned the value true.

Character type

The char type represents a single Unicode character. Unicode is a standardized character encoding system designed to support the representation of text and symbols from virtually all written languages, as well as technical and special characters, ensuring consistent and universal text handling across different platforms and systems. Because it has a 16-bit value and can hold any letter found in the Unicode norm, it may be used in multinational projects that handle numerous characters and dialects. For example:

```
char letter = 'A';
```

In this example, 'letter' is a char variable that stores the character **'A'**. The **'char'** type is essential for working with individual characters in strings, performing text manipulation, and handling user input in various applications.

Type conversions

Shifting value from one data type to another is known as type conversion. Understanding how type conversions work helps avoid mistakes that may arise from converting incompatible data types.

Implicit conversions are automatic and do not require special syntax. They occur when a value may be safely converted by the compiler between different types without any chance of incompatibility or loss of information. Usually, implicit conversions are permitted when the intended type can accept an instance of the original type. For example, in the code below, the integer '**number**' is implicitly converted to a double '**doubleNumber**'. This conversion is safe and can be performed since a double can hold all possible integer values plus fractional values:

```
int number = 10;
double doubleNumber = number; // Implicit conversion from int to double
```

When an implicit conversion is impossible, an explicit conversion is an option. Explicit conversions require a cast operator. These conversions are necessary when data loss or a runtime error might occur when converting between types. Explicit conversions are indicated by placing the target type in parentheses before converting the value. In this example, the double '**doubleNumber**' is explicitly converted to an integer '**number**'. The fractional part (**.8**) is truncated in this process, illustrating why explicit conversions are needed to indicate that potential data loss is acceptable. Explicit casting clarifies the programmer's intent, ensuring that conversions are intentional and managed carefully:

```
double doubleNumber = 9.8;
int number = (int)doubleNumber; // Explicit conversion from double to int
```

When the conversion requires a more complicated process, for example, converting the string **123** to the integer **123**, which requires understanding the meaning of the string and applying the rules to create numbers, a conversion method can be used. The **Convert** class in the .NET framework includes a variety of functions for converting between base data types.

The example below shows how the variable **number** is transformed into an integer variable **number** with the help of the **ToInt32** function of the **Convert** class. This method works especially well for transforming the types that need to be parsed or validated, like user input from a text box, to numbers that can be processed further. Conversion methods provide a robust way to handle type conversions, including error-handling capabilities through exception management.

In the following code snippet, we have a string representation of a number that needs to be converted into an integer for numerical operations. This is a common requirement when dealing with data input in text format that needs to be processed as a number. The following code demonstrates how to use the **Convert.ToInt32** method in C# to achieve this conversion:

```
string number = "2622";
int number = Convert.ToInt32(number);
```

Operators in C#

Operators are symbols that determine which actions should be carried out on variables. They are important in C# as they allow for various data manipulations such as numerical computations, analogies, and logical operations. Recognizing how to utilize operators properly is essential for creating concise and understandable code. C# has a comprehensive collection of operators, each intended to execute a certain sort of action, and mastering these operators will considerably improve your coding abilities.

Operators are classified into numerous groups, including mathematical operations, comparison, and logic. Every group of operators serves a specific function and has a range of operators suitable for various tasks. Mastering these groups and their operators enables programmers to conduct multiple tasks with minimal effort.

Operator precedence controls the priority of operators, meaning which operator will be executed first. Precedence describes the criteria for evaluating mathematical statements without using parentheses, resulting in uniform and predictable outcomes. Operators with greater priority are executed before the operators with low priority. When operators have equal priority, they are executed from left to right or right to left, depending on the operator.

For instance, in **'2 + 8 * 4'**, multiplication has greater priority than addition so that the evaluation will be like **'2 + (8 * 4)'**, making it **'2 + 32'**, equal to '**34**'.

```
int outcome = (2 + 8) * 4;// outcome is equal to 40
```

Arithmetic operators

These operators handle fundamental basic mathematical operations. Common operators in this category are **+, -, *, /**, and **%**. The operator **%**, modulus, yields the remainder from a division process. The codes these operators use are as follows:

```
// Define and assign values to the variables
int x = 16;
int y = 4;
// This is '+' operation int add = x + y;
Console.WriteLine($"{x} + {y} = {x + y}");
// This is '-' operation int subtract = x - y;
Console.WriteLine($"{x} - {y} = {x - y}");
// This is '*' operation int multiply = x * y;
Console.WriteLine($"{x} * {y} = {x * y}");
// This is '/' operation int divide = x / y;
Console.WriteLine($"{x} / {y} = {x / y}");
// This is '%' operation int modulus = x % y;
Console.WriteLine($"{x} % {y} = {x % y}");
```

This C# code shows the use of basic arithmetic operators:

- **Addition (+)**: The + operator adds two operands. The line **int add = x + y** adds the values of **x** and **y** and assigns the result to the variable add.

- **Subtraction (-)**: The - operator subtracts the second operand from the first. The line **int subtract = x - y** subtracts y from x and assigns the result to the variable subtract.

- **Multiplication (*)**: The * operator multiplies two operands. In the line **int multiply = x * y**, it multiplies **x** and **y** and assigns the result to the variable multiply.

- **Division (/)**: The / operator divides the first operand by the second. The line **int divide = x / y** divides **x** by **y** and assigns the result to the variable divide. Note that since **x** and **y** are integers, this will perform integer division.

- **Modulus (%)**: The **%** operator calculates the remainder of the division of the first operand by the second. The line **int modulus = x % y** calculates the remainder of **x** divided by **y** and assigns the result to the variable modulus.

Each of these operations is then printed to the console with **Console.WriteLine()**, which displays the operation and the result. For example, **Console.WriteLine($"{x} + {y} = {add}");** will print something like "**16 + 4 = 20**" to the console.

Comparison operators

Comparison operators are employed to verify two variables and return a Boolean value. Popular operators in this category include **==, !=, >, <, >=,** and **<=**. This code illustrates the use of these operators:

```
// Defining and initializing variables
int a = 7;
int b = 5;
// Using the '==' operation
Console.WriteLine($"{a} equals {b}? {a == b}");
// Using the '!=' operation
Console.WriteLine($"{a} does not equals {b}? {a != b}");
// Using the '>' operation
Console.WriteLine($"{a} greater than {b}? {a > b}");
// Using the '<' operation
Console.WriteLine($"{a} less than {b}? {a < b}");
// Using the '>=' operation
Console.WriteLine($"{a} greater than or equals {b}? {a >= b}");
// Using the '<=' operation
Console.WriteLine($"{a} less than or equals {b}? {a <= b}");
```

This C# code shows the use of basic comparison operators:

- **Equality (==)**: The == operator checks if two operands are equal. In the line `Console.WriteLine($"is {a} equals {b}? {a == b}");`, it checks if **a** is equal to **b**.

- **Inequality (!=)**: The != operator checks if two operands are not equal. In the line `Console.WriteLine($"is {a} does not equals {b}? {a != b}");`, it checks if a is not equal to b.

- **Greater than (>)**: The > operator checks if the first operand is greater than the second. In the line `Console.WriteLine($"is {a} greater than {b}? {a > b}");`, it checks if **a** is greater than **b**.

- **Less than (<)**: The < operator checks if the first operand is less than the second. In the line `Console.WriteLine($"is {a} less than {b}? {a < b}");`, it checks if **a** is less than **b**.

- **Greater than or equal to (>=)**: The >= operator checks if the first operand is greater than or equal to the second. In the line `Console.WriteLine($"is {a} greater than or equals {b}? {a >= b}");`, it checks if **a** is greater than or equal to **b**.

- **Less than or equal to (<=)**: The <= operator checks if the first operand is less than or equal to the second. In the line `Console.WriteLine($"is {a} less than or equals b}? {a <= b}");`, it checks if **a** is less than or equal to **b**.

Each of these operations is then printed to the console with `Console.WriteLine()`, which displays the operation and the result. For example, `Console.WriteLine($"is {a} equals {b}? {a == b}");` will print something like **"is 7 equals 5? False"** to the console.

Logical operators

These operators are used to perform logical operations on Boolean values. Common operators in this category are: **&&, ||**, and **!**. Here is an example of using these operators:

```
using System;
namespace DemonstratingLogicalOperators
{
    class Logical
    {
        static void Main(string[] args)
        {
            // Defining and initializing boolean variables
            bool a = true;
            bool b = false;
```

```
            // This is the Boolean AND operation bool andResult = a && b;
            Console.WriteLine($"{a} && {b} = {a && b}");
            // This is the Boolean OR operation bool orResult = a || b;
            Console.WriteLine($"{a} || {b} = {a || b}");
            // This is the Boolean NOT operation bool notResultA = !a;
            Console.WriteLine($"!{a} = {!a}");
            Console.WriteLine($"!{b} = {!b}");
        }
    }
}
```

This preceding C# code shows the basic logical operators:

- **Logical AND (&&)**: The **&&** operator returns true if both operands are true and false otherwise. The line bool **andResult = a && b;** checks if both **a** and **b** are true. Since a is true and b is false, **andResult** will be false.

- **Logical OR (||)**: The **||** operator returns true if at least one of the operands is true and false otherwise. The line **bool orResult = a || b** checks if either **a** or **b** (or both) are true. Since a is true, **orResult** will be true.

- **Logical NOT (!)**: The **!** operator returns true if the operand is false, and false if the operand is true. In the lines **bool notResultA = !a;** and **bool notResultB = !b**, it negates the value of a and b. So, **notResultA** will be false, and **notResultB** will be true.

Each of these operations is then printed to the console with **Console.WriteLine()**, which displays the operation and the result. For example, **Console.WriteLine($"{a} && {b} = {andResult}");** will print something like **"True && False = False"** to the console.

The operators **&&** and **||** are short-circuit operators. These operators assess the second input only when required. This approach notably improves efficiency by eliminating unnecessary calculations, especially if the right side requires complicated or costly actions. The **&&** (AND) operator returns 'true' when both the inputs are 'true'. If the first input is 'false', the whole statement cannot be 'true', hence the second input is not considered, and this logic is called "short-circuiting."

Similarly, the **||** (OR) operator returns 'true' when inputs are 'true'. If the first input is 'true', the entire statement is 'true', but the subsequent input is not processed. This short-circuiting characteristic is advantageous when just one of several requirements must be satisfied.

Example

Here, we will look at a real-life example of using variables and operators:

Problem: When shopping, a customer purchases multiple items of the same type, each at the same price. The customer wants to know the total cost of the items purchased and the average cost per item.

Solution: A program calculates the total cost by multiplying the number of items by the cost per item. It then calculates the average cost per item by dividing the total cost by the number of items. The results are displayed to the user, providing clear and immediate information about their purchase.

Here is the implementation:

```csharp
using System;

class Example
{
    static void Main()
    {
        // Variable declaration
        int numberOfItems, costPerItem, totalCost;
        float averageCost;

        // Initialization
        numberOfItems = 10; // Let us say we bought 10 items
        costPerItem = 5;    // Each item costs $5

        // Using arithmetic operators
        totalCost = numberOfItems * costPerItem; // Total cost is number of
items times cost per item
        averageCost = (float)totalCost / numberOfItems; // Average cost is
total cost divided by number of items

        // Displaying results
        Console.WriteLine("The total cost for " + numberOfItems + " items
is $" + totalCost);
        Console.WriteLine("The average cost per item is $" + averageCost);

        // End of program
    }
}
```

In this program:

- **num1** and **num2** are integer variables initialized with the values **10** and **5**, respectively.

- The **sum** variable stores the result of adding **num1** and **num2** using the **+** operator.

- The **product** variable stores the result of multiplying **num1** and **num2** using the ***** operator.

- The division variable stores the result of dividing **num1** by **num2** using the **/** operator. Note that we cast **num1** to float to perform floating-point division.

The results are then printed to the console using **Console.WriteLine()**.

Conclusion

In conclusion, this chapter has provided a foundational understanding of C#, a versatile and robust programming language developed by Microsoft. We explored the basic syntax rules, such as case sensitivity, the importance of semicolons and curly braces, and using comments to improve code readability. Additionally, we covered the structure of a C# program, emphasizing the significance of the Main function as the entry point. Understanding these elements is crucial for writing clear and maintainable code. The chapter also delved into the fundamental concepts of variables and data types, highlighting the importance of strong typing in C# and how it ensures error identification at compile time. Mastering these basics is essential for anyone aspiring to develop efficient and reliable C# programs.

As we progress to subsequent chapters, we will build upon this knowledge by exploring more advanced concepts and practical applications of C#. Future topics will include control structures, exception handling, and object-oriented programming principles, vital for creating sophisticated software solutions. By continuing to build on this foundational understanding, you will develop the skills necessary to tackle real-world programming challenges and leverage the full potential of C# in various platforms such as desktop, web, and mobile applications. With a firm grasp of these basics, you are well on your way to becoming proficient in modern software development using C#.

Multiple choice questions

1. **What is the entry point of a C# program?**

    a. Class

    b. Method

    c. Main function

    d. Namespace

2. **Which of the following is NOT a basic data type in C#?**

    a. int

    b. string

    c. float

    d. array

3. **Which symbol is used to denote a single-line comment in C#?**

    a. //

    b. /* */

    c. #

    d. –

4. **In C#, what does the 'static' keyword indicate when used in a method declaration?**

    a. The method belongs to an instance of the class

    b. The method returns a value

    c. The method belongs to the class itself

    d. The method is private

5. **Which of the following statements about the 'int' data type in C# is true?**

    a. It represents a 64-bit signed integer

    b. It can store decimal numbers

    c. It represents a 32-bit signed integer

    d. It is not a value-type

Answers

1. (c) Main function
2. (d) array
3. (a) //
4. (c) The method belongs to the class itself
5. (c) It represents a 32-bit signed integer

Practice problems

1. A driver wants to calculate the total fuel cost for a trip and the average cost per mile. The driver knows the total distance of the trip in miles, the fuel efficiency of the car in miles per gallon, and the fuel cost per gallon.

Solution: Write a program to multiply the total distance by the cost per gallon and divide by the miles per gallon to get the total cost. The average cost per mile could be calculated by dividing the total cost by the total distance.

2. A shopper buys multiple types of groceries each week, each grocery type having a different cost. The shopper wants to know the total cost of the groceries and the average cost per type.

   Solution: Write a calculation of the total cost by summing up the cost of each type of grocery item. It could then calculate the average cost per type of grocery by dividing the total cost by the number of types of groceries.

Join our book's Discord space

Join the book's Discord Workspace for Latest updates, Offers, Tech happenings around the world, New Release and Sessions with the Authors:

https://discord.bpbonline.com

CHAPTER 3
Introduction to Control Structures

Introduction

Control structures are essential components in computer programming, directing the execution process of a program. In C#, these structures facilitate decision-making processes, repeating activities, and changing the execution sequence in response to certain conditions. Control structures, including conditional statements, loops, and branching techniques, are the foundational components of C# development. Mastering these structures will allow you to create efficient, intuitive, and maintainable programs. This chapter will review the various control structures in C#, preparing you to handle multiple programming challenges.

Structure

This chapter covers the following topics:

- Understanding conditional statements
- Exploring looping structures
- Interrupting looping structures
- Exception handling in C#
- Best practices for using control structures
- Real-world example of control structures

Objectives

This chapter aims to understand control structures in C#. It aims to equip you with the knowledge and skills needed to effectively use these structures to manage the flow of their programs. The chapter covers various types of control structures, including conditional statements (if, else if, else, switch), looping constructs (for, while, do-while, for each), and branching statements (break, continue, return, goto). It also discusses best practices for using control structures to write efficient, readable, and maintainable code and includes real-world examples to illustrate the practical application of these concepts.

Understanding conditional statements

Conditional statements are essential in coding because they allow the computer to take multiple execution routes depending on specified conditions. They render the code more flexible and responsive to events and conditions. This section reviews many conditional, including if, else if, else, and switch, and explains how each is used.

if statement

The **if** statement allows the application to run instructions only if certain criteria are met. This functionality is critical for developing dynamic and collaborative applications responding to various inputs and conditions. Understanding the proper usage of this conditional statement is crucial to any C# writer since it acts as the basis for more complex decision-making in programs.

The following is the basic syntax of an **if** statement:

```
if (condition)
{
    //This body will be executed if the condition stated in the if
statement is true
}
```

The condition may be true or false. If true, the body of the if statement executes; otherwise, it is ignored.

For example:

```
int number = 15;
if (number < 20)
{
    Console.WriteLine("The number is less than 20");
}
```

The output is as follows:

```
The number is less than 20
```

This program reads an integer and checks it through the **if** statement to determine whether it is less than 20. Since the number is 15, the body of the **if** statement is executed, and the message **The number is less than 20** is displayed.

Nested if

Nesting **if** statements allows developers to handle many levels of conditions. This method allows for more sophisticated decision-making procedures.

For example:

```
if (number > 0)
{
    if (number < 50)
    {
        Console.WriteLine("The number is greater than 0 and less than 50");
    }
}
```

The output is as follows:

The number is greater than 0 and less than 50

This program reads an integer value and then verifies it through the **if** statements to see if it is between 0 and 50. Since both if conditions are satisfied, "**The number is greater than 0 and less than 50**" is displayed.

Conditions must be defined to prevent frequent errors while utilizing if statements. Common mistakes include faulty logic in the condition, missing the parentheses around the condition, and missing braces. C# allows single-line statements with no braces; it is best to use braces to avoid ambiguity and potential errors, especially in complex code.

else statement

This statement is used with the **if** statement. It defines a separate set of code to be run when the **if** condition is false, guaranteeing that the application can handle both situations.

The syntax for the '**else**' statement is as follows:

```
if(Condition)
{
    // This body will be executed if the condition specified by the if
statement is true
}
else
{
```

```
    // This body will be executed if the condition specified by the if
statement is false
}
```

For example:

```
int number = 60;
if (number > 0)
{
    if (number < 50)
    {
        Console.WriteLine("The number is between 0 and 50");
    }
    else
    {
        Console.WriteLine("The number is not between 0 and 50");
    }
}
```

The output is as follows:

The number is not between 0 and 50

The condition number > 0 in the preceding example is valid. The condition number < 50 is false. The control moves to the **else** and displays this message: "**The number is not between 0 and 50**".

These **if** and **else** statements can be nested to create complex decision-making systems. This gives the developers an extensive intuition into how the program flows depending on various conditions.

For example:

```
int number = 6;
if (number >= 0)
{
    if (number % 3 == 0)
    {
        Console.WriteLine("The number is positive and divisible by 3");
    }
    else
    {
        Console.WriteLine("The number is positive and not divisible by 3");
    }
```

```
}
else
{
    Console.WriteLine("The number is negative");
}
```

The output is as follows:

The number is positive and divisible by 3

Here, the first **if** statement tests the number if it is positive. Then, the control moves to the nested **if** statement, which tests whether the number is divisible by 3. Since the number is 6, the nested if statement is executed, which displays "**The number is positive and divisible by 3**" on the screen.

Understanding and successfully using other statements can guarantee that the C# applications tackle every prospective outcome of conditional tests, resulting in more robust and dependable code.

else if statement

The **else if** statement expands the basic if and else control structure. It enables the sequential validation of various conditions, resulting in a more adaptable and understandable method for handling complex decision-making. Using the **else if** statements, you can assess a sequence of conditional expressions and execute different sections of code dependent on the criterion that is met first. This strategy simplifies the code and enhances its readability and reliability, both critical for complicated program logic.

The syntax of the else if statement is as follows:

```
if(firstCondition)
{
    // This body will be executed if the first condition is true
}
else if (secondCondition)
{
    // This body will be executed if the second condition is true
}
else if (thirdCondition)
{
    // This body will be executed if the third condition is true
}
else
```

```
{
    // This body will be executed if none of the conditions are true
}
```

For example:

```
int score = 85; // Example score

if (score >= 90)
{
    Console.WriteLine("Grade: A");
}
else if (score >= 80)
{
    Console.WriteLine("Grade: B");
}
else if (score >= 70)
{
    Console.WriteLine("Grade: C");
}
else if (score >= 60)
{
    Console.WriteLine("Grade: D");
}
else
{
    Console.WriteLine("Grade: F");
}
```

The output is as follows:

Grade: B

This program determines a student's grade based on their test score using a series of **if** and **else if** statements. The score is compared against predefined thresholds: if the score is **90** or above, it outputs "**Grade: A**"; if it is between **80** and **89**, it outputs "**Grade: B**"; if between **70** and **79**, it outputs "**Grade: C**"; if between **60** and **69**, it outputs "**Grade: D**"; and for scores below **60**, it outputs "**Grade: F**". The conditions are evaluated in sequence, and once a proper condition is found, the corresponding grade is printed, with subsequent conditions being ignored, ensuring that only one grade is assigned based on the highest applicable threshold.

switch statement

The '**switch**' block is a tool for managing distinct outcomes based on the given value of a variable. Instead of using many if-elseif blocks like above, the '**switch**' statement is more straightforward and usually more efficient in running alternative code based on the handled data. It verifies the value and switches to the appropriate case, making the program easier to understand and maintain. This is especially handy for designing menus, maintaining multiple states, or dealing with enumerations requiring handling many individual variables.

The syntax of the switch statement is as follows:

```
switch (variable)
{
    case FirstValue:
        // This block of code will be executed if the variable is equal to
the first value
        break;
    case SecondValue:
        // This block of code will be executed if the variable is equal to
the second value
        break;
    default:
        // This block of code will be executed if none of the values
matches the variable
        break;
}
```

Each **case** in this syntax represents a potential value for the **variable**, and the corresponding code section executes if the **variable** equals that value. When the case value matches the variable, the **break** statement terminates the given case and leaves the **switch** block. The default case is only executed when neither of the provided cases fits the variable.

For example:

```
int day = 2;

switch (day)
{
    case 0:
        Console.WriteLine("This is Sunday");
        break;
```

```
    case 1:
        Console.WriteLine("This is Monday");
        break;
    case 2:
        Console.WriteLine("This is Tuesday");
        break;
    case 3:
        Console.WriteLine("This is Wednesday");
        break;
    case 4:
        Console.WriteLine("This is Thursday");
        break;
    case 5:
        Console.WriteLine("This is Friday");
        break;
    case 6:
        Console.WriteLine("This is Saturday");
        break;
    default:
        Console.WriteLine("Not a day of the week");
        break;
}
```

The output is as follows:

This is Tuesday

Here, the variable **day** is initialized with the value **2**. The switch statement matches this value to the third case, displaying "**This is Tuesday**" on the screen. The compiler will run the '**default**' statement, displaying "**Not a day of the week**" if the given day value is less than 0 or more than 6. The '**break**' statement is used at the end of each case to avoid executing all the cases unnecessarily. Additionally, programmers need to be careful with the compatibility of the variable type and the case value.

Exploring looping structures

Looping structures are essential in any programming language, including C#, because they allow the programmer to run a section of code iteratively under conditions. These structures make automating repetitive processes easier, handling large amounts of data efficiently and executing sophisticated algorithms. Understanding loops enables you to create more robust and effective programs capable of handling large datasets and performing iterative actions seamlessly. This section will explain several looping structures in C#, including for, while, do-while, and 'for each' loops, and how to utilize them with examples.

for loop

The **'for'** loop is popular in C# due to its adaptability and simplicity. Knowing how many repetitions the loop will perform is particularly beneficial. The **'for'** loop allows developers to define a counting variable, giving an expression to keep the loop running, and increment/decrement the counting variable all on the same line, making it a simple and efficient iteration tool.

The syntax of the **'for'** loop is as follows:

```
for (initialize the count; boolean expression; increment/decrement the count)
{
    // This code will execute on each cycle
}
```

The components of the for loop are:

- **Initialization of count**: This part executes only at the beginning of the loop, generally to define and initialize the loop counter.

- **Expression**: This statement is evaluated before each cycle execution. If true, the loop body continues; otherwise, the loop terminates.

- **Increment**: This part is executed after every repetition of the loop body, usually to modify the counter.

For example:

```
for (int i = 1; i <= 5; i++)
{
    Console.WriteLine(i);
}
```

The output is as follows:

```
1
2
3
4
5
```

The first step in the preceding example, '**i**', is set to **1**. Before every repetition, the expression '**a <= 5**' is checked. Then, after every loop, the statement '**i++**' increments '**i**' by **1**. This prints the digits 1 to 5 on the display.

while loop

This is another essential iterative C# component that runs a particular code based on a specific condition. Unlike the '**for**' loop, the '**while**' loop works best when the number of repetitions can be determined during execution. It tests its condition preceding every round of iteration, which makes it a pre-test loop.

The syntax of the '**while**' loop is as follows:

```
while (conditional expression)
{
    //This block of code will be executed if the condition is true
}
```

The conditional expression is validated before every looping cycle. If the expression is true, the loop's body will execute. Otherwise, the loop will terminate.

For example:

```
int i = 1;
while (i <= 5)
{
    Console.WriteLine(i);
    i++;
}
```

The output is as follows:

```
1
2
3
4
5
```

In the preceding example, the loop starts with '**a**' equal to **1**. Before every repetition, it verifies whether '**i <= 5**'. The line "**Console.WriteLine(i)**" prints the present value of '**i**'. The statement '**i++**' increases '**i**' by one after every cycle. The loop repeats itself until '**i**' is more than **5**, displaying the integers from **1** to **5**. The '**while**' loop can be nested to handle more complicated repeating operations. This approach is suitable for manipulating multidimensional arrays or performing numerous iteration levels.

For example:

```
int row = 5;
int column = 5;
int a = 1;
while (a <= row)
{
    int b = 1;
    while (b <= column)
    {
        Console.Write(" * ");
        b++;
    }
    Console.WriteLine();
    a++;
}
```

The output is as follows:

```
*   *   *   *   *
*   *   *   *   *
*   *   *   *   *
*   *   *   *   *
*   *   *   *   *
```

In this case, the external loop executes for the given number of rows, while the nested loop executes for the specified number of columns, displaying asterisks '*' on the line. After completing every nested loop, "**Console.WriteLine()**" moves the pointer to the next row.

do-while loop

This looping construct guarantees that the loop body is executed once before the specified condition is evaluated. Since the conditional expression is checked after the first iteration is completed, the do-while structure is beneficial because the loop body must execute before the criterion is tested.

The syntax of the do-while loop is as follows:

```
do
{
    // This block of code will execute once and then check the condition if
true; this will repeat itself
}
```

```
while (condition);
```

The condition is a Boolean expression that is checked after every loop repetition. If it is true, the loop body repeats; otherwise, it terminates.

For example:

```
int i = 1;
do
{
    Console.WriteLine(i);
    i++;
}
while (i <= 5);
```

The output is as follows:

1

2

3

4

5

In the preceding example, the loop starts with '**i**' equal to **1**. Its body executes, displaying the present value of '**i**', and the statement '**i++**' increases '**5**' by **1**. Once the loop body concludes, the expression '**i <= 5**' is tested. As long as the condition is satisfied, the loop repeats itself; otherwise, it terminates. The resulting digits from digits from **1** up to **5** are displayed.

The do-while loop is helpful for dynamic circumstances in which the loop body must execute before the condition is evaluated. It is beneficial for activities such as retrieving information from a stream, where you must read first before determining whether you have reached the end.

for-each loop

In C#, the '**for each**' looping structure is a simple and effective method for iterating across collections and arrays. It simplifies reading every object in a collection, providing a more precise and succinct syntax than typical '**for**' or '**while**' structures. This loop is convenient when you must iterate across every component in an array consecutively without changing it.

The syntax for each loop is as follows:

```
for each (element in the collection)
{
    // This block of code will be executed for each element in the array
```

```
}
```

The "**element**" is the current element of the array or collection during a single iteration, and the "**array/collection**" is the intended collection being iterated.

For example:

```
string[] vegetables = { "Tomato", "Potato", "Onion" };
foreach (string vegetable in vegetables)
{
    Console.WriteLine(vegetable);
}
```

The output is as follows:

Tomato

Potato

Onion

In the preceding example, the '**foreach**' statement iterates over every item in the '**vegetables**' array, reporting the vegetable name to the display. In every repetition, the '**variable**' vegetable keeps the current element. The '**foreach**' structure helps navigate across collections, such as dictionaries, lists, and other data structures that follow the **IEnumerable** interface, making it an adaptable tool for multiple collections. In dictionaries, the '**foreach**' structures can iterate over key-value pairs and conveniently retrieve both keys and values within the loop body. One important characteristic of '**foreach**' is that it grants read-only access to the items, preventing developers from modifying them inside the loop. If changes need to be made, developers can consider utilizing a typical for loop or an alternative way.

Interrupting looping structures

In C# development, sometimes you must interrupt loops as they execute. Interrupting loops may be necessary when controlling particular situations, optimizing execution, and increasing the application's performance. Many loop interruption statements are used in C#, such as '**break**,' '**continue**,' '**return**,' and '**goto**.' Understanding a suitable use of these statements enables you to control loop execution easily.

The break statement

In C#, the break statement is applied to terminate a loop or switch statements immediately and go to the code that comes after it. It is handy for terminating loops early when a specific condition is fulfilled, allowing the program to execute more effectively by eliminating unnecessary repetitions. The '**break**' is used in **switch** statements to avoid the unintentional execution of several instances. By using '**break**,' developers can make the program easier to read and ensure that it works as intended, pausing activities only when necessary.

For example:

```csharp
char[] letters = {'a', 'b', 'c', 'd', 'e', 'f', 'g', 'h'};
char goal = 'e';
bool present = false;
for (int a = 0; a < letters.Length; a++)
{
    if (letters[a] == goal)
    {
        present = true;
        Console.WriteLine($"The letter {goal} is present at index {a}.");
        break;
    }
}
if (!present)
{
    Console.WriteLine($"The letter {goal} is not present in the array");
}
```

The output is as follows:

```
The letter e is present at index 4.
```

The preceding program searches for a letter in the array "**letters**". The '**break**' statement terminates the '**for**' loop right after discovering the '**goal**' letter, eliminating needless iterations.

The '**break**' statement can also be used in nested loops where it only terminates the loop in which it resides. Additional '**break**' statements will be needed for other loops to terminate.

continue statement

The continue statement in C# is a helpful feature that allows a developer to bypass an ongoing loop's current iteration and go to the next iteration. Unlike the **break** statement, which terminates the loop entirely, '**continue**' avoids the remaining code in the currently running iteration and tests the loop's condition while initiating another iteration. This is particularly handy when a coder wants to skip some iterations depending on specific criteria without terminating the entire loop.

For example, the following program displays the odd integers from 1 to 20:

```
for (int a = 1; a <= 20; a++)
{
    if (a % 2 == 0)
    {
        continue; // This statement will skip the iteration here if the
current value of a is divisible by 2
    }
    Console.WriteLine(a);
}
```

The output is as follows:

1   3   5   7   9   11   13   15   17   19

The continue statement works similarly in while and do-while loops, allowing the developer to ignore the remainder of the current repetition and go to the following one. In nested loops, its behavior is similar to the '**break**' statement, which only affects the innermost loop in which it resides. This gives developers robust control over the progression of specific repetitions within nested loops.

return statement

In C#, the **return** statement causes the program to leave a function body and, potentially, returns an output to the caller. It immediately terminates the processing of the current function and returns control to the calling function. This is critical for controlling the execution sequence and guaranteeing that methods provide the intended results. The **return** statement is beneficial in calculating numbers, resolving errors, or doing activities that need feedback from the caller context.

For example:

```
int Sum(int x, int y)
{
    return x + y; // The return statement is used to send the sum to the caller
}
number1 = 4;
number2 = 6;
int addition = Sum(number1, number2); // This is the caller
Console.WriteLine($"{number1} + {number2} = {addition}");
```

The output is as follows:

4 + 6 = 10

The preceding example uses a return statement to return the sum of numbers to the function call. The effective use of the '**return**' statement necessitates that the output type is the same as the return type specified in the function declaration.

When using the **return** keyword, checking that the outcome matches the intended type in the function's declaration is critical to avoid compilation issues. Moreover, do not put any code after a return statement, as it will not be executed and could result in warning messages during compilation. It is also critical to include a return statement in all achievable code paths for functions that return an outcome; otherwise, it leads to compilation issues. By successfully utilizing the return statement, developers may control the execution sequence of their functions and ensure that their code runs smoothly and efficiently.

goto statement

In C#, the '**goto**' statement enables unconditional control transfer to a designated statement inside the same function. Although powerful, its regular use could result in a code that is hard to comprehend and maintain; therefore, it is best used sparingly.

The '**goto**' statement sends control to a label with a proper name followed by a colon.

For example:

```
Console.WriteLine("This line is before the 'goto' statement");
goto Label;
Console.WriteLine("This line will be skipped");
Label:
Console.WriteLine("This line is after the 'goto' statement");
```

The output is as follows:

```
This line is before the 'goto' statement
This line is after the 'goto' statement
```

In the preceding example, the '**goto**' statement shifts the control to the '**Label**'. As a result, the line "**Console.WriteLine("This line will be skipped");**" is skipped.

The '**goto**' statement may be used in nested loops to exit multiple loops simultaneously, whereas the **break** statement only exits the loop in which it is located. Similarly, with **switch** conditional statements, the '**goto**' statement may be used to skip numerous cases at once, as opposed to the **break** statement, which only breaks out of the case in which it is present.

While '**goto**' might help simplify some control flows, other organized alternatives should always be considered first to ensure code readability and maintainability.

Exception handling in C#

Exception handling is an essential component in programming and enables programmers to control runtime errors. C# has a variety of mechanisms for this purpose, including the try-catch-finally block and the throw statement. These strategies help developers spot mistakes, cope with unexpected situations, and ensure their systems run smoothly. Proper error management guarantees that applications recover from errors before collapsing, resulting in greater user satisfaction and safer applications. This section will investigate the details of managing exceptions in C#, demonstrating how to integrate effective error-handling techniques into your code.

The try-catch block

The try-catch block has two parts. The try block includes a piece of code that can produce an error, which will be handled by the code in the catch block. This is an effective strategy for error handling. By discovering and managing errors, programmers may prevent their applications from crashing, provide useful information to the user, and make necessary adjustments.

Following is the structure of the try-catch block:

```
try
{
// This block contains the code that might produce an error
}
catch
{
// This block contains the code that describes how to handle the error
}
```

For example:

```
try
{
    int[] integers = { 5, 6, 7 };
    Console.WriteLine(integers[4]); // This line produces an error that the
index is out of range
}
catch (IndexOutOfRangeException ex)
{
    Console.WriteLine("Error: " + ex.Message);
}
```

The output is as follows:

```
Error: Index was outside the bounds of the array.
```

In the preceding example, attempting to get to the wrong array index yields an "**Index Out Of Range Exception**". The **catch** block identifies and handles this error, keeping the application from crashing.

Developers can use several catch blocks to handle different sorts of errors independently. Each catch block aims to deal with a specific type of exception.

For example:

```
try
{
    // This block has the code that can potentially throw different exceptions
}
catch (ArgumentOutOfRangeException ex)
{
    Console.WriteLine("Error: " + ex.Message);
}
catch (IndexOutOfRangeException ex)
{
    Console.WriteLine("Error: " + ex.Message);
}
catch (NullReferenceException ex)
{
    Console.WriteLine("Error: " + ex.Message);
}
```

The preceding example handles specific exceptions such as "**ArgumentOutOfRangeException**", "**IndexOutOfRangeException**", and "**NullReferenceException**" individually.

finally block

The '**finally**' block is implemented following the 'try-catch' blocks to ensure that the program runs irrespective of whether an error occurs. It helps with clean-up operations such as closing files and resetting states.

For example:

```
try
{
    // This block has the code that can potentially throw different
exceptions
}
```

```
catch (Exception ex)
{
    Console.WriteLine("Error: " + ex.Message);
}
finally
{
    Console.WriteLine("This line of code will be executed irrespective of
the try-catch block");
}
```

The output is as follows:

This line of code will be executed irrespective of the try-catch block.

The '**finally**' block executes irrespective of whether an error was thrown, which makes it ideal for cleaning activities. While not mandatory, it is highly suggested for resource management. It is essential to understand that the '**finally**' block cannot handle exceptions; if one happens within it, it will propagate up the call stack.

throw statement

The throw statement in C# indicates that an error was encountered during the program's execution. Raising an exception means that a relevant catch block in the code may handle an exception or unexpected situation. This method is critical for reasonable exception handling since it allows for transparent and consistent code to cope with unforeseen events.

The '**throw**' statement declares an exception explicitly. It can throw a preset exception or the one defined during the code.

For example:

```
void Division(int dividend, int divisor)
{
    if (divisor == 0)
    {
        throw new DivideByZeroException("divisor must be non-zero");
    }
    Console.WriteLine($"{ dividend}/{ divisor} = { dividend / divisor}");
}


try
{
    Division(10, 2); // Valid division
```

```
    Division(10, 0); // Invalid division, will throw exception
}
catch (DivideByZeroException ex)
{
    Console.WriteLine($"Error: { ex.Message}");
}
```

The output is as follows:

10 / 2 = 5

Error: divisor must be a non-zero number

Here, a function is used to test and verify that the denominator is a non-zero number, or it will raise an error. The '**Main**' method has two calls to that function, one with a valid '**divisor**' and the other with an invalid '**divisor**'. The invalid '**divisor**' produces an error, handled by the '**catch**' block with the error message.

The '**throw**' statement helps develop simple, maintainable, resilient error handling in C# applications. This guarantees that unusual situations are adequately controlled and that the program handles the errors appropriately.

Best practices for using control structures

Control structures are fundamental components of C# development, enabling programmers to manage how their programs run. It is critical to use these structures properly to preserve code simplicity, reliability, and performance. The following are some best practices for utilizing control structures in C#:

- **Simplicity and clarity:**
    - ○ **Avoid excessive layering**: Complex loops and conditional statements layered on top of each other can confuse code, making it difficult to understand and update. Use methods to break down complex reasoning into smaller, more understandable components.
    - ○ **Choose descriptive names**: Use specific and relevant names for variables and methods to clarify the objective of the control structures.

- **Appropriate exception handling:**
    - ○ **Try-catch**: Utilizing try-catch blocks for handling exceptions will allow the program to deal with errors and avoid crashes effortlessly.
    - ○ **Managing specific errors**: Instead of using a general Exception catch block, use specific exception catch blocks. This strategy simplifies debugging and makes it easier to grasp the problems encountered.

- **Right loop for the right task:**

- o **'for' loop**: Use 'for' loops when a program requires a certain number of repetitions or access to an iteration counter.

- o **'while' loop**: Use 'while' loops when the total number of repetitions is not fixed, and the looping process should continue until a criterion is met.

- o **'foreach' loop**: Use 'foreach' loops to simplify syntax and reduce mistakes when traversing collections.

Avoid using 'goto' in favor of organized control flow techniques such as 'loops' and 'conditional statements', making the code better to handle. Use the 'Using' statement to manage resources that need to be disposed of, such as file descriptors or links to databases, to ensure appropriate release. Keep standardized structuring and indentation throughout the code to improve visibility and reliability. Use utilities such as code formatters and linters to ensure consistency.

By adopting these best practices, developers can produce C# code that is efficient, simple to understand, maintain, and troubleshoot while also assuring smooth program execution and resistance to mistakes and unanticipated conditions.

Real-world example of control structures

Create a number-guessing game in which the computer randomly selects a number between 1 and 10, and the player has to guess it. The game should provide feedback to the player indicating whether their guess is too low, too high, or correct. The game should continue until the player correctly guesses the number. The following code presents a commented solution to this problem:

```csharp
using System

class ControlStructures
{
    public static void Main()
    {
        // Create an instance of the Random class to generate random numbers
        Random randomNums = new Random();

        // Generate a random number between 1 and 10
        int randomguess = randomNums.Next(1, 11);

        // Variable to store the user's guess initialized to 0
        int GuessbyUser = 0;

        // Inform the user about the game
```

```csharp
        Console.WriteLine("This is a Number Guessing Game");
      Console.WriteLine("I chose a number between 1 and 10. Can you identify
it?");

        // Loop until the user guesses the correct number
        while (GuessbyUser != randomguess)
        {
            // Prompt the user to enter their guess
            Console.Write("What is your guess? ");

            // Read the user's input
            string? enter = Console.ReadLine();

            // Try to parse the user's input to an integer
            if (int.TryParse(enter, out GuessbyUser))
            {
                // Check if the user's guess is lower than the random number
                if (GuessbyUser < randomguess)
                {
                    Console.WriteLine("Lower than mine! Guess again");
                }
                // Check if the user's guess is higher than the random number
                else if (GuessbyUser > randomguess)
                {
                    Console.WriteLine("Higher than mine! Guess again");
                }
                // If the user's guess is correct
                else
                {
                    Console.WriteLine("Great! You got the number");
                }
            }
            // If the user's input is not a valid number
            else
            {
                Console.WriteLine("Your guess must be between 1 and 10");
            }
        }
    }
}
```

The output is as follows:

```
This is a Number Guessing Game
I chose a number between 1 and 10. Can you identify it?
What is your guess:
Your guess must be between 1 and 10
What is your guess? 7
Higher than mine! Guess again
What is your guess? 3
Lower than mine! Guess again
What is your guess? 5
Great! You got the number
```

Conclusion

This chapter has thoroughly explored the essential control structures used in C#, including conditional statements like if, else, if, else, and switch statements, looping constructs such as for, while, do-while, and for each, and branching techniques. Branching statements, including break, continue, return, and goto, that give developers fine-grained control over the flow of their programs.

Exception handling is another crucial aspect covered in this chapter. Adhering to best practices is critical to writing clear, maintainable, and efficient code. This chapter discusses some best practices, including avoiding excessive nesting, descriptive names, handling exceptions appropriately, and choosing the right loop for the task.

In the next chapter, we will explore C# Methods, a core concept that enhances code organization and reusability. You will learn how to define, call, and utilize methods effectively, including topics such as parameters, return types, and method overloading. This chapter will equip you with the skills to write cleaner, more efficient, and maintainable C# code, paving the way for more advanced programming techniques.

Multiple choice questions

1. **Which of the following control structures is used to handle multiple execution paths based on the value of a variable in C#?**

    a. if statement

    b. for loop

    c. switch statement

    d. while loop

2. **What is the primary purpose of the continue statement in a loop?**
    a. To exit the loop immediately.
    b. To skip the current iteration and proceed with the next iteration.
    c. To return a value from a method.
    d. To handle exceptions.

3. **Which of the following is true about the final block in exception handling?**
    a. It executes only if an exception is thrown.
    b. It executes only if no exception is thrown.
    c. It executes regardless of whether an exception is thrown or not.
    d. It must contain a return statement.

4. **When should you use a foreach loop in C#?**
    a. When you know the exact number of iterations beforehand.
    b. When you need to iterate over each element in a collection or array without modifying it.
    c. When you need to act until a specific condition is met.
    d. When you need to exit a loop early.

5. **What will be the output of the following C# code snippet?**

```
int number = 15;
if (number < 20)
{
    Console.WriteLine("The number is less than 20");
}
```

    a. No output
    b. Compilation error
    c. "The number is less than 20"
    d. "The number is not less than 20"

Answers

1. (c) switch statement
2. (b) To skip the current iteration and proceed with the next iteration
3. (c) It executes regardless of whether an exception is thrown or not

4. (b) When you need to iterate over each element in a collection or array without modifying it

5. (c) "The number is less than 20"

Practice problems

1. Write a C# program that acts as a simple calculator, allowing the user to perform basic arithmetic operations (addition, subtraction, multiplication, and division) based on user input.

   Instructions:

   - Create a console application in C#.
   - Prompt the user to enter two numbers.
   - Prompt the user to choose an operation: +, -, *, or /.
   - Use a switch statement to perform the chosen operation on the two numbers.
   - Display the result of the operation to the user.

   For example:

   ```
   Enter the first number: 10
   Enter the second number: 5
   Choose an operation (+, -, *, /): /
   Result: 2
   ```

2. Write a C# program that generates a random number between 1 and 100 and prompts the user to guess the number. The program should provide feedback to the user on whether their guess needs to be lowered or corrected.

   Instructions:

   - Create a console application in C#.
   - Generate a random number between 1 and 100.
   - Use a while loop to repeatedly prompt the user to guess the number until they guess correctly.
   - Use if, else if, and else statements to provide feedback to the user which are as follows:

     o If the guess is too high, print "Too high! Try again".

     o If the guess is too low, print "Too low! Try again".

     o If the guess is correct, print "Congratulations! You've guessed the number".

   - Use int.TryParse to validate the user input and ensure it is a valid number.

For example:

```
I have chosen a number between 1 and 100. Can you guess it?
Your guess: 50
Too high! Try again.
Your guess: 25
Too low! Try again.
Your guess: 37
Congratulations! You've guessed the number.
```

Join our book's Discord space

Join the book's Discord Workspace for Latest updates, Offers, Tech happenings around the world, New Release and Sessions with the Authors:

https://discord.bpbonline.com

CHAPTER 4
Introduction to Methods in C#

Introduction

In programming, writing complex code often involves significant repetition and potential errors if not properly organized. In C#, this challenge is met by utilizing fundamental building blocks for creating clean, efficient, and maintainable code. Methods allow developers to encapsulate functionality into reusable and modular pieces, significantly improving code readability and reducing redundancy.

This chapter delves into the core concepts of methods in C#. It begins by exploring what methods are and how they are defined. We will then cover the various types of methods, including instance methods and static methods, highlighting their distinct uses and advantages. Furthermore, we will examine method overloading, which enables multiple methods with the same name to coexist as long as they have different parameter lists.

The chapter also emphasizes the importance of method parameters, including value, reference, output, and parameter arrays, each serving different purposes in method calls. You will learn the best practices for writing methods, such as ensuring single responsibility, maintaining concise and clear code, and employing meaningful naming conventions.

We will discuss debugging and testing strategies to ensure your methods are robust and reliable. These include setting breakpoints, walking through code, inspecting variables, and writing unit tests. We will also cover common errors encountered in methods and how to handle them effectively.

By the end of this chapter, you will have a comprehensive understanding of how to create, use, and maintain methods in C#. This knowledge is crucial for developing efficient, scalable, and maintainable C# applications, enabling you to tackle complex coding tasks easily and confidently.

Structure

This chapter covers the following topics:

- Concept of methods
- Defining methods
- Scope and lifetime of variables in methods
- Overloading methods
- Best practices for writing methods
- Debugging and testing methods

Objectives

This chapter introduces methods in C#, focusing on their role in creating modular and organized code. You will learn how to define methods, understand the scope and lifetime of variables within them, and use method overloading to enhance flexibility. Best practices for writing efficient, readable methods will be discussed, along with techniques for debugging and testing to ensure reliability. Real-world examples will illustrate these concepts, helping you apply them effectively in your programming projects.

Concept of methods

A method is a set of code instructions that work together to perform a particular task. Methods or functions in C# are specified within classes or structures and then invoked to accomplish their objectives. Every function declaration contains its name, return type, and a list of parameters. The return type identifies the type of output that the method will produce, whereas the parameter list describes the inputs needed for the technique to execute.

Methods are divided into various kinds based on their functionality and usage. They are as follows:

- **Instance methods**: These methods work on the objects created from the class and have access to their properties and other methods.

- **Static methods**: These methods are usually employed for utility or supplementary actions that do not require instance-specific data. They can be invoked without establishing a class object and have access to static variables and other static methods only, whereas Instance methods can access both static and non-static items.

Reasons for using methods

Methods are essential in C# programming for various reasons, including increased code efficiency, visibility, and maintainability. The following are the main advantages of utilizing methods in C# applications:

- **Re-use**: Methods allow for reusing code across a program. This lowers the repetition, minimizes errors, and makes modifications easier. Instead of repeating code in various locations, you can call the method as needed.

- **Modularity**: Methods simplify complex tasks and organize code into logical chunks. Every method serves a unique purpose, making the entire program's structure simpler and easier to comprehend.

- **Maintainability**: Methods simplify code maintenance and updates. If a modification is required, you may alter the method in a single location rather than changing several instances of the code. This decreases the chance of errors and simplifies debugging.

- **Readability**: Using methods improves code readability. Descriptive method names serve as documentation, defining what each method accomplishes. This helps the readers understand the logic and flow of the software easily.

- **Encapsulation**: Methods can conceal internal code from other portions. This approach promotes data integrity and enables a clear separation of concerns in programming.

- **Abstraction**: Methods allow developers to focus on their operation rather than the implementation. This abstraction enables them to manage complicated activities without being mired in specifics.

- **Parameterization**: Methods take parameters, allowing for data-driven processes. This adaptability enables methods to manage a variety of tasks and conditions.

Structure of a C# method

The key components that define a method are:

- **Method signature**: In C#, each method has a signature with these elements:

    o **Access modifier**: Specifies the method's visibility (public, private, protected, or internal).

    o **Modifiers**: Functions can be static, virtual, abstract, async, or overridden, along with public and private access modifiers. These modifiers provide extra features and adaptability depending on the software's requirements.

    o **Return type**: Determines the type of value the method returns after execution. If the method does not return anything, it is specified as '**void**'.

    o **Method name**: This uniquely identifies the method within its class or struct.

      o   **Parameter list**: This is an optional list of input parameters enclosed in parentheses. Each parameter specifies both a data type and a parameter name.

- **Method body**: The method body is enclosed in curly braces '**{}**' that comprises statements specifying the method's behavior when invoked. This is where developers write the code to accomplish the method's specified purpose.

- **Return statement**: Any method with a non-void return type must have a return statement inside its body. It concludes the function's execution and, possibly, returns the result to the caller. A void method can also use return to exit.

Understanding these properties of a function is critical for writing clean and efficient code. By adequately designing methods and utilizing suitable modifiers and arguments, you may improve the readability, maintainability, and general usefulness of your C# programs.

Defining methods

In C#, a method signature consists of various components describing how it works within a class or structure. Following is how a common method signature appears and what every component represents:

```
public int CalculateProduct (int x, int y)
```

The parts of the declaration are as follows:

- **Public**: This indicates the method's accessibility from the other parts of the program. When a function is marked as '**public**', it can be invoked from anywhere inside the application.

- **int**: This is the return type. In this example, '**int**' specifies that the method '**calculateProduct**' returns an integer.

- **CalculateProduct**: This unique name distinguishes the method inside its class or structure. When developers want to utilize the method elsewhere in their application, they refer to it by this name. Selecting an appropriate name that accurately represents the method's unique purpose or calculation is critical.

- **(int x, int y)**: This is the list of parameters enclosed in parentheses '**()**' and represents the variables the method intends to receive when invoked. Parameters serve as storage for the data that is used in the function. In the given signature, '**calculateProduct**' requires two arguments, '**x**' and '**y**', which are of '**int**' type.

The method signature is a blueprint for how a method operates and interacts with other program sections.

Examples of method definitions

The following are some examples of simple method declarations in C# that show how methods may be created to perform simple tasks. The following example continues the preceding example, where we implement the **CalculateProduct** method:

```
int CalculateProduct(int x, int y)
{
    int product = x * y;
    return product;
}


int multiply = CalculateProduct(5, 6);
Console.WriteLine($"Result: {multiply}");
```

The method '**CalculateProduct**' accepts two '**int**' parameters: '**x**' and '**y**'. Inside the body, it finds the product of '**x**' and '**y**' and stores the result in the '**product**' variable. Then, the '**return**' statement returns the computed product to the code section that invoked the method, that is, "**double multiply = CalculateProduct (5,6);**".

The following example is a method that prints a welcome message:

```
void PrintWelcome(string Name)
{
    Console.WriteLine($"Hello {Name}!");
}


PrintWelcome("John");
```

In this example, the '**PrintWelcome**' method has a single parameter, '**Name**', which is a string. The technique utilizes '**Console.WriteLine**' to show a personalized welcome message on the console, greeting the user by name. The method's return type is '**void**,' resulting in no output values. The following example determines if a number is even or odd:

```
bool IsEven(int number)
{
    return number % 2 == 0;
}
Console.WriteLine(IsEven(5));
```

The '**IsEven**' function takes an integer input named '**integer**'. The method then verifies if the integer is even by employing the modulus operator '**%**'. The function's return type is '**bool**', meaning it returns either '**true**' or '**false**' depending on whether the integer is even.

Calling methods

In C#, methods are executed using their names and any required arguments in parentheses. Here are the steps to call a function:

- **Identify the function**: Find the function you want to utilize within the class or structure where it is declared.

- **Specify the method name**: Write the name of a function followed by parenthesis to invoke it. For example, a function '**CalculateProduct**' would be called '**CalculateProduct()**'.

- **Add parameters**: If the function requires any parameters, insert them in parentheses. For example, if '**CalculateProduct**' takes two integers, you would pass them as arguments like this: **CalculateProduct(3, 8)**.

- **Store the result**: If the function has a non-void return type, you can save it by assigning the function call to a variable of the relevant type. For instance: **int result = CalculateProduct(3, 8);**

Understanding parameters

Parameters work like variables and are defined in a method's parameter list. They are enclosed in parenthesis '**()**' inside the method's signature. Every parameter has a data type and a name, indicating the data type the function will receive and how it might be utilized inside the method's code. There are multiple types of parameters. The main types are as follows:

- **Value parameters**: C# parameters are often supplied as values. This signifies that a copy of the argument's value is passed to the method. Alterations made to the parameter inside the method do not affect the original argument. Structures are passed by value by default.

- **Reference parameters**: The method can alter the original information supplied as input by using the '**ref**' keyword with the parameter. Object class types are passed by reference by default.

- **Output parameters**: Similar to '**ref**', '**out**' parameters include a reference to the argument. However, the method must assign a value to the argument before returning.

- **Parameters (params)**: The 'params' keyword allows methods to take multiple arguments of the same type.

Here is an example of the different types of parameters:

```
// Method that uses value parameter
void ValueParameterExample(int number)
{
    number = 10; // This change will not affect the original variable
    Console.WriteLine($"Inside ValueParameterExample: {number}");
}
```

```csharp
// Method that uses ref parameter
void RefParameterExample(ref int number)
{
    number = 20; // This change will affect the original variable
    Console.WriteLine($"Inside RefParameterExample: {number}");
}

// Method that uses out parameter
void OutParameterExample(out int number)
{
    number = 30; // The out parameter must be assigned before the method ends
    Console.WriteLine($"Inside OutParameterExample: {number}");
}

// Method that uses params parameter
void ParamsParameterExample(params int[] numbers)
{
    Console.WriteLine("Inside ParamsParameterExample:");
    foreach (int number in numbers)
    {
        Console.WriteLine(number);
    }
}

int a = 5;

// Using value parameter
Console.WriteLine($"Before ValueParameterExample: {a}");
ValueParameterExample(a);
Console.WriteLine($"After ValueParameterExample: {a}");

// Using ref parameter
Console.WriteLine($"Before RefParameterExample: {a}");
RefParameterExample(ref a);
Console.WriteLine($"After RefParameterExample: {a}");
```

```
// Using out parameter
int b; // No need to initialize before passing to out parameter
OutParameterExample(out b);
Console.WriteLine($"After OutParameterExample: {b}");


// Using params parameter
ParamsParameterExample(1, 2, 3, 4, 5);
```

The value parameter is demonstrated in the **ValueParameterExample** method, which takes an integer parameter by value. When this method is called, it creates a copy of the variable passed to it. Any modifications made to the parameter inside the process does not affect the original variable. This is evident when the variable a retains its original value after the method call, despite the method changing the parameter to 10.

The **ref** parameter is illustrated in the **RefParameterExample** method, which takes an integer parameter by reference using the **ref** keyword. Unlike the value parameter, this method operates directly on the original variable passed to it. Any changes made to the parameter inside the process will affect the original variable. This is shown when the variable a is modified to 20 after the method call. It is important to note that the variable must be initialized before being passed to a method using ref.

The out parameter is used in the **OutParameterExample** method, which also takes an integer parameter by reference but uses the **out** keyword. The critical difference with the 'ref' keyword is that the method must assign a value to the parameter before it returns. This ensures that the parameter is initialized within the method. The variable does not need to be initialized before being passed to the method. After the method call, the variable b is assigned the value 30, demonstrating how out parameters ensure the variable gets a value from the method.

Lastly, the params parameter is showcased in the **ParamsParameterExample** method. This method takes a variable number of integer parameters using the params keyword, allowing it to accept a comma-separated list of integers or an array of integers. This flexibility is helpful for methods that must handle an undetermined number of arguments. The process iterates through the provided integers and prints them, showing how params can simplify method calls that require multiple arguments of the same type.

Void methods

Void methods are mainly employed for tasks that involve actions such as displaying output, modifying data, or interacting with external systems. These methods encapsulate a series of operations designed to accomplish a particular task. Void methods are identified by the keyword **void** in their method signature, signaling that they do not yield any return value. For instance:

```
void PrintNote(string note)
{
    Console.WriteLine(note);
}
```

Scope and lifetime of variables in methods

In C#, local variables are defined within a method, a constructor, or a block of code and can only be accessed inside that block. Mastering the use of local variables and their scope is critical for effective data handling and preventing unwanted consequences in coding. A thorough description of local variables in C# is provided in the following example

Local variables are specified within a function following the syntax '**[type] [variableName];**'. where '**[type]**' represents the data type of the variable and '**[variableName]**' its name. They are typically initialized either when defined or subsequently inside the same block. For example:

```
void DisplayTheTotal()
{
    int x = 6; // Definition and initialization at the same time
    int y; // Definition without initialization
    y = 6; // Later Initialization
    int total = x + y; // Local variables are used
    Console.WriteLine($"The total = {total}");
}
```

Local variables

Local variables can only be accessed inside the block '**{}**' where they are defined. They cannot be accessed outside of this scope. In C#, the scope and length of the function's execution determines the variable's lifespan. Understanding the idea of a variable lifetime is essential for good memory management and ensuring that your application works appropriately. Local variables are typically defined and loaded within the function's body. Their lives begin when the function is called upon and its execution hits the declaration point.

In this example, we will walk through a simple method in C# that demonstrates how to declare and use variables within a method's scope to perform a basic arithmetic operation. The method, named **CalculateProduct**, calculates the product of two integers and outputs the result to the console. The scope and lifetime of the variables are confined within the method, showcasing how local variables are created and destroyed within a block of code. Let us explore how this is done:

```
void CalculateProduct ()
{
    int x = 3; // The lifetime of 'x' starts here
    int y = 6;
    int Product = x * y;
    Console. WriteLine ($»The product = {Product}»);
} // The lifetime of 'x' and 'y' end here
```

A local variable's scope is confined to the function body in which it is declared. They are out of range when the control goes out of the function body.

Method parameters

Function parameters are variables supplied to a function when it is invoked. These variables are initialized with the values or references sent in as arguments by the function's caller. In C#, function arguments have a lifespan corresponding to the time the method is executed, with the exception of **'ref'** and **'out'**, where the parameters do not disappear when the function ends.

They are created when the function is invoked with particular arguments and disappear after the function has completed its execution. In this example, we will examine a simple method in C# that demonstrates how to use a parameter passed into a method. The method, named **PerformOperation**, takes an integer parameter named data and outputs its value to the console. This example illustrates the concept of method parameters and their scope, showing how a parameter is accessible only within the method where it is defined. Once the method execution is complete, the parameter goes out of scope. Let us take a closer look:

```
void PerformOperation (int data)
{
  Console. WriteLine(data); // Here 'data' is a parameter of type 'int'
} // Here the parameter 'data' is out of scope
```

Block-scope variables

When a variable is defined in nested blocks (loops, conditionals, or other types of blocks) within a function, it is called a block-scope variable. These variables are only valid within the block where they are defined, and their scope expires when the block action is completed.

In this example, we will explore a method in C# that showcases how to work with conditional statements and variable scope within an if block. The method, named **TestNumber**, takes an integer parameter called number and checks if it is positive. If the condition is met, a local string variable named **outcome** is created and initialized with the value "**Positive**". This variable exists only within the if block, illustrating how variables can have a limited scope within specific code blocks. Once the block is exited, the variable goes out of scope. Let us examine the code:

```
void TestNumber(int number)
{
    if (number > 0)
    {
        string outcome = "Positive"; // The lifetime of 'outcome' is inside
this 'if' block
        Console.WriteLine(outcome);
    } // Here the 'outcome' is out of scope
}
```

Block-scope variables have a lifetime limited to the block of code where they are defined. They are initialized when the control flow hits the block and disappear when it departs.

Handling variable lifespan appropriately implies that the storage space is utilized optimally and assists in preventing difficulties such as retrieving variables that are no longer accessible or making unintentional data changes.

Default parameters

Providing default parameter values enables programmers to specify values allocated to parameters if no argument is supplied during the function call. This feature improves flexibility and facilitates function calls by giving a backup value when needed. Some main features of establishing default values for parameters:

- Default parameter values are specified in the function signature by initializing the parameter at the time of declaration.

- The default value sets the parameter's initial value if no argument is sent to the function

Here is an example:

```
void PrintNote1(string note = "Welcome")
{
    Console.WriteLine(note);
}


PrintNote1(); // The output is: Welcome
PrintNote1("Hello"); // The output is: Hello
```

In the preceding instance, the '**PrintNote**' function creates a parameter '**note**' initialized with **"Welcome"**. When the function is called without specifying an argument for '**note**', it utilizes the preset value. If an argument is passed along with the function call, the given value precedes the default value.

When specifying a default parameter value, they must appear after the non-default arguments in the function signature. This guarantees that function calls are plain and unambiguous, especially when specific parameters are omitted. Moreover, preset values must be compile-time constants, which means they can only contain primitive types like integers, strings, and '**enums**'. This limitation guarantees that the predefined parameters are predictable and may be assessed during compilation time.

Setting default parameter values in C# streamlines function calls by reducing the need for function overloads or conditionals inside the function body to handle multiple argument scenarios. This strategy improves code comprehension by clearly stating the predefined parameters, making the function's signature more descriptive and understandable to programmers evaluating or using the function.

When defining preset parameter values, it is essential to pick them carefully to avoid ambiguity or unexpected results in function calls. Consistency between function overloads is critical to ensuring that the predefined parameters match the function's intended operation, enabling clarity and predictability in how programmers use and understand functions.

Benefits of default parameters

Setting predefined values for parameters helps programmers minimize the number of function overloads needed, simplifying the API. Functions with predefined parameters are also easier to call since unnecessary arguments may be skipped, leading to cleaner, more legible code. Finally, providing predefined values in function signatures clearly defines the intended behavior, improving code readability.

Named arguments

In C#, naming parameters when calling functions allows coders to provide parameter names and values directly. This approach improves code comprehension and maintainability by explicitly stating the objective of each argument in function calls. When calling a function, users can pass named parameters in the '**parameterName: value**' pattern. It enables users to supply arguments in any order determined by parameter names rather than their position in the function signature. For example, suppose a method '**DisplayPersonalData**' takes parameters '**name**', '**age**', and '**address**', like:

```
void DisplayPersonalData(string name, int age, string address)
{
    Console.WriteLine($"Name is: {name}, Age is: {age}, Address is: {address}");
}
```

```
// Calling the method using named arguments
DisplayPersonalData(address: "123 street", name: "Stacy", age: 45);
```

In the preceding instance, the '**DisplayPersonalData**' function is used with named parameters, and the values for '**age**', '**name**', and '**address**' are supplied in a different order than defined in the function.

Benefits of named arguments

Providing explicit argument names with named arguments demonstrates each parameter's purpose, which is especially useful in functions with several parameters of the same type or many parameters. Named arguments allow developers to send parameters to functions in any order, providing flexibility in function calls. Named arguments assist in reducing errors by clearly labeling each value with a parameter name, lowering the potential for misinterpretation of argument order.

Combined benefits

Using default parameters and named arguments simultaneously simplifies function calls by enabling programmers to eliminate extraneous arguments while explicitly stating which ones are required. In this example, we will delve into the use of named arguments and default parameters in C#. These features allow for more flexibility and clarity when calling methods. The code demonstrates two key concepts: first, calling a method with named arguments, and second, combining both default and specified arguments when invoking a method.

The first part of the example shows how to call a method using named arguments, which can enhance readability and make it clear what values are being assigned to each parameter:

```
// Calling the method using named arguments
DisplayPersonalData (address: "123 street", name: "Stacy", age: 45);
```

Next, the **ReportText** method is defined with a combination of required and optional parameters. The severity parameter has a default value of "**info**", and the **toFile** parameter defaults to false. This method can be called with different combinations of arguments, utilizing both the default values and explicitly specified arguments to control its behavior:

```
void ReportText (string content, string severity = "info", bool toFile =
false)
{
    // Implementation code
}


// Combining both default and specified arguments
```

```
ReportText ("Informative message.");
ReportText ("Warning message", severity: "Warning");
ReportText ("Error message", severity: "Error", toFile: true);
```

Overloading methods

Function overloading allows developers to create many functions with the same name in a single class, as long as their argument lists differ in number, type, or order. This feature enhances code readability and usefulness by allowing functions to handle identical tasks using various inputs. Overloaded methods require different parameter lists. For example, this can be accomplished by changing the number of parameters, their types, or their sequence:

```
// Display function with a string parameter
void Display1(string note) { }
// Display function with an integer parameter
void Display1(int digit) { }
// Display function with two parameters
void Display1(string note, int digit) { }
```

Function overloading is a form of compile-time polymorphism. The compiler selects the function to invoke based on its name and parameter list. The **return** type alone cannot distinguish between overloaded functions; the argument list must be distinct:

```
// Sum function with integer return type and two integer parameters
int Sum1(int x, int y) { return x + y; }
// Sum function with double return type and two double parameters
double Sum1(double x, double y) { return x + y; }
```

Rules for overloading methods

In C#, overloaded functions must have distinct argument lists to be correctly recognized and utilized by the compiler. While it is permissible for the return types of these functions to vary, the return type alone cannot be relied upon to distinguish between them. Additionally, the access modifiers (public, private, etc.) and function modifiers (static, virtual, etc.) can differ among overloaded functions. However, these modifiers do not influence the resolution of which overloaded function is called, as the compiler relies solely on the distinct argument lists to differentiate between them.

Examples of overloaded methods

The following example demonstrates function overloading:

```csharp
class OverloadExample
{
    // Method with no parameters
    public static void Display()
    {
        Console.WriteLine("Display method with no parameters.");
    }

    // Overloaded method with one integer parameter
    public static void Display(int number)
    {
        Console.WriteLine("Display method with one integer parameter: " +
number);
    }

    // Overloaded method with one string parameter
    public static void Display(string text)
    {
        Console.WriteLine("Display method with one string parameter: " +
text);
    }

    // Overloaded method with two parameters: an integer and a string
    public static void Display(int number, string text)
    {
        Console.WriteLine($"Display method with two parameters: integer =
{number}, string = {text}");
    }

    static void Main1()
    {
        // Calling the overloaded methods
        Display();
        Display(42);
        Display("Hello, world!");
        Display(42, "Hello, world!");
    }
}
```

In this example of method overloading in C#, the **Program** class contains several overloaded versions of the **Display** method, each with a different parameter list. The first **Display** method takes no parameters and prints a message. The second **Display** method takes a single integer parameter and prints a message that includes the integer. The third **Display** method takes a single string parameter and prints a message that consists of the string. The fourth **Display** method takes two parameters, an integer, and a string, and prints a message that includes both. When the **Main** method calls each version of the **Display** method, the compiler distinguishes between them based on the unique parameter lists. This illustrates how method overloading allows multiple methods with the same name to coexist by varying the parameters they accept.

Best practices for writing methods

Creating clean, maintainable, and intelligible code requires keeping functions focused and straightforward. A focused method achieves a specific aim, rendering it easier to understand and debug. This principle aligns with the **Single Responsibility Principle** (**SRP**) of object-oriented programming, which proposes that a method should only have one reason for change. Implementing this notion makes methods more adaptive and reusable, improving code quality and reliability.

The following are some valuable recommendations to keep the functions focused and straightforward:

- **Limit scope**: Each function should target only one unique capability. If a function seems to fulfill multiple objectives, consider breaking it into smaller, more specific functions.

- **Keep it concise**: Minimize function length. Extended functions may be challenging to read and comprehend. If a function has more statements, consider dividing it into lesser, more manageable sections.

- **Reduce side effects**: Functions should not abruptly change the system's state. If side effects are required, they should be carefully documented to avoid misinterpretation or unexpected consequences.

Naming conventions for methods

To ensure the code is legible and easy to maintain, functions must be named clearly and meaningfully. Effective naming approaches include the following:

- Use verbs in function names to explain their behavior. Samples include: `'GetPersonalData'`, `'CalculateProduct'`, and `'UpdateTheDatabase'`.

- Keep a consistent name style across the codebase, such as `'camelCase'` or `'PascalCase'`, to increase readability and understanding.

- Choose informative and straightforward labels that communicate the function's objective. Avoid using acronyms unless they are commonly utilized inside your team or domain to ensure clarity for everyone analyzing the code.

- Follow the established name standards used by the C# community and your company. For example, 'PascalCase' is used for **public** methods, while 'camelCase' is used for private and protected methods.

Documenting methods with comments

Providing explicit and valuable annotations for functions is critical to ensure that your code is understandable and convenient for current and future coders. Effective practices of documentation include the following:

- Use XML documentation comments to overview the function's capabilities briefly. Tools can analyze these annotations to build API documentation, which helps comprehend the function's purpose:

```
/// <summary>
/// Determines the total cost of all goods in the shopping basket
/// </summary>
/// <param name = "items"> List the products in the purchasing
basket </param>
/// <returns>Total price of all the products</returns>
public decimal CalculateTotal (List<Item> items)
{
    // Method implementation
}
```

- In the function documentation, provide precise descriptions of each argument and the **return** value. This will help other programmers understand what arguments are anticipated and what results the function produces:

```
class OverloadComments
{
    /// <summary>
    /// Displays a default message.
    /// </summary>
    public static void Display()
    {
        Console.WriteLine("Display method with no parameters.");
    }
```

```
/// <summary>
/// Displays a message that includes an integer.
/// </summary>
/// <param name="number">An integer to be included in the
display message.</param>
public static void Display(int number)
{
    Console.WriteLine("Display method with one integer
parameter: " + number);
}

/// <summary>
/// Displays a message that includes a string.
/// </summary>
/// <param name="text">A string to be included in the display
message.</param>
public static void Display(string text)
{
    Console.WriteLine("Display method with one string parameter:
" + text);
}

/// <summary>
/// Displays a message that includes an integer and a string.
/// </summary>
/// <param name="number">An integer to be included in the
display message.</param>
/// <param name="text">A string to be included in the display
message.</param>
public static void Display(int number, string text)
{
    Console.WriteLine($"Display method with two parameters:
integer = {number}, string = {text}");
}

static void Main()
{
    // Calling the overloaded methods
```

```
            Display();
            Display(42);
            Display("Hello, world!");
            Display(42, "Hello, world!");
        }
    }
```

- Include inline comments to illustrate complex functionality or highlight critical decisions in function implementation. Avoid annotations that reiterate apparent code:

```
public void HandleOrder(Order order)
{
    // Test the validity of the order before handling
    if (!order.IsValid)
    {
        throw new InvalidOperationException("The order is invalid");
    }

    // Process the order here
}
```

- Regularly modify comments to reflect changes made to the function. Outdated comments can mislead programmers and cause misconceptions, so ensure they represent the function's present state correctly.

By following these best practices, programmers can successfully develop functions that fulfill their purpose and are transparent, maintainable, and simple to utilize throughout the codebase.

Debugging and testing methods

Debugging is an essential skill for discovering and fixing errors in the code efficiently. To identify and solve issues, it is necessary to thoroughly trace through code, examine variables, and comprehend how the code works. Using fundamental debugging strategies guarantees that the functions work as expected and improves the overall state of the code.

These practices include the following:

- **Creating breakpoints**: Place breakpoints throughout the code to pause execution at specific points. This enables you to monitor the status of variables and assess conditions in real time.

- **Walking through code**: During debugging sessions, use commands such as step into (*F11*), step over (*F10*), and step out (*Shift + F11*) to move across lines of code, passing over functions and blocks to investigate the way they are executed.

- **Variable inspection**: Utilize resources like the *Locals* window or watch variables to keep track of the contents of variables and expressions when debugging. This aids in comprehending how data changes across the code execution.

- **Logging**: Use logging statements like "`Console.WriteLine`" or "`Debug.WriteLine`" to display the application's state and control flow details. This strategy gives useful insights into the operation sequence and aids in problem identification.

Writing unit tests for methods

Unit testing is critical for confirming function correctness and guaranteeing reliable operation under various scenarios. It entails writing automated tests targeting individual functions in isolation from the larger codebase.

The following are some fundamental techniques for good unit testing:

- **Test case design**: Create thorough test cases covering a range of conditions, such as edge cases and everyday use patterns.

- **Framework selection**: Given the project needs and team choices, pick an appropriate unit testing platform such as NUnit, MSTest, or xUnit.

- **Arrange-Act-Assert (AAA) design**: Use the AAA pattern to structure tests: Arrange (put up test data and prerequisites), Act (call on the function being tested), and Assert (check expected results).

- **Spoofing dependencies:** Use mocking platforms like 'Moq' to build fake objects that mimic dependencies, allowing for isolated analysis of the function under consideration.

- **Constant integration**: Incorporate unit tests into your **continuous integration/ continuous development (CI/CD)** pipeline for automated testing during the development process, ensuring that the function behavior is validated as code changes.

Handling common errors in methods

Effectively handling common failures in functions is critical for developing solid and trustworthy programs capable of gracefully recovering from unanticipated problems. These problems frequently include null reference exceptions, index out-of-range exceptions, and division by zero exceptions.

The following are some strategies for dealing with these typical errors:

- **Input validation**: Before execution, verify function arguments to ensure they fit the requirements and prevent oversights.

- **Error handling**: To handle errors properly, use the 'try-catch' blocks. Logging exceptions aids debugging, whereas clear error messages improve the user experience.

- **Defensive coding**: This approach helps detect potential errors. This includes evaluating inputs, verifying assumptions, and guaranteeing reliable exception handling.

- **Fallback mechanisms**: Use fallback techniques or default settings to keep the program stable in the face of failures or unexpected situations.

- **Unit testing edge cases**: Create unit tests that consciously test conditions likely to result in errors. This guarantees that functions handle errors effectively while maintaining the intended behavior.

By incorporating these methods into the debugging and testing procedures, programmers may improve function reliability, performance, and error tolerance. This strategy considerably enhances the overall quality and durability of software programs.

Conclusion

This chapter explored the fundamental concepts and practical applications of methods in C#. We learned the importance of methods in creating an organized, modular, and reusable code. We delved into the structure of methods, covering its essential components.

We also examined method overloading, highlighting how it allows multiple methods with the same name to coexist as long as they have distinct argument lists. The discussion on method parameters provided insights into the different types of parameters, including value, reference, output, and parameter arrays, and their specific uses.

Furthermore, we covered the scope and lifetime of variables within methods. The chapter also introduced default parameters and named arguments, demonstrating how they can simplify method calls and improve code readability. We concluded with the best practices for writing methods.

By mastering these concepts, you can write efficient, maintainable, and scalable methods in C#, laying a solid foundation for developing high-quality software applications.

In the next chapter, we will delve into the world of **object-oriented programming (OOP)** by introducing C# classes and objects. This is where we will learn to model real-world entities, encapsulate data and behavior, and apply the principles of OOP to create more complex, reusable, and maintainable code.

Multiple choice questions

1. **Which of the following is a primary benefit of using methods in C#?**

    a. Increase code size.

    b. Reduce code readability.

    c. Promote code reuse and modularity.

    d. Decrease code maintainability.

2. **What is the correct way to define a public method in C# that returns an integer and takes two integer parameters?**

    a. public int CalculateSum(int x, int y)

    b. public void CalculateSum(int x int y)

    c. int CalculateSum(int x, int y)

    d. public int CalculateSum(void x, void y)

3. **Which keyword is used to pass a parameter so that the method can use and modify the original variable in C#?**

    a. out

    b. ref

    c. in

    d. params

4. **How does the C# compiler distinguish between different overloaded methods in method overloading?**

    a. By the return type of the methods

    b. By the names of the methods

    c. By the access modifiers of the methods

    d. By the distinct argument lists of the methods

5. **Which of the following statements about the void return type in C# methods is true?**

    a. It indicates the method returns a string.

    b. It indicates the method returns an integer.

    c. It indicates the method does not return any value.

    d. It indicates the method returns a Boolean.

Answers

1. (c) Promote code reuse and modularity
2. (a) public int CalculateSum(int x, int y)
3. (b) ref
4. (d) By the distinct argument lists of the methods
5. (c) It indicates the method does not return any value

Practice problems

1. You must create a Calculator class in C# demonstrating your understanding of methods, method overloading, parameters, and best practices. The Calculator class should provide the following functionalities:

   - **Addition**:
     - Method that takes two integers and returns their sum.
     - Overloaded method that takes three integers and returns their sum.
     - Overloaded method that takes an array of integers using params and returns their sum.

   - **Documentation**: Provide XML documentation for each method, including descriptions of parameters and return values.

   - **Requirements**:
     - Define the Calculator class with the necessary methods for addition.
     - Implement method overloading for the Add method.
     - Ensure all methods follow best readability, maintainability, and documentation practices.
     - Demonstrate the use of value and params parameters.
     - Write the main method to test all the functionalities of the Calculator class with various inputs.

   The example usage is as follows:

```
public static void Main()
{
    Calculator calculator = new Calculator();

    int sum2 = calculator.Add(5, 10);
    int sum3 = calculator.Add(1, 2, 3);
```

```
int sumArray = calculator.Add(1, 2, 3, 4, 5);

calculator.PrintResult("Addition of two numbers", sum2);
calculator.PrintResult("Addition of three numbers", sum3);
calculator.PrintResult("Addition of an array of numbers",
sumArray);
}
```

Instructions:

- Implement the Calculator class with the methods for addition as described.

- Use the provided example usage to test your class.

- Ensure your code is well-documented and follows best practices for readability and maintainability.

2. Create a MessagePrinter class in C# that demonstrates your understanding of method parameters, scope, and lifetime of variables. The MessagePrinter class should provide the following functionalities:

- **Print welcome message**: Method that takes a string parameter (name) and prints a welcome message using that name.

- **Print custom message**: Method that takes two parameters: a string (message) and an integer (number of times to print the message) and prints the message the specified number of times.

- **Print detailed message**: Method that takes a string parameter (message) and a params array of strings (details), printing the message followed by each detail on a new line.

- **Documentation**: Provide XML documentation for each method, including descriptions of parameters and return values.

The requirements are:

- Define the MessagePrinter class with the necessary methods.

- Implement methods with different parameter types, including value and params parameters.

- Ensure all methods follow best readability, maintainability, and documentation practices.

- Write a main method to test all the functionalities of the MessagePrinter class with various inputs.

The example usage is as follows:

```
public static void Main()
{
    MessagePrinter printer = new MessagePrinter();

    printer.PrintWelcome("Alice");
    printer.PrintCustomMessage("Hello, world!", 3);
    printer.PrintDetailedMessage("Important Update", "Detail 1",
"Detail 2", "Detail 3");
}
```

The instructions are as follows:

- Implement the MessagePrinter class with the methods as described.

- Use the provided example usage to test your class.

- Ensure your code is well-documented and follows best practices for readability and maintainability.

Join our book's Discord space

Join the book's Discord Workspace for Latest updates, Offers, Tech happenings around the world, New Release and Sessions with the Authors:

https://discord.bpbonline.com

CHAPTER 5
Classes and Objects in C#

Introduction

Understanding the foundational principles of programming is crucial for developing efficient and maintainable software. This chapter delves into the core concepts of classes and objects within the C# programming language. These concepts form the backbone of **object-oriented programming** (**OOP**), a paradigm that facilitates the creation of modular, reusable, and scalable code. By exploring how classes and objects are defined and utilized, this chapter provides a comprehensive overview of the mechanisms that allow developers to model real-world entities and abstract concepts in their applications.

Whether you are new to programming or looking to deepen your understanding of C#, this chapter will equip you with the essential knowledge to leverage the full potential of OOP in your software development projects. You will gain insights into the significance of encapsulation, inheritance, polymorphism, and abstraction through detailed explanations and practical examples, all of which are pivotal in building robust and flexible software systems.

Structure

This chapter covers the following topics:

- Defining classes and objects
- Understanding classes in C#

- Understanding objects in C#
- Encapsulation in C#
- Practical applications

Objectives

By the end of this chapter, you will understand core OOP concepts and how they are implemented in C# through classes and objects. You will learn to define classes, create objects, and apply principles like encapsulation, inheritance, polymorphism, and abstraction. You will also manage properties, methods, constructors, access modifiers, static members, and nested/partial classes. Finally, you will apply these skills to build practical applications, establishing a strong foundation in C# OOP for developing scalable and maintainable software.

Defining classes and objects

A class outlines the characteristics and behaviors of objects, encompassing data and methods to manipulate that data. It typically includes variables, properties (getters and setters), processes (functions), and events. An object represents an instance of a class, with memory allocated upon creation. An object has three primary properties: state (data stored in fields), behavior (functions to manipulate data), and identity (unique differentiation even among identical objects).

Classes and objects form the cornerstone of C#'s OOP approach. The following vital advantages highlight their significance:

- **Encapsulation**: Classes group variables and functions into a single entity, concealing internal workings and presenting a straightforward interface for interaction, enhancing code organization and manageability.

- **Modularity**: By dividing complex tasks into smaller components, each class focuses on a specific solution aspect, simplifying writing, testing, and maintaining code. This modular design promotes code reuse across program areas or future projects.

- **Reusability**: Once defined, a class can be reused to create multiple objects, saving time and effort while ensuring consistency and reducing errors.

- **Inheritance**: C# supports inheritance, allowing new classes to derive from existing ones, enhancing and customizing functionality while inheriting properties and methods. This promotes code reuse and supports a hierarchical structure that improves code organization and readability.

- **Polymorphism**: Classes provide polymorphism, enabling objects to be treated as instances of their base class, even if they originate from different subclasses. This flexibility makes generic algorithms compatible with various objects, enhancing code scalability and adaptability.

- **Abstraction**: Classes model real-world items and abstract concepts, allowing developers to focus on defining core qualities and behaviors without delving into unnecessary details. This clear separation of elements facilitates code comprehension and maintenance.

In summary, classes and objects are vital in C# for logically organizing code, promoting reusability and maintainability, and supporting the development of complex yet organized software solutions. Embracing OOP principles enables developers to create robust, scalable applications.

Understanding classes in C#

Understanding classes in C# is fundamental to object-oriented programming, as classes serve as the blueprints for creating objects. A class defines the properties (fields) and behaviors (methods) that its objects will have. It encapsulates data and functionality, allowing you to organize and structure your code more effectively. In C#, classes can include various elements like constructors for object initialization, access modifiers to control visibility, and static members for shared data. By mastering how to create and use classes, you will be able to model real-world entities and abstract concepts efficiently, leading to more modular, maintainable, and reusable code.

Structure of a class

A class typically includes the following elements:

- **Class declaration**: It begins with the keyword class, followed by the class name and optional access modifiers like **public** or **private** to control visibility.

- **Fields/variables and properties**: Fields store data or the state of objects created from the class, while properties provide controlled access to these fields. They allow external code to read (**get**) or modify (**set**) values while keeping internal workings hidden.

- **Methods or functions**: Define an object's behavior, comprising code that executes specific tasks or actions.

- **Constructors**: Special methods that initialize objects upon creation, sharing the class name and typically initializing fields or properties.

Additionally, classes can include events (notifications), indexers (access elements like arrays), and other advanced features tailored to specific application requirements. Each component within a class shapes object behavior, forming the foundational principles of OOP.

Creating a class in C#

The following is an example of a class in C#:

```
public class Bike
{
    // Fields
    public string Model { get; set; }
    public string MadeIn { get; set; }
    public int ReleaseYear { get; set; }

    // Methods
    public void BikeStart()
    {
        // Implementation
    }

    public void BikeStop()
    {
        // Implementation
    }

    // Constructor
    public Bike()
    { }

    public Bike(string model, string madeIn, int releaseYear)
    {
        Model = model;
        MadeIn = madeIn;
        ReleaseYear = releaseYear;
    }
}
```

The provided class **Bike** in C# is a blueprint for creating bike objects, encapsulating relevant properties and behaviors. It defines three public fields: **Model**, **MadeIn**, and **ReleaseYear**, each with auto-implemented properties allowing easy access and modification of the bike's model, country of manufacture, and release year. The class also includes two methods, **BikeStart** and **BikeStop**, which represent actions that a motorcycle can perform, although their implementations are not detailed in the preceding code. These methods illustrate how behavior can be encapsulated within a class, allowing objects created from the class to perform specific actions.

Additionally, the **Bike** class features a parameterized constructor, enabling the initialization of bike objects with specific values for **Model**, **MadeIn**, and **ReleaseYear** when they are created. This constructor ensures that every instance of the Bike class starts with a defined state. The class's design highlights fundamental principles of OOP, such as encapsulation, where data and behaviors are bundled together, and abstraction, where implementation details are hidden from the user, providing a simplified interface for interaction. Through this structure, the **Bike** class demonstrates how OOP facilitates the creation of modular, reusable, and maintainable code.

Properties in C# classes

Properties in C# offer a flexible way to read, write, or compute the values of private fields. They act like fields that manage access while preserving data integrity and encapsulation. They encapsulate a private field by providing public methods to get and set its value, allowing controlled access. This control ensures that the internal state of an object can be accessed or modified only in predefined ways, which enhances data security and integrity.

One of the key advantages of using properties is that they maintain backward compatibility with older code. When you switch from public fields to properties, the external interface remains the same, meaning the code that uses your class does not need to change. Properties support both get and set accessors. The get accessor returns the property value, while the set accessor assigns a new value. Using these accessors, you can introduce logic that runs when the property is accessed or modified, such as validation or transformation of the data.

Additionally, properties can be made read-only or write-only. A read-only property contains only a get accessor, ensuring the value can be retrieved but not modified. Conversely, a write-only property contains only a set accessor, allowing the value to be set but not read. This flexibility helps enforce constraints and rules on how data is accessed and manipulated:

```
public class Student
{
    private string stdname;
    public string StdName
    {
        get { return stdname; }
        set { stdname = value; }
    }
}
```

Auto-implemented properties

C# also offers auto-implemented properties, providing a concise syntax for defining properties without needing explicit backing fields. The compiler automatically generates the backing field, reducing boilerplate code and enhancing readability. These properties can be initialized either directly when they are declared or within the class's constructors, offering further flexibility in managing the state of objects.

Here is a simple example of how to define a class in C# that models a student. This **Student** class includes properties for the student's name and ID, and a constructor to initialize the ID. The **StdName** property has both **public get** and **set** accessors, while the **StdID** property restricts its **get** accessor to private, ensuring encapsulation. This demonstrates how to manage access control for class members in C#:

```
public class Student
{
    public string StdName { get; set; } = "Amelia";
    public int StdID { private get; set; }

    public Student(int stdId)
    {
        StdID = stdId;
    }
}
```

Methods in C# classes

Methods in C# are vital components that define the behaviors and actions of objects, encapsulating reusable code for specific tasks, data manipulation, or computations. They promote modular design by hiding implementation details, enhancing code reusability, and allowing for parameterization and return of values, thus providing flexibility in performing operations. Access modifiers can control methods, enabling encapsulation and secure data handling. Additionally, method overloading allows multiple methods with the same name but different parameters, improving code readability and flexibility. Understanding and effectively using methods is crucial for building robust, maintainable object-oriented applications.

Creating and calling methods

In the following code, the **Arithmetic** class defines two **Multiply** methods, showcasing method overloading by having methods with the same name but different parameter types. The first **Multiply** method takes two integers, **x** and **y**, multiplies them, and returns the result as an integer. The second **Multiply** method takes two doubles, **a** and

b, performs the multiplication, and returns the result as a double. In the **Main** method, an instance of the **Arithmetic** class, named calculate, is created. The integer version of the **Multiply** method is then called with the arguments **5** and **8**, and the result is stored in the variable product. Finally, the result is printed to the console using **Console.WriteLine**, demonstrating how to call methods, pass parameters, and handle return values in C#. This example illustrates the flexibility and reusability of methods in C# through encapsulation and method overloading.

In C#, method overloading allows you to define multiple methods with the same name but different parameter types or numbers. Here is an example with a class called **Arithmetic** that demonstrates the overloading of the **Multiply** method. The first **Multiply** method accepts two integers, while the second accepts two doubles. This allows for flexible use of the method with different data types, showcasing polymorphism in action. Following is the implementation:

```
public class Arithmetic
{
    public int Multiply(int x, int y)
    {
        return x * y;
    }

    public double Multiply(double a, double b)
    {
        return a * b;
    }
}


Arithmetic calculate = new Arithmetic();
int product = calculate.Multiply(5, 8);
Console.WriteLine($"Product = {product}");
```

Constructors in C#

Constructors are unique methods in C# designed to initialize objects when they are created. They play a crucial role in setting up an object's initial state by assigning values to its fields or properties. Constructors come in two primary forms: default constructors and parameterized constructors.

A default constructor initializes objects without requiring any parameters. It is automatically generated by the C# compiler if no other constructors are explicitly defined in the class. This type of constructor ensures that the object is created and its fields are set to default values (for example, zero for numeric types, null for reference types). In the following example, the **Student** class includes an explicit default constructor:

```
public class Student
{
    public Student() { }
}
```

On the other hand, a parameterized constructor allows initializing objects with specific values at the time of their creation. This type of constructor takes parameters, which are used to set the initial values of the object's fields or properties. Parameterized constructors offer greater flexibility and control over the object's initialization process. The following example illustrates a student class with a parameterized constructor:

```
public class Student
{
    public string StdName { get; set; }
    public int StdId { get; set; }

    public Student(string stdname, int stdid)
    {
        StdName = stdname;
        StdId = stdid;
    }
}
```

Understanding objects in C#

Creating and manipulating objects involves understanding how to instantiate and interact with class instances effectively. Using the **Bike** class from the previous section:

```
// Object Creation
Bike myBike = new Bike("Altis", "Japan", 2022);

// Accessing Members
myBike.Model = "Altis";
myBike.BikeStart();
```

Object initializers

Object initializers in C# provide a concise and readable way to initialize an object's properties without directly invoking a constructor for each property assignment. This feature is particularly beneficial when dealing with classes that have multiple properties, allowing you to set values in a more streamlined manner.

Object initializers allow you to assign values to an object's properties using a special syntax at the time of creation. This approach simplifies the initialization process, making the code cleaner and easier to read. Here is an example using the **Bike** class:

```
Bike mybike = new Bike()
{
    Model = "Altis",
    MadeIn = "Japan",
    ReleaseYear = 2022
};


myBike.BikeStart();
```

Object initializers can also be used with parameterized constructors, providing additional flexibility. This combination allows you to initialize some properties through the constructor while setting or overriding other properties using the object initializer. Here is an example demonstrating this usage:

```
Bike myBike1 = new Bike("Altis", "Japan", 2022)
{
    Model = "Corolla",
    // Additional properties can be set or overridden here
};


myBike1.BikeStart();
```

Encapsulation in C#

Encapsulation is a fundamental principle of OOP that involves bundling data and methods that operate on that data within a single class, restricting direct access to some of the object's components. By making fields private and providing public methods (getters and setters) to access and modify them, encapsulation ensures that an object's internal state can only be controlled. This data-hiding mechanism prevents unauthorized access and modifications, thus maintaining the integrity of the data. For instance, validation logic can be incorporated into setter methods to ensure that only valid data is assigned to the fields, enhancing data security and consistency.

Moreover, encapsulation enhances code maintainability and abstraction. By presenting a simplified interface through public methods, encapsulation hides a class's complex internal implementation details from the outside world, making the code easier to understand and use. This abstraction allows developers to interact with an object based on what it does rather than how it does. Additionally, encapsulation facilitates modular design, where changes to the internal workings of a class can be made without affecting other parts of the program that rely on the class as long as the public interface remains unchanged. This modularity simplifies debugging and allows for flexible and extensible code, making it easier to update and maintain as the system evolves.

Access modifiers

In C#, access modifiers are used to control the accessibility of class members, such as fields, properties, and methods, determining which parts of the code can interact with these members. Access modifiers are essential for encapsulation, security, and code organization. There are four primary access modifiers in C#, which are described as follows.

Members declared as public are accessible from any other class or assembly. This means that public members can be accessed from anywhere in the code, providing the broadest level of accessibility. Public access is helpful when you want to expose certain functionalities or data to other parts of your or external applications.

The following example illustrates a simple **Library** class in C#. The class contains a property **Name** to store the library's name, and a method **OpenLibrary()** that will handle the logic for opening the library (though the implementation is not provided in this snippet). This class demonstrates how to define properties and methods in C#, allowing future expansion as needed for more complex functionality:

```
public class Library
{
    public string Name { get; set; }
    public void OpenLibrary()
    {
        // Implementation
    }
}
```

In this example, the **Name** property and the **OpenLibrary** method are accessible from any other class.

Members declared as private are accessible only within the same class, the most restrictive access level. Private members cannot be accessed or modified from outside the class, which is useful for hiding implementation details and protecting an object's internal state.

In the following example, the **Library** class demonstrates how to encapsulate internal data and behavior using private members. The **libraryCode** field is marked private, meaning it can only be accessed and modified within the class itself. Additionally, the **GenerateLibraryCode()** method, which will contain the logic for generating a unique library code, is also private, ensuring that this functionality is hidden from outside classes. This encapsulation is a key principle of object-oriented programming, helping to protect and manage data within the class:

```
public class Library
{
    private string libraryCode;
    private void GenerateLibraryCode()
    {
        // Implementation
    }
}
```

The **libraryCode** field and the **GenerateLibraryCode** method are only accessible within the **Library** class.

Members declared as protected are accessible within the same class and any derived classes (subclasses). This access level is practical when allowing subclasses to access and modify certain base class members while keeping them hidden from other application parts.

In the following example, we demonstrate the concept of inheritance and access modifiers in C#. The **Library** class has a **Location** property that is marked as protected, meaning it can only be accessed by the class itself and any derived classes. The **PublicLibrary** class inherits from **Library** and can access the **Location** property because of the protected modifier. The **SetLocation()** method in **PublicLibrary** allows setting the **Location** value, demonstrating how a derived class can interact with protected members of its base class:

```
public class Library
{
    protected string Location { get; set; }
}


public class PublicLibrary: Library
{
    public void SetLocation(string location)
    {
        Location = location;
    }
}
```

In this example, the **Location** property is accessible within the **Library** class and its subclass, **PublicLibrary**.

Members declared as internal are accessible only within the same assembly (or module). This access level helps organize code within a single project, ensuring that certain members are not exposed outside the assembly.

In the following example, the **Library** class uses the internal access modifier, which restricts access to the current assembly (or project). The **Address** property is also marked as internal, meaning it can only be accessed by other classes within the same assembly. This provides a way to encapsulate members while still allowing access to related classes within the same application or library, but not from external assemblies:

```
internal class Library
{
    internal string Address { get; set; }
}
```

Here, the **Address** property is accessible only within the same assembly as the **Library** class.

Static members in C#

Static members belong to the class itself, shared across all instances. They are defined with the **static** keyword and include fields, properties, methods, and events.

In the following example, the **Multiply** method within the **Arithmetic** class is defined as **static**, meaning it belongs to the class itself rather than to a specific instance of the class. This allows the method to be called directly on the class without needing to create an object. Static methods are useful when the behavior does not depend on instance data and is shared across all instances:

```
public class Arithmetic
{
    public static int Multiply(int x, int y)
    {
        return x * y;
    }
}
```

Static classes

Static classes cannot be instantiated and contain only static members, ideal for utility or helper methods.

In the following example, we define a **MathToolkit** class as static, which means it cannot be instantiated, and all its members must also be static. The **Pi** constant is declared as **static**, allowing it to be shared across all methods in the class. The **FindCircumference** method calculates the circumference of a circle using the formula **2 * Pi** * radius. Since both the class and its members are static, you can call the method directly without creating an instance of the class:

```
public static class MathToolkit
{
    public static double Pi = 3.141593;

    public static double FindCircumference(double radius)
    {
        return 2 * Pi * radius;
    }
}
```

Nested classes in C#

Nested classes are defined within another class and help organize related classes or encapsulate helper classes closely tied to their parent class.

In the following example, the **MainClass** contains a nested class called **SubClass**. The **SubClass** has a method **Show()** that displays a message. Nested classes in C# allow grouping logically related classes together, which can help in organizing and encapsulating code. The **SubClass** is defined inside **MainClass**, meaning it is only accessible through an instance of **MainClass** or directly if the outer class allows it:

```
public class MainClass
{
    public class SubClass
    {
        public void Show()
        {
            Console.WriteLine("This message is from the nested class");
        }
    }
}
```

Use nested classes for solid relationships with the parent class, logical grouping, and encapsulation of helper functionality.

Partial classes in C#

Partial classes allow splitting a class definition across multiple files, enhancing code organization and maintainability. Each part must use the **partial** keyword.

In the following example, the **PartialClass** is defined using the **partial** keyword, which allows its implementation to be split across multiple files. This is useful when you want to organize a large class across different files for better maintainability and clarity.

Both File 1 and File 2 contain parts of the same class, each defining different methods. When the program is compiled, these parts are combined into a single class:

```
// File 1: PartialClass1.cs
public partial class PartialClass
{
    public void Part1Method()
    {
        Console.WriteLine("This method belongs to File 1");
    }
}


// File 2: PartialClass2.cs
public partial class PartialClass
{
    public void Part2Method()
    {
        Console.WriteLine("This method belongs to File 2");
    }
}
```

Practical applications

You are tasked with creating an application to manage buyers and their purchases in an e-commerce platform. Each buyer can have multiple purchases, and you need to keep track of the details of each purchase and the buyer's information. Your application should allow you to add purchases for a buyer and display the buyer's details along with all their purchases.

Requirements:

- Create a **Purchase** class with the following properties and methods:
  - **Properties:**
    - **PurchaseId (int):** A unique identifier for each purchase.
    - **ItemName (string):** The name of the purchased item.
    - **Cost (decimal):** The cost of a single item unit.
    - **ItemCount (int):** The number of items purchased.
  - **Constructor:**
    - Initializes the **PurchaseId, ItemName, Cost**, and **ItemCount** properties.

o Methods:

- **NetCost()**: Calculates and returns the total purchase cost (**Cost * ItemCount**).

- Create a **Buyer** class with the following properties and methods:

  o **Properties:**

    - **BuyerName (string):** The name of the buyer.
    - **BuyerEmail (string):** The email address of the buyer.
    - **Purchases (List<Purchase>):** A list of purchases the buyer makes.

  o **Constructor:**

    - Initializes the **BuyerName** and **BuyerEmail** properties and initializes the purchases list.

  o **Methods:**

    - **OrderPlacement(Purchase purchase):** This function adds a new purchase to the buyer's list of purchases and prints a confirmation message.
    - **ShowBuyerInformation():** Displays the buyer's name, email, and details of all their purchases, including the total cost of each purchase.

- Write a **program** class that:

  o Creates an instance of the **Buyer** class.
  o Creates several purchase objects and adds them to the buyer's list.
  o Displays the buyer's information along with all their purchases.

Solution code:

The following code meets the preceding requirements and provides a complete solution to the problem:

```
using System;
using System.Collections.Generic;

public class Purchase
{
    public int PurchaseId { get; set; }
    public string ItemName { get; set; }
    public decimal Cost { get; set; }
    public int ItemCount { get; set; }
```

```csharp
    public Purchase(int purchaseId, string itemName, decimal cost, int
itemCount)
    {
        PurchaseId = purchaseId;
        ItemName = itemName;
        Cost = cost;
        ItemCount = itemCount;
    }

    public decimal NetCost()
    {
        return Cost * ItemCount;
    }
}

public class Buyer
{
    public string BuyerName { get; set; }
    public string BuyerEmail { get; set; }
    public List<Purchase> Purchases { get; set; }

    public Buyer(string buyerName, string buyerEmail)
    {
        BuyerName = buyerName;
        BuyerEmail = buyerEmail;
        Purchases = new List<Purchase>();
    }

    public void OrderPlacement(Purchase purchase)
    {
        Purchases.Add(purchase);
        Console.WriteLine($"Order placed for {purchase.ItemName} by
{BuyerName}");
    }

    public void ShowBuyerInformation()
    {
        Console.WriteLine($"Buyer Name: {BuyerName}");
```

```
            Console.WriteLine($"Buyer Email: {BuyerEmail}");
            Console.WriteLine("Purchases:");
            foreach (var purchase in Purchases)
            {
                Console.WriteLine($"  Purchase Id: {purchase.PurchaseId}");
                Console.WriteLine($"  Product: {purchase.ItemName}");
                Console.WriteLine($"  Cost: ${purchase.Cost}");
                Console.WriteLine($"  ItemCount: {purchase.ItemCount}");
                Console.WriteLine($"  Total: ${purchase.NetCost()}");
                Console.WriteLine();
            }
        }
    }
}


public class Exanmple
{
    public static void Main(string[] args)
    {
        Buyer buyer1 = new Buyer("Cynthia", "Cynthia@example.com");
        Purchase order1 = new Purchase(1, "Tablet", 539.99m, 2);
        Purchase order2 = new Purchase(2, "Earbuds", 299.99m, 3);

        buyer1.OrderPlacement(order1);
        buyer1.OrderPlacement(order2);

        Console.WriteLine();
        buyer1.ShowBuyerInformation();
    }
}
```

Output:
```
Order placed for Tablet by Cynthia
Order placed for Earbuds by Cynthia

Buyer Name: Cynthia
Buyer Email: Cynthia@example.com
Purchases:
  Purchase Id: 1
```

```
Product: Tablet
Cost: $539.99
ItemCount: 2
Total: $1079.98

Purchase Id: 2
Product: Earbuds
Cost: $299.99
ItemCount: 3
Total: $899.97
```

Explanation:

- **Purchase class**: Defines the structure for a purchase, including properties for the purchase ID, item name, cost, and item count. It also includes a method to calculate the total cost of the purchase.

- **Buyer class**: This defines the structure for a buyer, including properties for the buyer's name, email, and list of purchases. It also includes methods to add a purchase to the list and display the buyer's information along with all their purchases.

- **Program class**: Demonstrates the creation of a **Buyer** object, adds several purchase objects to the buyer's list, and displays the buyer's information, including the details of all purchases.

Conclusion

In this chapter, we have explored the foundational concepts of classes and objects within the C# programming language, which are central to OOP. We began by understanding how classes serve as blueprints for objects, encapsulating data and behavior into a single entity. This encapsulation is critical for creating organized, modular code that is easier to manage and maintain. By examining the structure of a class, including fields, properties, methods, and constructors, we learned how to define and utilize these components to model real-world entities and abstract concepts effectively.

Furthermore, we learned the principles of OOP, such as encapsulation, inheritance, polymorphism, and abstraction, highlighting their importance in building robust and scalable software. We also explored static members, nested classes, and partial classes, which provide additional tools for organizing and sharing code within and across applications. Through practical examples, we saw how these concepts are applied in real-world scenarios, demonstrating their utility in various domains, from software systems to business applications. This chapter has equipped you with the essential knowledge to leverage OOP in C#, paving the way for developing more sophisticated and maintainable software solutions.

As we move into the next chapter, we will explore two powerful concepts in C#: interfaces and polymorphism. These concepts are essential for designing flexible, maintainable, and scalable applications. Interfaces allow us to define a contract that ensures consistency across classes, while polymorphism enables objects to be treated as instances of their parent types, allowing for dynamic and flexible behavior. By understanding and leveraging these tools, you will gain the ability to write more modular and reusable code, setting the stage for advanced software design patterns and practices.

Multiple choice questions

1. **What is the primary purpose of a class in C#?**

    a. To define a data structure for storing variables only

    b. To encapsulate data and behavior into a single unit

    c. To execute a specific sequence of code

    d. To manage the memory allocation for applications

2. **Which of the following keywords defines a class in C#?**

    a. struct

    b. object

    c. class

    d. public

3. **What is encapsulation in OOP?**

    a. The ability of different classes to inherit methods and properties from a base class.

    b. The process of hiding the internal state and requiring all interactions to be performed through an object's methods.

    c. The ability to create multiple methods with the same name but different parameters.

    d. The concept of using the same method name in different classes.

4. **Which of the following correctly describes a constructor in C#?**

    a. A method that is called explicitly to destroy an object.

    b. A special method used to initialize objects when they are created.

    c. A method used to perform repetitive tasks within a class.

    d. A method that defines the behavior of an object.

5. **In C#, how do you access a public property named Model of an object myBike of the class Bike?**

   a. myBike.getModel()

   b. myBike->Model

   c. myBike.Model

   d. myBike["Model"]

Answers

1. (b) To encapsulate data and behavior into a single unit

2. (c) class

3. (b) The process of hiding the internal state and requiring all interactions to be performed through an object's methods.

4. (b) A special method used to initialize objects when they are created.

5. (c) myBike.Model

Practice problems

1. You are tasked with creating a simple application to manage a library of books. Each book has a title, author, publication year, and a method to display its details. Additionally, you need to create a library class that can hold a collection of books and provide functionality to add new books and display the details of all books in the library.

   Requirements:

   Create a Book class with the following properties and methods:

   a. **Properties:**

       i.   Title (string)

       ii.   Author (string)

       iii. PublicationYear (int)

   b. **Methods:**

       i.   **DisplayDetails()**: This method should print the book's title, author, and publication year.

   Create a Library class with the following properties and methods:

   a. **Properties:**

       i.   Books (a collection of Book objects)

b. **Methods:**

    i.   **AddBook(Book book)**: This method should add a new book to the library's collection.

    ii.   **DisplayAllBooks()**: This method should iterate through the collection of books and call DisplayDetails() for each book to print its details.

Write a program that creates an instance of the Library class, adds a few books to the library, and displays the details of all the books in the library.

Your code should enable the execution of the following:

```
using System;

class Program
{
    static void Main(string[] args)
    {
        Library library = new Library();

        Book book1 = new Book("1984", "George Orwell", 1949);
        Book book2 = new Book("To Kill a Mockingbird", "Harper Lee",
1960);
        Book book3 = new Book("The Great Gatsby", "F. Scott
Fitzgerald", 1925);

        library.AddBook(book1);
        library.AddBook(book2);
        library.AddBook(book3);

        library.DisplayAllBooks();
    }
}
```

2. You are tasked with creating a simple application to manage a fleet of vehicles. Each vehicle has a make, model, year of manufacture, and a method for displaying its details. Additionally, you need to create a garage class that can hold a collection of vehicles, provide the functionality to add new vehicles and display the details of all vehicles in the garage.

Requirements:

Create a Vehicle class with the following properties and methods:

a. **Properties:**

   i.   Make (string)

   ii.   Model (string)

   iii. YearOfManufacture (int)

a. **Methods:**

   i.   **DisplayDetails()**: This method should print the vehicle's make, model, and year of manufacture.

Create a Garage class with the following properties and methods:

a. **Properties:**

   i.   Vehicles (a collection of Vehicle objects)

b. **Methods:**

   i.   **AddVehicle(Vehicle vehicle)**: This method should add a new vehicle to the garage's collection.

   ii. **DisplayAllVehicles()**: This method should iterate through the collection of vehicles and call DisplayDetails() for each vehicle to print its details.

Write a program that creates an instance of the Garage class, adds a few vehicles to the garage, and display the details of all the vehicles in the garage.

Your code should run with the following.

```
using System;

class Program
{
    static void Main(string[] args)
    {
        Garage garage = new Garage();

        Vehicle vehicle1 = new Vehicle(«Toyota», «Camry», 2019);
        Vehicle vehicle2 = new Vehicle(«Honda», «Civic», 2018);
        Vehicle vehicle3 = new Vehicle(«Ford», «Mustang», 2020);

        garage.AddVehicle(vehicle1);
        garage.AddVehicle(vehicle2);
        garage.AddVehicle(vehicle3);

        garage.DisplayAllVehicles();
    }
}
```

CHAPTER 6

C# Interfaces and Polymorphism

Introduction

This chapter explores the concepts of interfaces and polymorphism in C#. These features are crucial for creating flexible, reusable, and maintainable code. Interfaces in C# act as contracts, defining methods and properties that a class must implement without providing any implementation details, allowing different classes to implement the same functionalities uniquely. Polymorphism enables objects of different classes to be treated as objects of a common superclass or interface, allowing a single interface to represent different underlying forms.

Mastering interfaces and polymorphism is not just about understanding abstract concepts. It is about creating modular and manageable code that can be easily extended and reused. These concepts are vital for developing scalable applications requiring plugins, dependency injection, or other forms of extensibility. This chapter will not only cover the structure and declaration of interfaces but also show you how to implement them in classes and the types of polymorphism in C#, as well as provide practical examples in real-world applications. You will also learn how to combine interfaces and abstract classes for flexible design, making your code more adaptable and robust.

By the end of this chapter, you will understand how to define and use interfaces, leverage polymorphism to write adaptable code, and apply these concepts in various programming scenarios, preparing you to tackle more advanced C# programming challenges and design robust software systems

Structure

This chapter covers the following topics:

- Introducing interfaces in C#
- Implementing an interface in a class
- Understanding polymorphism
- Abstract classes and methods
- Using interfaces for polymorphism
- Casting and type checking with interfaces
- Applications of interfaces and polymorphism

Objectives

By the end of this chapter, you will be able to understand the purpose and structure of interfaces in C# and declare and implement interfaces in your classes. You will also recognize the importance of polymorphism and how it enhances code flexibility and reusability. You will learn how to differentiate between compile-time and run-time polymorphism and implement both in your code, and utilize abstract classes alongside interfaces to create robust and maintainable software designs.

Introducing interfaces in C#

An interface in C# is a binding agreement that describes a class's requirements to implement some methods or properties. Unlike classes, interfaces never have any code to implement those; they only specify the members' names that must be implemented by classes, saying that they adhere to these particular contracts. When you think about an interface, imagine the blueprint that outlines what specific capabilities an object must have, but does not dictate how these capabilities should be achieved by the class implementing it.

For example, consider an interface '**IShape**' that might define a method '**Draw**'. Any class implementing '**IShape**' would need to provide its version of the '**Draw**' method:

```
public interface IShape
{
    void Draw();
}

public class Circle : IShape
{
    public void Draw()
```

```
    {
        Console.WriteLine("Drawing a Circle");
    }
}
```

Here, '**Circle**' implements the '**IShape**' interface by providing code for the '**Draw**' method.

Interfaces in C# are potent tools defining a class's capabilities. This framework lets programmers write for agreements without specifying exactly how those agreements must be met. This section describes an interface structure and how it is declared and implemented in class.

Structure of an interface

An '**interface**' is defined using the keyword '**interface**'. It has methods, properties, events, or indexers declared but no implementation. Here is the basic structure of an interface:

```
public interface IExample
{
    void MethodA();
    int PropertyB { get; set; }
}
```

The preceding example contains an interface called '**IExample**' and two members, '**MethodA**' and '**PropertyB**'. Any class that implements this interface must implement each of these members.

Declaring an interface

Declaring an interface in C# is straightforward. You use the '**interface**' keyword followed by the interface name. By convention, interface names in C# start with an uppercase "**I**" to distinguish them from classes and other types.

Here is an example of declaring an interface:

```
public interface IAnimal
{
    void MakeSound();
    void Move();
}
```

This sample defines an interface called '**IAnimal**' with two methods: '**MakeSound()**' and '**Move()**'.

Implementing an interface in a class

Once the interface is defined, all classes that implement it should contain some actual implementation. This is done using the : '**InterfaceName**' syntax in the class declaration.

Here is an example of a class implementing the '**IAnimal**' interface:

```csharp
public class Dog : IAnimal
{
    public void MakeSound()
    {
        Console.WriteLine("Bark");
    }

    public void Move()
    {
        Console.WriteLine("Run");
    }
}
```

As we can see, the class '**Dog**' has implemented the '**IAnimal**' interface using the '**MakeSound**' and '**Move**' methods. Here, the idea of an abstract class arises when a class does not implement all the members of an interface. So, that should be marked as an **abstract** class. For instance:

```csharp
public abstract class AbstractAnimal : IAnimal
{
    public abstract void MakeSound();
    public void Move()
    {
        Console.WriteLine("Abstract animal moving");
    }
}
```

Here, '**AbstractAnimal**' is provided with the '**Move**' implementation, while the '**MakeSound**' method is left as an abstract method, which has to be implemented by any non-abstract derived class.

Implementing interfaces allows the creation of classes that adhere to a specific contract, ensuring consistency and predictability in how those classes behave. This facilitates polymorphism, through which different classes can be used interchangeably if they implement the same interfaces, thereby improving the flexibility and scalability of your code.

Interface properties

In C#, interfaces can include properties and methods that classes or structs must implement. Understanding how to define and enforce these members is crucial for leveraging the power of interfaces. Properties within interfaces are similar to properties within classes but only have property signatures without any actual implementations. A property in an interface can be read-only, write-only, or read-write.

Consider the following example of an interface with properties:

```
public interface IVehicle
{
    string Make { get; set; }
    string Model { get; set; }
    int Year { get; }
}
```

The '**IVehicle**' interface contains three properties: '**Make**,' '**Model**,' and '**Year**,' where '**Make**' and '**Model**' are read-write and '**Year**' is read-only.

These properties must be implemented by a class that implements the following interface:

```
public class Car : IVehicle
{
    public string Make { get; set; }
    public string Model { get; set; }
    public int Year { get; private set; }

    public Car(string make, string model, int year)
    {
        Make = make;
        Model = model;
        Year = year;
    }
}
```

The '**Car**' class provides concrete implementations for the '**Make**,' '**Model**,' and '**Year**' properties in this implementation.

Methods in interfaces

Methods in interfaces are declared similar to properties. They include the method signature without the implementation, and the implementing class must provide the body for these methods.

Here is an example of an interface with methods:

```
public interface IPrinter
{
    void Print(string document);
    void Scan(string document);
}
```

The 'IPrinter' interface specifies two methods in this example: 'Print' and 'Scan'.

A class implementing this interface must specify the method's specific implementation.

Here is an example of how a class can implement an interface in C#. The Printer class implements the IPrinter interface, providing concrete implementations for the Print and Scan methods, which ensure that any class implementing this interface adheres to the contract defined by the interface:

```
public class Printer : IPrinter
{
    public void Print(string document)
    {
        Console.WriteLine($"Printing: {document}");
    }

    public void Scan(string document)
    {
        Console.WriteLine($"Scanning: {document}");
    }
}
```

In this implementation, the 'Printer' class provides concrete implementations for the 'Print' and 'Scan' methods.

Explicit interface implementation

Explicit interface implementation is another feature of C#. This feature is used to implement multiple interfaces with the same name of methods or properties. Explicit implementation allows the class to provide separate implementations for each interface.

Here is an example of explicit interface implementation:

```
public interface IWriter
{
    void Write(string text);
}
```

```csharp
public interface IFileWriter
{
    void Write(string filePath);
}

public class DocumentWriter : IWriter, IFileWriter
{
    void IWriter.Write(string text)
    {
        Console.WriteLine($"Writing text: {text}");
    }

    void IFileWriter.Write(string filePath)
    {
        Console.WriteLine($"Writing to file: {filePath}");
    }
}
```

In this example, **'DocumentWriter'** implements both interfaces, **'IWriter'** and **'IFileWriter'**. The **'Write'** method is implemented explicitly for each of them, ensuring the right method calls, depending on which one of the implemented interfaces is being referred to.

Interface members can be implemented explicitly if you want to control how they are accessed through the implementing class or avoid naming conflicts.

Understanding polymorphism

Polymorphism is an object-oriented programming technique in which objects of different types can be treated as a single super-type. In the case of C#, polymorphism mainly involves inheritance and interfaces. This increases the adaptability and reusability of code by allowing developers to create methods that can interact with objects of different types.

In C#, these concepts are essential for the following reasons:

- **Code flexibility and reusability**: By defining interfaces, you create a set of rules that multiple classes can follow, making your code more flexible and reusable. Therefore, you can change the implementations without modifying the code based on them.

- **Loose coupling**: Interfaces help reduce dependencies between classes. When classes rely on interfaces instead of specific implementations, they are less tightly coupled, which makes the code easier to maintain and modify.

- **Enhancing testability**: Using interfaces can make unit testing easier. By using mock object implementations of the interfaces, you can test classes for their interaction without relying on the real implementation.

- **Facilitating polymorphism**: Interfaces enable polymorphic behavior. Code can be written to work with different objects, implementing a familiar interface and making it more general and versatile.

In the following sections, we will discuss how to define and use interfaces in C#, examine several types of polymorphism, and examine practical examples that help illustrate these concepts.

Polymorphism in C#

Polymorphism, in simple terms, is creating a single interface for entities of many types. C# implements polymorphism by function overloading, function overriding, operator overloading, and shadowing. In general, it might be categorized into the following two categories inside C#:

- Static or compile-time polymorphism is the type of polymorphism that is resolved during compilation. It is achieved through method overloading and operator overloading.

- Dynamic or run-time polymorphism is resolved at runtime. It is achieved through method overriding and interface implementation.

Compile-time or static polymorphism

It may be accomplished by declaring many methods in a class with the same name but distinct signatures. This is known as method overloading. The correct method to call is determined at compile time based on the method signature.

Here is an example of method overloading:

```
public class MathOperations
{
    public int Add(int a, int b)
    {
        return a + b;
    }

    public double Add(double a, double b)
    {
        return a + b;
    }
}
```

In this example, the '`MathOperations`' class has two '**Add**' methods with different parameter types. The appropriate method is chosen depending on the arguments passed while calling the methods.

Another example of compile-time polymorphism is operator overloading. Here, operators are redefined to perform with user-defined data types. Here is a simple example:

```
public class Complex
{
    public int Real { get; set; }
    public int Imaginary { get; set; }

    public Complex(int real, int imaginary)
    {
        Real = real;
        Imaginary = imaginary;
    }

    public static Complex operator +(Complex x, Complex y)
    {
        return new Complex(x.Real + y.Real, x.Imaginary + y.Imaginary);
    }
}
```

This example adds two complex objects by overloading the '**+**' operator.

Run-time or dynamic polymorphism

Dynamic polymorphism is achieved by function overriding. In dynamic polymorphism, the base class defines a **virtual** or **abstract** method that is later overridden by one or more derived classes. The correct method to invoke is determined at runtime based on the object type.

Here is an example of method overriding:

```
public class Animal
{
    public virtual void MakeSound()
    {
        Console.WriteLine("Animal sound");
    }
}
```

```csharp
public class Dog : Animal
{
    public override void MakeSound()
    {
        Console.WriteLine("Bark");
    }
}

public class Cat : Animal
{
    public override void MakeSound()
    {
        Console.WriteLine("Meow");
    }
}
```

Here, '**MakeSound**' is defined in the base class '**Animal**' and is overridden by the derived classes '**Dog**' and '**Cat**'. At run time, the appropriate method is called based on the type of the object:

```csharp
Animal myDog = new Dog();
Animal myCat = new Cat();

myDog.MakeSound(); // Outputs: Bark
myCat.MakeSound(); // Outputs: Meow
```

Interfaces also facilitate run-time polymorphism. When a class implements an interface, it provides definite implementations for the interface methods, while the actual process is determined in the run-time.

Here is an example:

```csharp
public interface IShape
{
    void Draw();
}

public class Circle : IShape
{
    public void Draw()
    {
```

```
        Console.WriteLine("Drawing a Circle");
    }
}

public class Square : IShape
{
    public void Draw()
    {
        Console.WriteLine("Drawing a Square");
    }
}
```

With polymorphism, you can write code that works with the '**IShape**' interface, and at run time, the appropriate '**Draw**' method is called, based on the actual object type:

```
IShape shape1 = new Circle();
IShape shape2 = new Square();

shape1.Draw(); // Outputs: Drawing a Circle
shape2.Draw(); // Outputs: Drawing a Square
```

Abstract classes and methods

Abstract classes and methods in C# allow you to define a class's blueprint without providing a full implementation. They serve as a foundation for other classes, allowing you to establish common functionality while leaving specific details to derived classes.

Understanding abstract classes

An abstract class is one in which an instance cannot be created by itself but is intended to be inherited by other classes. You may have abstract methods, methods without body implementations, and fully implemented methods in an abstract class. It is one of the most common ways we carry out polymorphism, for instance, implementation. Abstract courses are practical when you want a standard base class that enforces specific methods or properties but allows derived classes to implement or override the method's functionality.

Here is an example of an **abstract** class:

```
public abstract class Animal
{
    public string Name { get; set; }

    public Animal(string name)
```

```
    {
        Name = name;
    }

    public void Eat()
    {
        Console.WriteLine($"{Name} is eating.");
    }

    public abstract void MakeSound();
}
```

In this example, the '**Animal**' class is abstract. It includes a concrete method, '**Eat**,' and an abstract method, '**MakeSound**.' Any class that inherits from '**Animal**' must implement the '**MakeSound**' method.

Declaring abstract methods

Abstract methods are declared within an abstract class and do not have an implementation. The derived class must provide the implementation for these methods. Declaring an **abstract** method ensures that all subclasses offer specific behavior for the process.

Here is how you declare an abstract method:

```
public abstract class Shape
{
    public abstract void Draw();
}
```

In the preceding example, class '**Shape**' declares an abstract method, '**Draw**.' All the classes that derive from '**Shape**' must implement the '**Draw**' method.

Implementing abstract methods

The abstract methods are implemented by the class derived from the abstract class. This is known as contracting, which requires the derived class to follow the contract established by the abstract class.

The following is an example that defines an **abstract** method:

```
public class Circle : Shape
{
    public override void Draw()
    {
```

```
            Console.WriteLine("Drawing a Circle");
    }
}

public class Square : Shape
{
    public override void Draw()
    {
        Console.WriteLine("Drawing a Square");
    }
}
```

In this example, classes '**Circle**' and '**Square**' are inherited from class '**Shape**' and override '**Draw.**'

Using interfaces for polymorphism

This section will explore how interfaces facilitate polymorphism, including implementing multiple interfaces and the benefits of interface-based polymorphism.

Implementing multiple interfaces

An essential advantage of interfaces is that a class can implement any number of different interfaces. This allows for the inheritance of behavior from multiple sources, increasing flexibility and code reusability.

Here is an example of a class implementing multiple interfaces:

```
public interface IPlayable
{
    void Play();
}

public interface IRecordable
{
    void Record();
}

public class MediaDevice : IPlayable, IRecordable
{
    public void Play()
```

```
    {
        Console.WriteLine("Playing media");
    }

    public void Record()
    {
        Console.WriteLine("Recording media");
    }
}
```

Here, the '**MediaDevice**' class has implemented the '**Play()**' and '**Record()**' defined by the '**IPlayable**' and '**IRecordable**' interfaces.

Interface-based polymorphism

Interface-based polymorphism allows objects to be treated as instances of their interface type, regardless of their specific class type. Relying on interfaces rather than specific implementations promotes flexibility and simplifies code maintenance.

Here is an example demonstrating interface-based polymorphism:

```
public interface IShape
{
    void Draw();
}

public class Circle : IShape
{
    public void Draw()
    {
        Console.WriteLine("Drawing a Circle");
    }
}

public class Square : IShape
{
    public void Draw()
    {
        Console.WriteLine("Drawing a Square");
    }
}
```

```
public class DrawingProgram
{
    public void DrawShape(IShape shape)
    {
        shape.Draw();
    }
}
```

In this instance, the '**DrawingProgram**' class features a method: '**DrawShape**', that takes any object subscribing to the '**IShape**' interface. It, therefore, makes it drawable in several shapes ('**Circle**,' '**Square**,' etc.) without genuinely being aware of the particular type and shape at compile time.

Benefits of interface-based polymorphism

Interface-based polymorphism offers several benefits in C# programming. They are as follows:

- **Flexibility**: Allows classes to implement multiple behaviors through interfaces, enabling diverse functionality within the same class hierarchy.

- **Code reusability**: Interfaces promote code reuse by defining common behaviors that can be implemented by multiple classes.

- **Loose coupling**: Reduces dependencies between classes, making the codebase more modular and easier to maintain.

- **Testability**: This feature facilitates unit testing by allowing interfaces to be mocked or stubbed, aiding in isolated testing of components.

Casting and type checking with interfaces

Casting and type checking with interfaces in C# are essential for working with polymorphic behavior and ensuring compatibility between types. This section will cover the fundamentals of casting with interfaces, using the '**is**' and '**as**' operators, and performing type checking.

Using 'is' and 'as' operators

In C#, the following operators are used for type checking and conversion when dealing with interfaces.

- The '**is**' operator checks whether an object is compatible with a specific type or interface at runtime. If the object is compatible, it returns true; otherwise, it returns false.

In the following example, the code checks if the **MediaDevice** object can be cast to the **IPlayable** interface using the is keyword. If the object implements the **IPlayable** interface, the condition is true, and the logic inside the if block can safely assume that the object can be treated as **IPlayable**, allowing the use of the methods or properties defined by the interface:

```
MediaDevice device = new MediaDevice();

if (device is IPlayable)
{
    // Object can be cast to IPlayable
}
```

- The 'as' operator performs a safe cast of an object to a specified type or interface. If the cast is successful, it returns the object as the specified type; otherwise, it returns 'null.' In the following example, the as keyword is used to attempt to cast the **MediaDevice** object to the **IPlayable** interface. If the cast is successful, the **playable** variable will not be **null**, and the **Play()** method can be called. This approach is a safe way to cast objects, as it avoids throwing exceptions if the object does not implement the **IPlayable** interface:

```
MediaDevice device = new MediaDevice();
IPlayable playable = device as IPlayable;

if (playable != null)
{
    // Successfully cast to IPlayable
    playable.Play();
}
```

Applications of interfaces and polymorphism

The concepts of interfaces and polymorphism are not just theoretical; they are precious and are found in most real-world software development. Here are some examples:

- **Plugin architectures**: Interfaces are pivotal in plugin architectures where applications must dynamically extend their functionality. Consider a text editor that supports various file formats through plugins. Each plugin can define the '**IFileFormatPlugin**' interface, which has methods like '**Open**,' '**Save**,' and '**Close**.' The process allows additional formats to be effortlessly introduced without affecting the basic editing logic.

- **Dependency injection (DI)**: DI frameworks rely heavily on interfaces to manage dependencies in modern software development. Interfaces define contracts that classes are supposed to adhere to and guarantee components of loose coupling. Example: An e-commerce application can define an '**IPaymentProcessor**' interface, encapsulating the methods, for example, to charge a payment and refund money. Then, different payment gateways—say, PayPal and Stripe—facilitate implementation given the interface, which allows a developer to switch among different providers easily.

- **Graphical user interface (GUI) programming**: Interfaces enable components such as buttons, text boxes, and menus to respond to user inputs. An '**IControl**' interface may provide methods such as '**OnClick**,' '**OnHover**,' and '**OnFocus**' to ensure uniform behavior across several UI components. This abstraction allows developers to create custom controls or themes that adhere to the same interface contract.

- **Database abstraction layers**: Abstracting database operations via interfaces enable applications to support multiple database engines transparently. An '**IDatabaseProvider**' interface can find definitions for methods such as '**ExecuteQuery**' and '**ExecuteNonQuery**,' and implementations for SQL Server, MySQL, and PostgreSQL can be conformed to that interface. The application can switch databases in real-time, either based on configuration or conditions at runtime.

- **Service integration**: Interfaces allow programmers to integrate with other external services or APIs. An '**IWeatherService**' interface may include methods like '**GetWeatherData**' and '**GetForecast**' to encapsulate the knowledge on how to contact multiple weather data sources. The interface might then be implemented by other weather API implementations (such as **OpenWeatherMap** and **Weather.com**), allowing the application to obtain weather data without directly linking to these providers.

- **Unit testing**: Interfaces improve the testability of code by enabling mock objects during unit testing. Mocking frameworks can create mock implementations of interfaces to simulate behavior, making it easier to isolate and verify the functionality of individual components without relying on complex dependencies or external systems.

Examples from real-world applications

Let us look at a couple of simplified examples to illustrate these concepts:

- **Example one**: Plugin architecture

  Imagine you are developing a media player application that supports different media formats. You could define an interface '**IMediaPlayer**' that all media player plugins must implement:

```
public interface IMediaPlayer
{
    void Play(string mediaFilePath);
    void Pause();
    void Stop();
}
```

Different plugins (for example, '**AudioPlayer**,' '**VideoPlayer**') would implement this interface with their specific logic for playing, pausing, and stopping media files.

- **Example two**: Dependency injection

    Assume a service that returns user data from a local database or a remote API. You can define an interface '**IUserDataService**':

```
public interface IUserDataService
{
    UserData GetUser(int userId);
}
public class LocalUserDataService : IUserDataService
{
    public UserData GetUser(int userId)
    {
        // Logic to fetch user data from the local database
        return new UserData();
    }
}
public class RemoteUserDataService : IUserDataService
{
    public UserData GetUser(int userId)
    {
        // Logic to fetch user data from remote API
        return new UserData();
    }
}
```

In the preceding example, you can switch between '**LocalUserDataService**' and '**RemoteUserDataService**' implementations based on configuration or runtime conditions without modifying the code that depends on '**IUserDataService**'.

Conclusion

In this chapter, we explored the pivotal concepts of interfaces and polymorphism in C#. Understanding these concepts is essential for creating flexible, reusable, and maintainable code. Interfaces define the contracts that classes must adhere to, ensuring consistency while allowing diverse implementations. Polymorphism, through both compile-time and run-time mechanisms, enables objects of different types to be treated uniformly, promoting code generalization and reuse. We also examined how to declare and implement interfaces, use abstract classes to complement interfaces and apply these concepts to real-world scenarios.

As you continue to advance your C# programming skills, remember the importance of interfaces and polymorphism in fostering modular and adaptable code. These principles will serve as a foundation for tackling more complex programming challenges and implementing sophisticated design patterns in your software projects.

In the upcoming chapter, we will explore the power of C# Collections and Generics, two essential features for managing and organizing data efficiently. Collections provide a way to store and manipulate groups of objects, whether you're dealing with lists, dictionaries, queues, or stacks. Generics, on the other hand, enable you to create reusable, type-safe code by allowing collections and methods to operate with any data type without sacrificing performance or flexibility. By mastering collections and generics, you will be equipped to handle complex data structures and write cleaner, more scalable code for a wide range of applications.

Multiple choice questions

1. **What is an interface in C#?**

    a. A class with implemented methods.

    b. A contract that defines methods and properties without implementation.

    c. A variable that stores data.

    d. A method that performs calculations.

2. **Which keyword is used to declare an interface in C#?**

    a. class

    b. interface

    c. implements

    d. inherit

3. **What must a class do if it implements an interface?**

   a. It must provide implementations for all the methods and properties defined in the interface.

   b. It must inherit from another class.

   c. It must be abstract.

   d. It must override the base class methods.

4. **What is polymorphism?**

   a. The ability of a class to have multiple constructors.

   b. The ability of objects of different types to be treated as objects of a common super-type.

   c. The ability to store multiple values in an array.

   d. The ability to define multiple methods with the same name but different parameters.

5. **How is compile-time polymorphism achieved in C#?**

   a. Through method overriding.

   b. Through interface implementation.

   c. Through method overloading.

   d. Through abstract classes.

6. **How is run-time polymorphism achieved in C#?**

   a. Through method overloading.

   b. Through method overriding.

   c. Through operator overloading.

   d. Through defining multiple constructors.

7. **Which of the following is true about abstract classes?**

   a. An abstract class can be instantiated.

   b. An abstract class cannot contain any implemented methods.

   c. An abstract class must implement all methods from an interface it implements.

   d. An abstract class can contain both abstract and implemented methods.

8. **What is the main benefit of using interfaces in C#?**

   a. To create multiple inheritance.

   b. To enforce a contract that multiple classes can implement, ensuring consistency and promoting code reuse.

    c.   To store global variables.

    d.   To handle exceptions more efficiently.

9. **Which operator can be used to check if an object implements a particular interface?**

    a.   is

    b.   as

    c.   new

    d.   typeof

10. **What is the purpose of using the virtual keyword in a base class method?**

    a.   To prevent the method from being overridden in derived classes.

    b.   To indicate that the method is abstract.

    c.   To allow the method to be overridden in derived classes.

    d.   To declare a method without any implementation.

Answers

1. (b) A contract that defines methods and properties without implementation

2. (b) interface

3. (a) It must provide implementations for all the methods and properties defined in the interface.

4. (b) The ability of objects of different types to be treated as objects of a common super-type.

5. (c) Through method overloading

6. (b) Through method overriding

7. (d) An abstract class can contain both abstract and implemented methods.

8. (b) To enforce a contract that multiple classes can implement, ensuring consistency and promoting code reuse.

9. (a) is

10. (c) To allow the method to be overridden in derived classes.

Practice problems

1. **Implementing an interface**: Create an interface called IMovable with two methods: void Move (int distance) and void Stop(). Then, implement this interface

in a class called Car. The Move method should display a message indicating the car is moving a specified distance, and the Stop method should display a message indicating the car has stopped.

a. **Steps**:

i. Define the IMovable interface.

ii. Create the Car class that implements the IMovable interface.

iii. Implement the Move and Stop methods in the Car class.

2. **Polymorphism with interfaces**: Create an interface called IShape with a method void Draw(). Then, create two classes, Circle and Square, that implement the IShape interface. In the Draw method of each class, display a message indicating the shape being drawn. Finally, create a method DrawShapes that takes a list of IShape objects and calls the Draw method on each object in the list.

a. **Steps**:

i. Define the IShape interface.

ii. Create the Circle and Square classes that implement the IShape interface.

iii. Implement the Draw method in each class.

iv. Create the DrawShapes method that takes a list of IShape objects and calls the Draw method on each object.

Join our book's Discord space

Join the book's Discord Workspace for Latest updates, Offers, Tech happenings around the world, New Release and Sessions with the Authors:

https://discord.bpbonline.com

CHAPTER 7

C# Collections and Generics

Introduction

In C# programming, collections, generics, and **Language Integrated Query** (**LINQ**) are essential tools for efficiently managing and manipulating data. Collections, such as lists, dictionaries, queues, and stacks, provide the foundation for storing and organizing groups of related objects. Each collection type offers unique advantages depending on the task, making them crucial for handling dynamic data in a structured way.

Generics, a key feature in C #, enhances the flexibility and safety of collections. They allow you to define classes, methods, and interfaces with placeholders for data types, reducing redundancy and improving performance. More importantly, they enable you to write reusable and type-safe code, a crucial aspect for creating versatile applications that can work with any data type while ensuring type safety.

LINQ, a powerful tool, simplifies data querying and manipulation by seamlessly integrating **Structured Query Language** (**SQL**)-like query capabilities directly into the C# language. It empowers you to filter, sort, group, and join data across various sources with minimal code. This chapter will guide you in using collections, generics, and LINQ in C#, equipping you with the knowledge to write more efficient and maintainable code.

Structure

This chapter covers the following topics:

- Collections and generics
- Introduction to lists
- Dictionaries in C#
- Queues
- Stacks
- Generics
- LINQ with collections

Objectives

By the end of this chapter, you will have a solid understanding of collections in C# and how they can be used to store, manage, and manipulate data efficiently. You will explore various collection types such as lists, dictionaries, queues, and stacks, learning when and how to use each. Additionally, you will delve into generics, which allow you to create flexible, type-safe classes and methods that work with any data type. Furthermore, you will learn to leverage LINQ to query, filter, and transform collections in a concise and expressive manner. With these tools, you will be able to write more efficient, scalable, and maintainable code that effectively handles complex data structures.

Collections and generics

Collections are data structures that can hold more than one element in C#. These elements may be of the same or different types. Collections make it easy to store, retrieve, and manipulate data. Among others, the.NET Framework has several built-in collection classes. For instance, lists, dictionaries, queues, and stacks fall into discrete use categories, each serving specific purposes for handling data. Collection simplifies how we deal with groups of related objects, thus allowing us to perform various tasks like adding, deleting, or finding items quickly within a group.

Generics allow the developer to assign a placeholder to classes, methods, and interfaces in C#, which the end-user of the class will later define. It mainly features implications for developing or setting up underlying component type-safety and reusability of code. Generics are declared by the angle brackets '<' and '>,' and the **type** parameter is specified. For instance, one could define a generic list as 'List<T>,' where 'T' would determine the type of list to store. These generics provide compile-time checking of the data type being inserted, reducing runtime errors and eliminating type casting.

Importance of collections and generics in C#

Collections and generics in C# are essential for a variety of reasons. They are as follows:

- **Type safety**: Generics provide explicit data typing and catches type mismatches during compile time, reducing runtime errors and, hence, developing reliable and maintainable code.

- **Code reusability**: Generics allow one to create reusable components of code that work with any data type, promoting code reuse and reducing redundancy.

- **Performance**: Collections provide the best data structures for storing and managing groups of objects. This enables efficient memory usage and fast execution of data manipulation operations.

- **Flexibility**: C# contains an extended set of built-in collection classes; from simple lists to complex dictionaries, flexibility prevails when using them.

- **Maintainability**: Collections and generics have been used to ensure the code is neat and clean, making it easier to read, understand, and thus maintain.

Any C# developer who wants to develop efficient, high-quality, and scalable applications needs to understand and effectively use collections and generics. This chapter describes various collection and generic types in detail, with examples and best practices for leveraging their potential in your C# programming projects.

Overview of collection types

C# has a variety of collection types for storing and managing groups of objects. Each type of collection has peculiar characteristics that make it suitable for specific uses; thus, developers can select the most appropriate one for their needs. Common collection types include arrays, lists, dictionaries, queues, and stacks.

Arrays

Arrays are among the most basic data structures used in C#. An array is an ordered sequence of elements (similarly typed) that is fixed in size. It is specified using square brackets '[]' during declaration, but its length cannot change once it is instantiated. Arrays have fast element access through indices, making them ideal where the number of elements is known or fixed beforehand.

For example:

```
int[] digits = new int[4];
digits[0] = 2;
digits[1] = 4;
digits[2] = 6;
digits[3] = 8;
```

Lists

Lists are flexible collections that can expand or contract in size as necessary. The '**List <T>**' class in C# provides a way of managing groups of objects that is elastic and computationally efficient. Unlike arrays, the lists do not need to be static. Thus, elements can be added or removed dynamically from them. They are suitable for situations where the number of items in the list is either unknown at design time or can change over time.

For example:

```
List<int> digits = new List<int>();
digits.Add(2);
digits.Add(4);
digits.Add(6);
digits.Add(8);
```

Dictionaries

It is a collection of key-value pairs with a unique value, meaning the key cannot be null while the value can. To build a dictionary, developers use the class '**Dictionary<TKey, TValue>**' where '**TKey**' stands for the type of key and '**TValue**' stands for the value type. Dictionaries can be used if the programmer needs to find pieces of information quickly by unique IDs.

For example:

```
Dictionary<int, string> employees = new Dictionary<int, string>();
employees.Add(1, "Cynthia");
employees.Add(2, "John");
employees.Add(3, "Alice");
employees.Add(4, "Michael");
```

Queues

Queues operate under the **first-in-first-out** (**FIFO**) principle; new objects will be sent into them from behind, while old ones will walk out through frontiers. The '**Queue <T>**' class in C# is used to create queues best suited for processing order matters, like task scheduling or buffering.

For example:

```
Queue<string> buffers = new Queue<string>();
buffers.Enqueue("Buffer 1");
buffers.Enqueue("Buffer 2");
buffers.Enqueue("Buffer 3");
buffers.Enqueue("Buffer 4");
```

Stacks

Stacks adhere to the **last-in-first-out** (**LIFO**) principle, meaning that elements added to them move right up the top while those removed also start from the top. A C# class '**Stack <T>**' is used for implementing stacks; these structures are handy whenever reverse order processing is required, such as undo operations and expression evaluation.

For example:

```
Stack<string> history = new Stack<string>();
history.Push("Page 1");
history.Push("Page 2");
history.Push("Page 3");
history.Push("Page 4");
```

Different types of collections have various advantages and other use cases. Choosing the appropriate collection type can enable developers to create readable and maintainable code.

Working with arrays

Arrays can be declared and initialized in several ways in C #. Examples that demonstrate each approach are as follows:

- **Declaration**: Here, we declare an array named '**digits**' without initializing it:

  ```
  int[] digits;
  ```

- **Initialization**: We then initialize the '**digits**' array with a size of **4**:

  ```
  digits = new int[4];
  ```

- Declaration and instantiation in one statement: This line declares and initializes the '**digits**' array, which has a size of **4**:

  ```
  int[] digits = new int[4];
  ```

- Arrays initialized with values upon declaration: This array is declared and directly initialized with specific values:

  ```
  int[] digits = new int[] { 1, 2, 3, 4 };
  ```

- **Simplified array initialization**: This is a shorthand for declaring and initializing the array with values:

  ```
  int[] digits = { 1, 2, 3, 4 };
  ```

In C#, the index of an array element determines how it can be accessed or modified. Array indices start at 0, meaning the first element is at index 0, the second at index 1, and so on. Accessing elements through their index is a very fast operation in Arrays. Examples of how to access and modify elements in an array are as follows:

- **Accessing**: Retrieves the value of the first element in the array:

```
int firstdigit = digits[0]; // accessing the first element of the array
```

- **Accessing**: Retrieves the value of the second element in the array:

```
int seconddigit = digits[1]; // accessing the second element of the
array
```

- **Modifying**: Sets the value of the first element in the array to **2**:

```
digits[0] = 2; // modifying the first element of the array
```

- **Modifying**: Sets the value of the second element in the array to **4**:

```
digits[1] = 4; // modifying the second element of the array
```

Using foreach loops

The foreach loop in C# iterates over a collection or array. It simplifies accessing each element in the collection without needing to manage the loop counter manually. In the following example, the loop iterates over an array called Digits and prints each digit to the console:

```
foreach (int digit in digits)
{
    Console.WriteLine(digit);
}
```

Multidimensional arrays

These arrays are commonly used for storing data in a matrix or table form (rows and columns). Depending on the developer's needs, they can be two-dimensional or more. The commonly used type are two-dimensional arrays. In C#, a two-dimensional array stores data in a grid format, where data is organized in rows and columns. An example of how to declare and initialize a two-dimensional array is as follows:

- **Declaration and initialization**: This creates a 3x3 two-dimensional array named '**table**':

```
int[,] table = new int[3, 3];
```

This line of code creates a 3x3 matrix, initializing the array with default values (0 for integers). The variety `table` now has three rows and three columns.

You can also initialize the two-dimensional array with specific values at the time of declaration:

  o Declaration and initialization with values directly initialize the '**table**' array with values:

```
int[,] table = new int[,]
{
    { 1, 2, 3 },
    { 4, 5, 6 },
    { 7, 8, 9 }
};
```

In this example, the array is initialized with values arranged into three rows and three columns. Each row is enclosed in curly braces `{}`.

You can access or modify specific elements in a two-dimensional array by specifying their row and column indices.

- **Accessing an element**: This retrieves the value in the first row and first column of the 'table' array:

```
int item = table[0, 0];
```

Here, the item in the first row and column is accessed.

- **Modifying an element**: Sets the value at the first row and first column to **10**:

```
table[0, 0] = 10;
```

The item present in the first row and the first column is modified. In the preceding examples, `table[0,0]` accesses or modifies the element at the intersection of the first row and the first column. Note that array indices in C# are zero-based, meaning the first row is at index 0.

You can use nested loops to iterate over all the elements in a two-dimensional array. The outer loop iterates through the rows, while the inner loop iterates through the columns.

In the following example, a two-dimensional array is iterated through using nested loops. The outer loop cycles through the rows, while the inner loop iterates over the columns, printing each element at the specified row and column indices:

```
// Iterating through the array using nested loops.
for (int a = 0; a < table.GetLength(0); a++) // The outer loop iterates
over rows.
{
    for (int b = 0; b < table.GetLength(1); b++) // The inner loop iterates
over columns.
    {
        Console.WriteLine(table[a, b]); // Prints the element at row 'a'
and column 'b'.
    }
}
```

In this code, `table.GetLength(0)` returns the number of rows, and `table.GetLength(1)` returns the number of columns. The `for` loops allow you to access each array element and perform operations, such as printing each value to the console.

Introduction to lists

C# class 'List <T>' is a list that contains strongly typed objects that can be accessed using indexes. The type of the elements in the list is represented by 'T' and resizes itself automatically when elements are included or removed. Like arrays, you can initialize a list with values at the time of declaration. For example, the following code declares and initializes a list of integers named `digits` in a single statement:

```
List<int> digits = new List<int> { 2, 4, 6, 8, 10 };
```

This list is populated with the values 2, 4, 6, 8, and 10. Alternatively, you can declare a list without initializing it with values, as shown in the following code:

```
List<string> names = new List<string>();
```

Here, the list `names` is declared as a list of strings but is initially empty and ready to be populated.

Adding elements to a list is straightforward in C#. The `Add` method allows you to append a single element to the end of the list, as in:

```
digits.Add(6);
```

This adds the value 6 to the `digits` list. If you need to add multiple elements simultaneously, you can use the `AddRange` method, like the following:

```
digits.AddRange(new int[] { 6, 7, 8 });
```

This method takes an array of integers and adds each element to the end of the `digits` list.

Regarding removing elements from a list, C# offers several methods. The `Remove` method removes the first occurrence of a specified value, as seen in:

```
digits.Remove(6);
```

This removes the value six from the list. You can use the `RemoveAt` method to remove an element by its index, such as in:

```
digits.RemoveAt(0);
```

This removes the first element of the list. If you want to clear the list entirely, leaving it empty, the following `Clear` method will remove all elements from the list:

```
digits.Clear();
```

Accessing and modifying elements in a list is done using their index. For instance:

```
int firstdigit = digits[0];
```

This the first element of the `digits` list and stores it in the variable `firstdigit`. You can also modify elements by assigning a new value to a specific index. The following line changes the value of the first element in the `digits` list to **8**:

```
digits[0] = 8;
```

You can use either a `for` loop or a `foreach` loop to iterate through all the elements in a list. The `for` loop lets you iterate over the list by index, providing precise control over the iteration process. For example:

```
for (int i = 0; i < digits.Count; i++)
{
    Console.WriteLine(digits[i]);
}
```

This iterates through the list, where `digits.Count` returns the number of elements in the list, and within the loop, the following code prints each element:

```
Console.WriteLine(digits[i]);
```

On the other hand, the `foreach` loop simplifies the iteration process by directly accessing each element without needing to manage the loop counter. In:

```
foreach (int digit in digits)
{
    Console.WriteLine(digit);
}
```

Each `digit` in the `digits` list is accessed and printed with the following:

```
Console.WriteLine(digit);
```

List methods and properties

The various methods available in the 'List `<T>`' class make it possible to manage and manipulate the elements of a list effectively. They are as follows:

- '**Contains**': Determines whether an element is present in the list:

  ```
  bool hasNumber = digits.Contains(8);
  ```

- '**IndexOf**': It returns the index of the first occurrence of an element in the list:

  ```
  int index = digits.IndexOf(8);
  ```

- '**Insert**': This function helps you insert a value into a defined point on the list:

  ```
  digits.Insert(0, 12);
  ```

- '**Sort**': This method will sort the elements of the list:

  ```
  digits.Sort();
  ```

- **'Reverse'**: Function used to reverse the order of list elements:

```
digits.Reverse();
```

- **'Count'**: This property is used to get the number of elements in a list:

```
int count = digits.Count;
```

- **'Capacity'**: This property allows developers to get or set the total number of elements the internal data structure can hold without resizing:

```
int capacity = digits.Capacity;
```

Dictionaries in C#

Dictionaries in C# are collections of key-value pairs that function similarly to hash tables. They allow quick access to values using their associated keys. Dictionaries are particularly useful for performing key-based lookups, insertions, and deletions, making them ideal for scenarios where data needs to be accessed through unique identifiers. This section will cover how dictionaries work, how to add or remove key-value pairs, and explore essential dictionary methods and properties.

To declare a dictionary, you can use the following syntax:

```
Dictionary<int, string> employees = new Dictionary<int, string>();
```

The preceding code declares a dictionary named employees where the keys are of type int, and the values are of type string. Another way to initialize a dictionary is by providing key-value pairs at the time of declaration:

```
Dictionary<int, string> employees = new Dictionary<int, string>
{
    { 1, "John" },
    { 2, "Cynthia" },
    { 3, "Sneha" }
};
```

In the preceding example, the employees' dictionary is initialized with three key-value pairs, where the keys are integers (**1, 2,** 3) and the corresponding values are names (**"John"**, **"Cynthia, "Sneha"**).

To add new key-value pairs to the dictionary, you can use the following **Add** method:

```
employees.Add(4, "Shabnam");
```

The preceding line adds a new entry to the dictionary with the key four and the value **"Shabnam"**. Alternatively, you can use the indexer to add or update a value in the dictionary:

```
employees[5] = "Emily";
```

The preceding line sets the value for key **5** to **"Emily"**. If key five already exists, this operation will update the existing value; otherwise, it will add a new key-value pair.

Removing elements from the dictionary can be done using the remove method, which removes the element with the specified key:

```
employees.Remove(4);
```

The preceding code removes the entry with the key four from the dictionary. If you want to clear all entries from the dictionary, you can use the following **Clear** method:

```
employees.Clear();
```

This operation empties the dictionary, removing all key-value pairs.

Accessing values in a dictionary is straightforward. You can retrieve the value associated with a specific key using the indexer:

```
string employeeName = employees[1];
```

In the previous example, **employeeName** is assigned the value associated with the key 1, **"John"**.

To iterate over all the key-value pairs in a dictionary, you can use a foreach loop:

```
foreach (KeyValuePair<int, string> employee in employees)
{
    Console.WriteLine($"ID: {employee.Key}, Name: {employee.Value}");
}
```

In the preceding loop, each **KeyValuePair<int, string>** represents an entry in the dictionary, allowing you to access both the key and the value. The code inside the loop prints the ID and name of each employee in the dictionary.

Dictionary methods and properties

The class that represents the dictionary has various methods to manage key-value pairs.

Some common methods are:

- 'ContainsKey': This method checks whether the dictionary contains an item with the specified key:

  ```
  bool hasKey = employees.ContainsKey(1);
  ```

- 'ContainsValue': This method checks whether the dictionary contains an item with a specified value:

  ```
  bool hasValue = employees.ContainsValue("Emily");
  ```

- The 'TryGetValue' method gets the value of a specified key if it exists:

```
if (employees. TryGetValue (1, out string name) )
{
Console. WriteLine(name);
}
```

- **'Keys'**: This method retrieves a collection containing the keys in the dictionary:

```
ICollection<int> keys = employees.Keys;
```

- **'Values'**: This method retrieves a collection containing the values in the dictionary:

```
ICollection<string> values = employees.Values;
```

- **'Count'**: This property is used to get the dictionary's total number of key-value pairs:

```
int count = employees.Count;
```

Queues

This section explores queues and stacks, focusing on their key operations and how each data structure supports them. Queues follow the FIFO principle, meaning the first item added to the queue is the first to be removed. This behavior makes queues particularly useful for scheduling tasks, buffering data, and any situation where the processing order is essential. To declare and initialize a queue, you can use the following syntax:

```
Queue<string> buffers = new Queue<string>();
```

This line declares a queue named `buffers`, where each element is of type `string`. The queue starts empty and is ready to accept elements. Adding elements to a queue is done using the `Enqueue` method. This method adds an element to the end of the queue:

```
buffers.Enqueue("Buffer 1");
buffers.Enqueue("Buffer 2");
```

In this example, **"Buffer 1"** is added first, followed by **"Buffer 2"**. Since queues operate on the FIFO principle, **"Buffer 1"** will be the first element to be removed.

To remove an element from the queue, you use the `Dequeue` method:

```
string buffer = buffers.Dequeue(); // "Buffer 1" is removed
```

This operation removes and returns the element at the front of the queue. In this case, **"Buffer 1"** is removed, as it was the first element added to the queue.

There are other useful methods available for working with queues. The `Peek` method, for example, allows you to look at the element at the front of the queue without removing it:

```
string buffer = buffers.Dequeue(); // "Buffer 1" is removed
```

Here, `Peek` returns **"Buffer 2"**, which is now at the front of the queue after **"Buffer 1"** was dequeued. However, **"Buffer 2"** remains in the queue.

Another important property of queues is the `Count` property, which returns the number of elements currently in the queue:

```
int count = buffers.Count;
```

This line stores the number of elements in the `buffers` queue in the `count` variable.

To iterate through all elements in a queue, you can use a `foreach` loop. This allows you to access each element in the order in which they were added:

```
foreach (string buffer in buffers)
{
    Console.WriteLine(buffer);
}
```

Each `buffer` in the `buffers` queue is accessed and printed in this loop. This iteration will process the elements in FIFO order, reflecting the natural order of the queue.

Understanding queues and their operations is crucial for managing tasks where order matters. They are widely used in scenarios such as task scheduling, buffering data streams, and managing any sequence where the first-in item must be processed.

Stacks

Stacks are collections that process elements in the reverse order they were added, following the LIFO principle. They are helpful for scenarios requiring reverse order processing, such as undo operations and expression evaluation. Here is how a stack operates in C#, showcasing the declaration, initialization, and basic operations like Push and Pop:

- **Declaration and Initialization:**
    ```
    Stack<string> history = new Stack<string> ();
    ```

- **Push operation**: '**Push**' adds an element to the top of the stack:
    ```
    history.Push("Page 1");
    history.Push("Page 2");
    ```

- **'Pop' removes and returns the element at the top of the stack:**
    ```
    string lastPage = history.Pop(); // "Page 2"
    ```

Other useful methods include the following:

- **'Peek'**: Returns the element at the top of the stack without removing it:
    ```
    string currentPage = history.Peek(); // "Page 1"
    ```

- **'Count'**: Gets the number of elements in the stack:
    ```
    int count = history.Count;
    ```

- **Iterating through a stack:**

```
foreach (string page in history)
{
    Console.WriteLine(page);
}
```

Queues and stacks are essential data structures in C# for managing ordered collections of elements, each with unique characteristics and use cases.

Generics

Generics is a potent C# feature that lets you design type-safe algorithms and data structures. It enables developers to create classes, methods, or collections that work with all types of data and maintain type safety. Generics lets you build reusable code components that can work with any data. They are defined with type parameters, like placeholders for the actual data types that will be specified once the generic class or method is initiated.

The definition is as follows:

```
public class GenericClass<T>
{
    public T Value { get; set; }
}
```

The benefits of using generics include:

- **Type checking**: Generics allow for compile-time type checking that reduces the risk of runtime errors from type mismatches.

- **Simplicity**: Creating generic classes and methods can help prevent code duplication with multiple data types.

- **More speed due to high performance**: Boxing and unboxing need not be done when using generics on value types.

- **Maintainability**: Generics reduce the need for type casting, encourage code readability, and signify cleaner code with better maintainability.

Generic classes and methods

In C#, a generic class can operate with any data type. Generic courses have one or more type parameters, which are placeholders for specific data types specified when the class is instantiated. This allows for creating flexible and reusable code that can work with different data types without duplication.

To declare a generic class, you define a **type** parameter within angle brackets (`<>`) after the class name. This **type** parameter can then be used throughout the class as a placeholder for the data type provided during instantiation. Here is an example:

```
public class GenericClass<T>
{
    public T Value { get; set; }

    public GenericClass(T value)
    {
        Value = value;
    }

    public void Display()
    {
        Console.WriteLine($"Value: {Value}");
    }
}
```

In this example, `GenericClass<T>` is a generic class where `T` is the **type** parameter. The `T` can represent any data type, such as `int`, `string`, or even a custom class. The `Value` property is of type `T`, and the constructor takes a type `T` parameter. The `Display` method prints the value of the `Value` property to the console.

When you create an instance of this generic class, you specify the data type that `T` should represent. For example, to create an instance where `T` is an integer (`int`), you would do the following:

```
GenericClass<int> intInstance = new GenericClass<int>(10);
intInstance.Display(); // Output: Value: 10
```

In this case, `intInstance` is an instance of `GenericClass` where `T` is replaced with `int`. The `Display` method outputs **"Value: 10"** to the console, showing the integer value stored in the `Value` property.

Similarly, you can create an instance of the generic class where `T` is a string:

```
GenericClass<string> stringInstance = new GenericClass<string>("Hello");
stringInstance.Display(); // Output: Value: Hello
```

Here, `stringInstance` is an instance of `GenericClass` where `T` is replaced with `string`. The `Display` method outputs **"Value: Hello"** to the console, displaying the string value stored in the `Value` property.

Generic classes provide a powerful way to write flexible and type-safe code. Using type parameters, you can create a single class definition that works with any data type, reducing code duplication and increasing reusability. This makes generic classes a fundamental feature in C# for developing robust and maintainable applications.

Generic methods

In C#, a generic method can operate on different data types without being rewritten for each type. Unlike generic classes, which are entirely generic, a generic method can be defined within either a non-generic or a generic class. The **type** parameter for the generic method is specified after the method name in angle brackets (`<>`), allowing the method to accept arguments of various types.

To declare a generic method within a non-generic class, you define the method with a **type** parameter. This **type** parameter acts as a placeholder for the data type specified when the method is called. Here is an example:

```csharp
public class NonGenericClass
{
    public void Display<T>(T value)
    {
        Console.WriteLine($"Value: {value}");
    }
}
```

In this example, the `Display` method is defined within a non-generic class named `NonGenericClass`. The method is generic, as indicated by the `<T>` following the method name. The `T` type parameter allows the `Display` method to accept any argument. The method then prints the value of the argument to the console.

When you use a generic method, specify the data type for the **type** parameter when calling the method. For example, if you want to call the `Display` method with an integer (`int`), you can do the following:

```csharp
NonGenericClass instance = new NonGenericClass();
instance.Display<int>(10); // Output: Value: 10
```

In this case, `Display<int>(10)` calls the `Display` method with `T` replaced by `int`, and the method outputs **"Value: 10"** to the console.

Similarly, you can call the `Display` method with a string by specifying `string` as the **type** parameter:

```csharp
instance.Display<string>("Hello"); // Output: Value: Hello
```

Here, `Display<string>("Hello")` calls the `Display` method with `T` replaced by `string`, and the method outputs **"Value: Hello"** to the console.

Generic methods provide flexibility by allowing a single method to handle multiple data types. This eliminates the need to create separate methods for each type, reducing code duplication and improving maintainability. By using type parameters, generic methods can adapt to the specific data types provided at runtime, making them a powerful tool in C# programming.

This explanation covers generic methods in C#, how they are defined within a non-generic class, and how they can be used flexibly to work with different data types.

Defining generic classes

The definition of a generic class in C# involves specifying one or more type parameters. These type parameters act as placeholders for actual data types, allowing the class to be used with different data types without creating separate classes for each type. When an object is instantiated from a generic class, the specific data types are provided, replacing the placeholders. For example, consider the following generic class with a single **type** parameter:

```
public class Container<T>
{
    public T Value { get; set; }
    public Container(T value)
    {
        Value = value;
    }
    public void Display()
    {
        Console.WriteLine($"Value: {Value}");
    }
}
```

In this example, `Container<T>` is a generic class where `T` is the **type** parameter. The `Value` property is of type `T`, and the constructor takes a type `T` parameter. The `Display` method prints the value of `Value` to the console. This generic class can be instantiated with different types:

```
Container<int> intContainer = new Container<int>(42);
intContainer.Display(); // Output: Value: 42


Container<string> stringContainer = new Container<string>("Hello, World!");
stringContainer.Display(); // Output: Value: Hello, World!
```

Here, `intContainer` is an instance of `Container` with `T` replaced by `int`, and `stringContainer` is an instance with `T` replaced by `string`.

A generic class can also have multiple type parameters, allowing it to work with multiple data types simultaneously, like:

```
public class Pair<T1, T2>
{
    public T1 First { get; set; }
    public T2 Second { get; set; }

    public Pair(T1 first, T2 second)
    {
        First = first;
        Second = second;
    }

    public void Display()
    {
        Console.WriteLine($"First: {First}, Second: {Second}");
    }
}
```

In this example, `Pair<T1, T2>` is a generic class with two type parameters, `T1` and `T2`. The class holds two values of different types and displays them. You can instantiate this class with different combinations of types, like:

```
Pair<int, string> pair = new Pair<int, string>(1, "One");
pair.Display(); // Output: First: 1, Second: One
```

Generic methods allow you to define type-safe methods that operate on different data types. A generic method can be defined in a non-generic and a generic class.

Generic collections

In C#, the .NET Framework has several built-in generic collection classes under the '`System.Collections.Generic`' namespace. These collections are intended to work with any data type, providing safety and better performance.

The standard generic collections include lists, dictionaries, queues, and stacks:

- The list represents a dynamic list of objects.
- The dictionary represents key-value pairs.
- The queue generic collection represents a FIFO collection.
- The stack generic collection represents a LIFO collection.

For example: Using a generic '`List<T>`':

```
List<string> names = new List<string> { "Michael", "Thomas", "John" };
names.Add("Alice");
```

```
names.Remove("Michael ");

foreach (string name in names)
{
    Console.WriteLine(name);
}
```

LINQ with collections

In C#, LINQ is a powerful feature that allows developers to query and update data collections with enhanced readability and efficiency. LINQ provides a unified syntax for querying different types of data sources, including arrays, lists, and other generic collections, as well as external data sources like databases and XML documents. By incorporating the power of querying directly into the C# language, LINQ enables developers to work with data using a familiar and expressive syntax.

LINQ supports two primary forms for writing queries: query syntax and method syntax. Query syntax is similar to SQL, making it intuitive for developers accustomed to working with SQL databases. This syntax is often preferred for its readability and ease of use when dealing with complex queries.

Here is an example of how LINQ can be used to query a simple array of integers:

```
int[] Digits = { 2, 4, 6, 8, 10 };
var evenDigits = from num in Digits
                 where num % 2 == 0
                 select num;
```

In this example, `Digits` is an array containing a series of integers. The LINQ query `from num in Digits where num % 2 == 0 select num;` filters the array to select only the even numbers. The `where` clause applies a condition (`num % 2 == 0`) that checks if each number is even. The `select` clause then returns the numbers that meet this condition.

The results of this LINQ query are stored in the variable `evenDigits`, which can be iterated over, using a `foreach` loop:

```
foreach (var num in evenDigits)
{
    Console.WriteLine(num); // This will display 2, 4, 6, 8, and 10, as all
of them are even
}
```

In this loop, each even number in `evenDigits` is printed to the console. The output will be `2`, `4`, `6`, `8`, and `10`; these are the even numbers in the original `Digits` array.

LINQ enhances the ability to work with data collections by providing a consistent, expressive, and powerful querying language integrated directly into C#. It allows developers to write commands that are both concise and similar to SQL, making data manipulation tasks more intuitive and maintainable. Whether you are querying in-memory collections like arrays and lists or external data sources, LINQ offers a versatile and efficient way to work with data in C#.

Method syntax

When using LINQ in C#, you often call extension methods provided by the `System.Linq` namespace. These extension methods allow you to perform operations such as filtering, selecting, and aggregating data concisely and readably. To utilize LINQ with arrays, lists, dictionaries, and other generic collections, you must include the `System.Linq` namespace in your project.

Consider the following example where LINQ is used with an array of integers:

```
int[] digits = { 6, 7, 8, 9, 10 };
var evenDigits = digits.Where(num => num % 2 == 0);
```

In the preceding code, `digits` is an array of integers. The `Where` method, a LINQ extension method, filters the array to select only the even numbers. The expression `num => num % 2 == 0` is called a Lambda expression that specifies the condition for filtering. The result, stored in `evenDigits`, includes the even numbers from the array.

You can then iterate over the filtered results using a `foreach` loop:

```
foreach (var num in evenDigits)
{
    Console.WriteLine(num); // This will display 6, 8, and 10
}
```

The loop outputs `6`, `8`, and `10`, the even numbers from the `digits` array.

LINQ can also be used with other generic collections, such as lists. Here is an example where LINQ filters a list of strings:

```
List<string> persons = new List<string> { "John", "William", "Joseph",
"Charles" };
var filteredPersons = persons.Where(person => person.StartsWith("J"));
```

In this case, `persons` is a list of names. The `Where` method filters the list to include only the names that start with the letter **"J"**. The result, stored in `filteredPersons`, can be iterated over as follows:

```
foreach (var person in filteredPersons)
{
    Console.WriteLine(person); // This will output 'John' and 'Joseph'
}
```

The loop outputs **"John"** and **"Joseph"**, which are the names in the list that start with **"J"**.

LINQ is also effective when working with dictionaries. Here is an example where LINQ is used to filter a dictionary based on the keys:

```
Dictionary<int, string> employees = new Dictionary<int, string>
{
    { 1, "Alice" },
    { 2, "Bob" },
    { 3, "Charlie" },
    { 4, "David" }
};
var filteredEmployees = employees.Where(employee => employee.Key % 2 == 0);
```

In this example, `employees` is a dictionary where the keys are integers and the values are employee names. The `Where` method filters the dictionary to include only the entries with even keys. The filtered results are stored in `filteredEmployees` and can be iterated over as follows:

```
foreach (var employee in filteredEmployees)
{
    Console.WriteLine($"{employee.Key}: {employee.Value}"); // Output: 2:
Bob, 4: David
}
```

The loop outputs `2: Bob` and `4: David`, the employees with even-numbered keys.

By including the `System.Linq` namespace, LINQ provides a powerful and expressive way to query and manipulate data in C#. Whether working with arrays, lists, dictionaries, or other collections, LINQ's extension methods simplify your code and improve readability, making data operations more intuitive and maintainable.

Common Language Integrated Query operations

LINQ in C# includes various query operators that allow you to perform multiple actions on collections. These operators make it easier to filter, project, sort, aggregate, group, and join data concisely and readably. Some commonly used LINQ operations are:

- Filtering with LINQ is straightforward using the `Where` operator, which filters elements in a collection based on a specified condition. For instance, if you want to find all even numbers in a collection, you can use the following code:

  ```
  var evenNumbers = numbers.Where(num => num % 2 == 0);
  ```

  Here, `evenNumbers` will contain only the even numbers from the `numbers` collection. Projection is another common operation where you transform each collection element into a new form using the `Select` operator. For example, to create a collection of squares from an array of numbers, you can use:

```
var squares = numbers.Select(num => num * num);
```

In this case, `squares` will contain the square of each number in the `numbers` collection.

Sorting is essential for organizing data, and LINQ offers the `OrderBy` and `OrderByDescending` operators for this purpose. To sort a collection of names in ascending order, you can write the following:

```
var sortedNames = names.OrderBy(name => name);
```

Alternatively, to sort the names in descending order, you would use the following code:

```
var sortedNamesDesc = names.OrderByDescending(name => name);
```

Aggregation in LINQ allows you to perform calculations across a collection. For example, to count the number of elements in a collection, you can use the `Count` operator:

```
int count = numbers.Count();
```

Similarly, to find the sum, average, maximum, or minimum value of elements in a collection, you can use the `Sum`, `Average`, `Max`, and `Min` operators respectively:

```
int sum = numbers.Sum();
double average = numbers.Average();
int max = numbers.Max();
int min = numbers.Min();
```

Grouping elements is made easy with the `GroupBy` operator, which groups elements in a collection that share a common attribute. For example, to group a list of names by their length, you can write the following:

```
var groupedNames = names.GroupBy(name => name.Length);
```

This creates groups of names based on their length. You can iterate through these groups as follows:

```
foreach (var group in groupedNames)
{
    Console.WriteLine($"Length: {group.Key}");
    foreach (var name in group)
    {
        Console.WriteLine(name);
    }
}
```

Joining is a powerful operation in LINQ that allows you to combine elements from two collections based on a related key. For instance, if you have a list of people and a list of their orders, you can join these lists by matching the `Id` from the people list with the `PersonId` from the orders list:

```
var people = new List<Person>
{
    new Person { Id = 1, Name = "Alice" },
    new Person { Id = 2, Name = "Bob" }
};
var orders = new List<Order>
{
    new Order { PersonId = 1, Product = "Book" },
    new Order { PersonId = 2, Product = "Pen" }
};
var personOrders = people.Join(orders,
                            person => person.Id,
                            order => order.PersonId,
                            (person, order) => new { person.Name,
order.Product });
```

The preceding code combines the `people` and `orders` collections into a new collection that associates each person with their corresponding order. You can then iterate through this combined collection to display the results:

```
foreach (var po in personOrders)
{
    Console.WriteLine($"{po.Name} ordered {po.Product}");
}
```

This would output the names of the people along with the products they ordered, such as **"Alice ordered Book"** and **"Bob ordered Pen"**.

These everyday LINQ operations provide powerful tools for manipulating and querying data in C#. Whether you are filtering, projecting, sorting, aggregating, grouping, or joining collections, LINQ simplifies complex data operations, making your code more readable and maintainable.

Conclusion

By the end of this chapter, you will have a solid understanding of C# collections and generics. You will explore various collection types like lists, dictionaries, queues, and stacks, and understand how to use them effectively to manage and organize data. Additionally, you will learn about generics, which provide a flexible way to create reusable, type-safe code for any data type. LINQ will also be covered, enabling you to manipulate collections efficiently through filtering, querying, and transforming data in a concise way. Mastering these concepts will help you write more scalable and maintainable code.

In the next chapter, we will dive into C# delegates and events, which are key to creating flexible and dynamic applications. You will learn how delegates enable methods to be passed as parameters, and how events allow for the implementation of event-driven programming, crucial for building interactive and responsive software.

Multiple choice questions

1. **Which of the following is not a collection type in C#?**
   a. List
   b. Dictionary
   c. Queue
   d. String

2. **What is the primary advantage of using generics in C#?**
   a. Faster execution
   b. Enhanced security
   c. Type safety and code reusability
   d. Simplified syntax

3. **In C#, which collection type operates on the FIFO principle?**
   a. Stack
   b. List
   c. Dictionary
   d. Queue

4. **Which LINQ operator filters elements in a collection based on a condition?**
   a. Select
   b. OrderBy
   c. Where
   d. GroupBy

5. **What is the purpose of the `List<T>` class in C#?**
   a. To store key-value pairs.
   b. To create a dynamic array that can resize automatically.

   c.   To process elements in reverse order.

   d.   To manage a fixed-size array of elements.

6. **Which LINQ operator would you use to group elements in a collection by a common attribute?**

   a.   Select

   b.   GroupBy

   c.   Join

   d.   Aggregate

7. **What does the `Peek` method do in a queue?**

   a.   Adds an element to the end of the queue.

   b.   Removes and returns the element at the front of the queue.

   c.   Returns the element at the front of the queue without removing it.

   d.   Counts the number of elements in the queue.

8. **How is a generic class defined in C#?**

   a.   public class GenericClass { }

   b.   public class GenericClass<T> { }

   c.   public class <T> GenericClass { }

   d.   public class GenericClass(T) { }

9. **Which methods can add a new key-value pair to a dictionary in C#?**

   a.   Add()

   b.   Push()

   c.   Enqueue()

   d.   Insert()

10. **In LINQ, which operator would you use to sort a collection in descending order?**

   a.   OrderBy

   b.   OrderByDescending

   c.   GroupBy

   d.   Select

Answers

1. (d) String
2. (c) Type safety and code reusability
3. (d) Queue
4. (c) Where
5. (b) To create a dynamic array that can resize automatically
6. (b) GroupBy
7. (c) Returns the element at the front of the queue without removing it
8. (b) public class GenericClass<T> { }
9. (a) Add()
10. (b) OrderByDescending

Practice problems

1. You are tasked with creating a generic class that can store a pair of related items and display their values. Additionally, you need to create a list of these pairs and sort them based on the first item in the pair. Complete the following:

   a. Define a generic class `Pair<T1, T2>` with two properties: `First` of type `T1` and `Second` of type `T2`.

   b. Implement a method `Display()` in the `Pair` class that prints the values of `First` and `Second`.

   c. Create a list of `Pair<int, string>` objects and add at least three pairs.

   d. Sort the list based on the `First` property (the integer) in ascending order.

   e. Iterate through the sorted list and display the pairs using the `Display()` method.

   An example of usage is:

```
Pair<int, string> pair1 = new Pair<int, string>(3, "Three");
Pair<int, string> pair2 = new Pair<int, string>(1, "One");
Pair<int, string> pair3 = new Pair<int, string>(2, "Two");
// Add pairs to a list, sort the list by `First`, and display each
pair.
```

2. You are given a list of students' names and their corresponding grades. Your task is to filter and display only students with a grade above 75 using LINQ.

Complete the following:

a. Create a `Dictionary<string, int>` where the key is the student's name (a string) and the value is their grade (an integer).

b. Populate the dictionary with at least five students and their grades.

c. Use a LINQ query to filter out students with a grade above 75.

d. Display the names and grades of the students who meet the criteria.

An example of usage is:

```
Dictionary<string, int> students = new Dictionary<string, int>
{
    { "Alice", 85 },
    { "Bob", 72 },
    { "Charlie", 90 },
    { "David", 65 },
    { "Eve", 78 }
};
// Use LINQ to filter students above 75 and display their names and grades.
```

Join our book's Discord space

Join the book's Discord Workspace for Latest updates, Offers, Tech happenings around the world, New Release and Sessions with the Authors:

https://discord.bpbonline.com

CHAPTER 8

C# Delegates and Events

Introduction

In C# programming, mastering delegates and events is crucial for understanding the language's event-driven architecture. Delegates are type-safe function pointers, allowing methods to be treated as first-class objects. This enables developers to pass methods as parameters, define callbacks, and implement design patterns like observer and strategy. Delegates encapsulate method signatures, allowing dynamic and safe invocation and enhancing code flexibility and reusability.

Events build on delegates, enabling structured communication between objects. They allow one object to notify others of specific actions or state changes, promoting a decoupled, maintainable design. Events are applicable when multiple subscribers must respond to a single event, such as user interactions or system changes.

This chapter covers the fundamentals of delegates and events, including delegate declaration, multi-cast delegates, anonymous methods, and Lambda expressions. It also explores event implementation with standard and custom event arguments, offering a comprehensive understanding of these concepts. By the end, you will be equipped to use delegates and events effectively to build interactive, event-driven C# applications.

Structure

This chapter covers the following topics:

- Delegates and events
- Delegate basics
- Anonymous methods and Lambda expressions
- Events basics
- Differences between delegates and events

Objectives

By the end of this chapter, you will be able to understand the concept and functionality of delegates and implement and manage events in C#. You will also learn to utilize anonymous methods and Lambda expressions in event handling and differentiate between delegates and events.

Delegates and events

A delegate is a type that represents references to methods with a specific parameter list and return type. In simpler terms, a delegate is like a pointer to a function. It enables functions to be supplied as arguments and called dynamically during execution. Delegates are declared with the '**delegate**' keyword and may be utilized to create callback functions, handle events, and apply design patterns such as observer and strategy.

An event is a communication given by an object that indicates the appearance of an action. Events are built on delegates and let a class alert other classes or objects when something happens. Events are declared using the '**event**' keyword, and the associated delegate specifies the signature of the methods that can handle the event.

Many reasons necessitate the use of delegates and events in C# programming and the .NET framework:

- **Method encapsulation**: Methods can be passed as parameters through delegates, thereby allowing flexible and reusable code. This aspect is indispensable in designing extensible APIs and implementing callbacks.

- **Event-driven programming**: Events are the perfect mechanism for building event-driven architectures where objects can communicate and respond to state or user action changes. Embodying this paradigm is critical for creating interactive applications that offer users responsiveness.

- **Decoupling of components**: Delegates and events promote loose coupling between components by allowing objects to interact without having direct references to each other. This decoupling enhances maintainability and scalability.

- **Design patterns implementation**: Several design patterns (observer, strategy, and command) are implemented using delegates and events to build robust software systems.

Delegate basics

In C#, delegates are powerful tools that allow methods to be treated as first-class objects. By encapsulating method signatures, delegates enable you to pass methods as parameters and define callback mechanisms.

The two major types of delegates are single-cast and multi-cast. A single-cast delegate holds a reference to a single method. This is the most straightforward type of delegate, where one delegate instance corresponds to one method. In this example, we will explore the concept of delegates in C#, a powerful feature that allows methods to be passed as parameters. Delegates are especially useful when you want to define a callback mechanism. We will start with a simple single-cast delegate designed to point to a single method. The following example will demonstrate how to declare a delegate, assign it to a method, and invoke it:

```
// Delegate declaration
public delegate void Notify(string message);
class ExampleProgram
{
    static void Main(string[] args)
    {
        // Assign the delegate to the method
        Notify notifyDelegate = ShowMessage;

        // Invoke the delegate
        notifyDelegate("Hello, Single-cast Delegate!");
    }

    // Method that matches the delegate signature
    static void ShowMessage(string message)
    {
        Console.WriteLine(message);
    }
}
```

A multi-cast delegate can hold references to multiple methods. When a multi-cast delegate is invoked, it calls all the methods in its invocation list in the order they were added. Multi-cast delegates are created by combining multiple delegate instances using the '**+**'

or '+=' operator. In C#, multi-cast delegates extend the concept of single-cast delegates by allowing a delegate to hold references to multiple methods. When a multi-cast delegate is invoked, it sequentially calls all the methods in its invocation list in the order they were added. This is particularly useful when performing multiple actions in response to a single event. Multi-cast delegates are easily created by combining various delegate instances using the **+** or **+=** operator. The following example illustrates how to create and use a multi-cast delegate:

```csharp
// Delegate declaration
public delegate void Notify(string message);
class ExampleProgram2
{
    static void Main(string[] args)
    {
        // Assign the delegate to the first method
        Notify notifyDelegate = ShowMessage;

        // Add another method to the delegate's invocation list
        notifyDelegate += ShowAnotherMessage;

        // Invoke the multi-cast delegate
        notifyDelegate("Hello, Multi-cast Delegates!");
    }
    // First method that matches the delegate signature
    static void ShowMessage(string message)
    {
        Console.WriteLine("First method: " + message);
    }
    // Second method that matches the delegate signature
    static void ShowAnotherMessage(string message)
    {
        Console.WriteLine("Second method: " + message);
    }
}
```

In this example, the '**notifyDelegate**' multi-cast delegate references both the '**ShowMessage**' and '**ShowAnotherMessage**' methods. When the delegate is invoked, both methods are called in sequence. Multi-cast delegates are helpful for event handling, where multiple subscribers might be interested in a single event. They enable a flexible and scalable way to notify numerous listeners about events or changes in state.

Combining and removing delegates

Delegates in C# can combine and remove delegate instances to form multi-cast delegates, which is one of their powerful features. This is extremely valuable when multiple methods need to be called whenever an event occurs.

Delegates can be combined using the '**+**' or '**+=**' operator. Invoking the delegate will call all methods in its invocation list when combined.

In this example, '**notifyDelegate**' combines '**ShowMessage**' and '**ShowAnotherMessage**'. When '**notifyDelegate**' is invoked, both methods are called in sequence.

Removing delegates

Delegates can be removed using the '**-**' or '**-=**' operator. This is useful for unsubscribing methods from events or reducing the invocation list. For example:

```
// Delegate declaration
public delegate void Notify(string message);


class ExampleProgram3
{
    static void Main(string[] args)
    {
        // Creating a delegate instance and assigning it to the ShowMessage
method
        Notify notifyDelegate = ShowMessage;

        // Adding another method to the delegate's invocation list
        notifyDelegate += ShowAnotherMessage;

        // Invoking the multi-cast delegate before removing any method
        notifyDelegate("Before removal.");

        // Removing the ShowAnotherMessage method from the delegate's
invocation list
        notifyDelegate -= ShowAnotherMessage;

        // Invoking the delegate after the removal to demonstrate the effect
        notifyDelegate("After removal.");
    }
```

```
// First method that matches the delegate signature
static void ShowMessage(string message)
{
    // Outputting the message from the first method
    Console.WriteLine("First method: " + message);
}

// Second method that matches the delegate signature
static void ShowAnotherMessage(string message)
{
    // Outputting the message from the second method
    Console.WriteLine("Second method: " + message);
}
}
```

'**ShowAnotherMessage**' is removed from '**notifyDelegate**' before the second invocation. As a result, only '**ShowMessage**' is called the second time.

Developers can effectively manage method invocations and implement event-driven programming patterns in C# by understanding how to create, invoke, combine, and remove delegates. This knowledge is foundational for working with more advanced concepts like events, which we will explore in the following sections.

Anonymous methods and Lambda expressions

This part introduces anonymous methods, shows how they can be used with delegates, and discusses Lambda expressions as a shorter option. Anonymous methods allow you to define inline method bodies without declaring a separate named method. They are helpful when the method body is brief and only required for a limited scope. Anonymous methods are created using the delegate keyword. Following is an example of using an anonymous method with a delegate:

```
// Delegate declaration
public delegate void Notify(string message);

class ExampleProgram4
{
    static void Main(string[] args)
    {
```

```
    // Anonymous method assigned to the delegate
    Notify notifyDelegate = delegate(string message)
    {
        // Outputting the message using the anonymous method
        Console.WriteLine(message);
    };


    // Invoking the delegate with the anonymous method
    notifyDelegate("Anonymous method invoked.");
    }
}
```

In this example, the '**notifyDelegate**' is assigned an anonymous method that prints the provided message to the console.

Using anonymous methods with delegates

Assigning delegates using anonymous methods provides a code that does less work but remains readable as regular methods would have done. They are instrumental when handling events or simple method logic that does not require reusability. In this example, we will explore anonymous methods in C#. Anonymous methods provide a way to define inline methods without declaring a separate method. They are handy for short, one-off operations closely tied to a delegate's invocation. Let us see how an anonymous method can be assigned to a delegate and invoked:

```
// Delegate declaration
public delegate void Notify(string message);


class ExampleProgram5
{
    static void Main(string[] args)
    {
        // Assigning an anonymous method to the delegate
        Notify notifyDelegate = delegate(string message)
        {
            // Outputting the message from the anonymous method
            Console.WriteLine("Anonymous method says: " + message);
        };


        // Invoking the delegate with the anonymous method
```

```
            notifyDelegate("Hello from an anonymous method!");
    }
}
```

This example demonstrates assigning an anonymous method to a delegate and invoking it. The anonymous method prints a message prefixed with the phrase **"Anonymous method says:"**.

Lambda expressions in delegates

Lambda expressions provide a more concise way to define inline methods. They are shorthand notations for anonymous methods and are defined using the '**=>**' syntax.

You can use a Lambda expression with a delegate through the following way:

```
// Delegate declaration
public delegate void Notify(string message);

class ExampleProgram6
{
    static void Main(string[] args)
    {
        // Lambda expression assigned to the delegate
        Notify notifyDelegate = (message) => Console.WriteLine(message);

        // Invoking the delegate with the lambda expression
        notifyDelegate("Lambda expression invoked.");
    }
}
```

Here, the '**notifyDelegate**' is given a Lambda expression that accepts and displays a '**message**' input.

Lambda expressions can also capture variables from the enclosing scope, allowing for a more flexible and powerful inline methods. For example:

```
// Delegate declaration
public delegate void Notify(string message);

class ExampleProgram7
{
    static void Main(string[] args)
    {
```

```
        // Local variable used within the lambda expression
        string prefix = "Lambda says: ";

        // Lambda expression assigned to the delegate, utilizing the local
variable
        Notify notifyDelegate = (message) => Console.WriteLine(prefix +
message);

        // Invoking the delegate with the lambda expression
        notifyDelegate("Hello from a lambda expression!");
    }
}
```

The preceding example demonstrates how a Lambda expression captures the '**prefix**' variable from its enclosing scope and uses it within its body.

Lambda expressions are shorter and clearer than anonymous methods. In C#, they are widely employed in **Language Integrated Query** (**LINQ**) and other functional programming constructs.

Events basics

Events are built on delegates and provide a way for objects to communicate in an event-driven architecture. Events are essentially special delegates that can only be invoked from within the class or struct where they are declared. Events offer a uniform approach for objects to deliver notifications and others to manage them. Events are commonly utilized when several objects are interested in a single occurrence, like user actions (clicks, key presses) or system status changes.

In C#, an event is declared by defining a delegate type and then declaring an event with that type. Events are declared using the '**event**' keywords, followed by the delegate type and event name.

First, we declare a delegate who will define the signature for the event handler. A delegate is a type that represents references to methods with a particular parameter list and return type.

An example of declaring and raising an event is as follows:

```
// Delegate declaration
public delegate void ProcessCompletedEventHandler (string message);
```

This delegate will be used to define the event signature in the **Process** class. It takes a string parameter and returns **void**. Next, we define the **Process** class, which will raise an event when a process is completed. This class contains the event declaration and the method to trigger the event:

```
// Event publisher class
class Process
{
    // Event declaration using the delegate
    public event ProcessCompletedEventHandler ProcessCompleted;
```

In this example, we demonstrate how to declare and raise an event in C#. The event **ProcessCompleted** is tied to a delegate **ProcessCompletedEventHandler**, which handles the communication between different parts of the program. When the **StartProcess** method is called, it simulates a process by pausing execution for three seconds. Once the process is completed, the event is raised using the **OnProcessCompleted** method to notify subscribers that the process has finished. Here is the code for simulating the process and triggering the event:

```
public event ProcessCompletedEventHandler ProcessCompleted;


public void StartProcess()
{
    // Simulate some processing work with a delay
    System.Threading.Thread.Sleep(3000);

    // Raise the event after the process is completed
    OnProcessCompleted("Process completed successfully!");
}


protected virtual void OnProcessCompleted(string message)
{
    // Check if there are any subscribers to the event
    ProcessCompleted?.Invoke(this, new ProcessCompletedEventArgs(message));
}
```

This code allows event subscribers to receive notifications when the process completes successfully, enhancing interactivity and responsiveness in C# applications.

In this example, the **StartProcess** method simulates a time-consuming operation by using **Thread.Sleep**. Once the operation is complete, the method triggers the **ProcessCompleted** event by calling the **OnProcessCompleted** method. The **OnProcessCompleted** method checks whether there are any subscribers before invoking the event to prevent potential errors. By making this method protected and virtual, we allow derived classes to override the behavior of event invocation if needed.

```
    // Protected method to raise the event
    protected virtual void OnProcessCompleted(string message)
```

```
    {
        // Invoke the event if there are any subscribers
        ProcessCompleted?.Invoke(message);
    }
}
```

In this example, the **OnProcessCompleted** method is designed to be flexible by making it protected and virtual. This allows derived classes to override and customize the way events are raised if needed. The method checks for any subscribers before invoking the **ProcessCompleted** event and passing a message to all handlers.

The **Program** class acts as the event subscriber. It subscribes to the **ProcessCompleted** event from the **Process** class and defines how to handle the event when it is raised. When the process completes, the subscribed event handler (**Process_ProcessCompleted**) is executed, which will output the completion message to the console.

Here is how the **Program** class is structured as an event subscriber:

```
// Event subscriber class
class ExampleProgram8
{
    static void Main(string[] args)
    {
        // Create an instance of the Process class
        Process process = new Process();

        // Subscribe to the ProcessCompleted event
        process.ProcessCompleted += Process_ProcessCompleted;

        // Start the process
        process.StartProcess();
    }
```

In the **Main** method, we create an instance of the **Process** class, subscribe to the **ProcessCompleted** event, and then start the process by calling **StartProcess**. The subscription uses the **+=** operator, linking the event to the **Process_ProcessCompleted** method.

Finally, we define the event handler method to be called when the **ProcessCompleted** event is raised. This method matches the signature of the **ProcessCompletedEventHandler** delegate:

```
    // Event handler method that matches the delegate signature
    static void Process_ProcessCompleted(string message)
```

```
    {
        // Output the event message to the console
        Console.WriteLine(message);
    }
}
```

The **Process_ProcessCompleted** method is the event handler executed when the event is triggered. It simply writes the received message to the console.

In the preceding example, the '**Process**' class declares an event '**ProcessCompleted**' of type '**ProcessCompletedEventHandler**'. The '**StartProcess**' method simulates some work and then raises the event by calling '**OnProcessCompleted**'. The event is raised using the '**?.Invoke**' syntax, which ensures that the event is only raised if there are any subscribers.

Event handlers

An event handler is a method called when an event is raised. Event handlers must match the delegate type used by the event. In the previous example, the '**Process_ ProcessCompleted**' event handler matches the '**ProcessCompletedEventHandler**' delegate type.

To subscribe to events with an event handler, the **+=** operator is used. This operator adds the specified method to the event's invocation list, meaning that the method will be called whenever the event is triggered. For example:

```
process.ProcessCompleted += Process_ProcessCompleted; // This is event
subscription
```

If you need to stop a method from handling an event, you can use the **-=** operator to unsubscribe from the event. This removes the method from the event's invocation list:

```
process.ProcessCompleted -= Process_ProcessCompleted; // Unsubscribing from
an event
```

In addition to subscribing named methods, event handlers can also be anonymous methods or Lambda expressions. An anonymous method is a method without a name, defined inline using the delegate keyword. Here is how you can use an anonymous method as an event handler:

```
process.ProcessCompleted += delegate(string message)
{
    Console.WriteLine("Anonymous method received: " + message);
};
```

Lambda expressions provide a more concise way to define inline methods. They are handy for short, simple event handlers. Here is how you can use a Lambda expression as an event handler:

```
process.ProcessCompleted += (message) =>
{
    Console.WriteLine("Lambda received: " + message);
};
```

These examples demonstrate the flexibility of C# events. You can use various types of methods—whether named, anonymous or defined using the Lambda expressions—as event handlers. This flexibility makes it easy to handle events in a way that best suits your coding style and your application's needs.

Event handling mechanisms

In C#, event handling is a powerful feature that allows objects to communicate and react to various actions or state changes. This communication is facilitated through event handler delegates, which defines the signature of the methods that can handle an event. These delegates are used to subscribe methods to events, ensuring type safety and consistency in the event-handling process. The most common event handler delegate is **EventHandler**, defined in the .NET Framework.

The **EventHandler** delegate is defined as follows:

```
public delegate void EventHandler(object sender, EventArgs e);
```

This delegate has two parameters:

- **sender**: The source of the event, typically the object that raised the event.

- **e**: An instance of the **EventArgs** class containing no event data.

Here is an example demonstrating the use of the **EventHandler** delegate. We begin by defining a **Publisher** class responsible for raising an event. The event is declared using the **EventHandler** delegate, a standard delegate in .NET for handling events:

```
public class Publisher
{
    // Event declaration using EventHandler
    public static event EventHandler ProcessCompleted;
```

Here, the **ProcessCompleted** event is declared using the **EventHandler** delegate. This event will be triggered when the process is completed. Next, we define the **StartProcess** method in the **Publisher** class, which simulates a process by sleeping for three seconds. Once the simulated process is complete, the **ProcessCompleted** event is raised as shown in the following code:

```
    public void StartProcess()
    {
        // Simulate some processing work
        System.Threading.Thread.Sleep(3000);
```

```
        OnProcessCompleted(EventArgs.Empty);
    }
```

In this method, **Thread.Sleep(3000)** is used to simulate some work being done. After the delay, the **OnProcessCompleted** method triggers the event—the **EventArgs.Empty** parameter is passed, indicating that no specific event data is associated with this event. The **OnProcessCompleted** method is responsible for raising the **ProcessCompleted** event. This method is protected and virtual, allowing derived classes to override it, as show in this code:

```
    protected virtual void OnProcessCompleted(EventArgs e)
    {
        ProcessCompleted?.Invoke(this, e);
    }
}
```

Here, the **ProcessCompleted** event is invoked using the **?.Invoke** syntax, which ensures that the event is only raised if there are any subscribers. This keyword refers to the current instance of the **Publisher** class, and **e** is the event data. Next, we define the **Subscriber** class, which will listen for the **ProcessCompleted** event raised by the **Publisher**. The **Subscribe** method is used to subscribe to the event, as shown here:

```
public class Subscriber
{
    public void Subscribe(Publisher publisher)
    {
        Publisher.ProcessCompleted += OnProcessCompleted;
    }
```

In the **Subscribe** method, the **OnProcessCompleted** method is attached to the **ProcessCompleted** event using the **+=** operator. This means that when the **ProcessCompleted** event is raised, the **OnProcessCompleted** method in this class will be called. The **OnProcessCompleted** class defines the **Subscriber** method to handle the event when it is raised. This method matches the signature of the **EventHandler** delegate, as shown in the following code:

```
    private void OnProcessCompleted(object sender, EventArgs e)
    {
        Console.WriteLine("Process completed event received.");
    }
}
```

When the event is triggered, this method is executed, and it simply outputs a message to the console indicating that the process has been completed. Finally, we bring everything together in the **Program** class, creating instances of **Publisher** and **Subscriber**. The

Subscriber subscribes to the Publisher's event, and the process starts. The code looks like the following:

```
class ExampleProgram8
{
    static void Main(string[] args)
    {
        Publisher publisher = new Publisher();
        Subscriber subscriber = new Subscriber();

        subscriber.Subscribe(publisher);
        publisher.StartProcess();
    }
}
```

The **Main** method creates a **Publisher** object and a **Subscriber** object. The **Subscriber** subscribes to the Publisher's **ProcessCompleted** event, and then the **StartProcess** method is called to initiate the process. After three seconds, the event is triggered, and the Subscriber handles it by printing a message to the console.

In this example, the **Publisher** class raises the **ProcessCompleted** event using the **EventHandler** delegate, and the **Subscriber** class handles the event. The **EventArgs. Empty** is passed to indicate that no specific event data is associated with this event.

The **EventArgs** class is the base class for classes containing event data. It is used when no specific data is needed to pass to the event handler. The **EventArgs** class is defined as follows:

```
public class EventArgs
{
    public static readonly EventArgs Empty;
}
```

Sometimes, additional data needs to be passed with an event. In such cases, custom event arguments can be created by defining a class that derives from **EventArgs** and contains properties for the extra data.

Here is an example of creating and using custom event arguments. We define a custom event arguments class, **ProcessEventArgs**, which derives from the **EventArgs** base class. This class allows us to pass additional information, such as a message, when an event is raised:

```
public class ProcessEventArgs : EventArgs
{
    public string Message { get; }
```

```
    public ProcessEventArgs(string message)
    {
        Message = message;
    }
}
```

The **ProcessEventArgs** class contains a single property, **Message**, which is initialized via the constructor. This message can then be accessed when subscribers handle the event. Next, we define the **Publisher** class, which raises an event when a process is completed. The event is declared using the **EventHandler<T>** delegate, with **ProcessEventArgs** as the **type** parameter as shown here:

```
public class Publisher
{
    // Event declaration using custom event arguments
    public event EventHandler<ProcessEventArgs> ProcessCompleted;
```

Here, the **ProcessCompleted** event is declared, and it uses the **ProcessEventArgs** class to pass additional information when the event is triggered. The **StartProcess** method in the **Publisher** class simulates a process and raises the event once the process is complete. This is done by invoking the **OnProcessCompleted** method with an instance of **ProcessEventArgs**, as shown:

```
    public void StartProcess()
    {
        // Simulate some processing work
        System.Threading.Thread.Sleep(3000);
        OnProcessCompleted(new ProcessEventArgs("Process completed
successfully!"));
    }
```

In this method, **Thread.Sleep(3000)** is used to simulate some work being done. After the delay, the **OnProcessCompleted** method passes in a **ProcessEventArgs** object with a success message and raises the **ProcessCompleted** event. It is protected and virtual, allowing for overriding in derived classes if needed, which is shown as follows:

```
    protected virtual void OnProcessCompleted(ProcessEventArgs e)
    {
        ProcessCompleted?.Invoke(this, e);
    }
}
```

This method checks if there are any subscribers to the **ProcessCompleted** event and, if so, invokes the event, passing along the current instance of the Publisher (**this**) and the event arguments (**e**). We then define the **Subscriber** class, which will listen for the **ProcessCompleted** event and handle it when it occurs. The Subscribe method attaches the **OnProcessCompleted** method to the event:

```
public class Subscriber
{
    public void Subscribe(Publisher publisher)
    {
        publisher.ProcessCompleted += OnProcessCompleted;
    }
```

In the **Subscribe** method, the **OnProcessCompleted** method is subscribed to the **ProcessCompleted** event using the **+=** operator. This ensures that the **OnProcessCompleted** method in this class will be executed when the event is raised. The **OnProcessCompleted** method is the event handler that will be called when the **ProcessCompleted** event is triggered. It matches the signature of the **EventHandler<ProcessEventArgs>** delegate, as shown here:

```
    private void  OnProcessCompleted(object sender, ProcessEventArgs e)
    {
        Console.WriteLine(e.Message);
    }
}
```

When the event is triggered, this method is executed, and the message from the **ProcessEventArgs** is printed to the console. Finally, we bring everything together in the Program class, where instances of **Publisher** and **Subscriber** are created, and the process is started. The code looks like the following:

```
class ExampleProgram9
{
    static void Main(string[] args)
    {
        Publisher publisher = new Publisher();
        Subscriber subscriber = new Subscriber();

        subscriber.Subscribe(publisher);
        publisher.StartProcess();
    }
}
```

The **Main** method creates a **Publisher** object and a **Subscriber** object. The **Subscriber** subscribes to the Publisher's **ProcessCompleted** event, and then the **StartProcess** method is called to initiate the process. After three seconds, the event is triggered, and the **Subscriber** handles it by printing the success message to the console.

Differences between delegates and events

Let us look at the details:

Definition:

- **Delegates**: Delegates are type-safe function pointers that can reference methods with a specific signature. They are used to create callback mechanisms and implement the observer design pattern.

- **Events**: Events are a higher-level abstraction built on delegates. They provide objects with a way of talking formally amongst themselves. When something interesting occurs, most scenarios use them as notifications for other objects.

Usage:

- **Delegates**: Directly invoke methods or chain multiple methods together (multi-cast delegates). They provide flexibility in method invocation and are commonly used for callback mechanisms.

- **Events**: Encapsulate delegates and provide a standardized way to subscribe to and handle notifications. They enforce encapsulation and decoupling between publishers and subscribers, promoting modular and maintainable code.

Syntax:

- **Delegates**: Declared using the '`delegate`' keyword and instantiated like a class.

- **Events**: Declared using the '**event**' keyword and restricts access to only add and remove operations outside the declaring class.

Conclusion

This chapter explored the powerful concepts of delegates and events in C#. We started by understanding delegates as type-safe function pointers that allow methods to be passed and invoked dynamically, enabling more flexible and reusable code. We then delved into creating and managing events, which build on delegates to provide a structured way for objects to communicate and respond to changes in an event-driven architecture. Along the way, we learned how to implement anonymous methods and Lambda expressions to simplify code and distinguish between the roles of delegates and events in different scenarios. Mastering delegates and events is essential for developing robust and interactive applications in C#. These tools enhance your code's flexibility and promote better separation of concerns, leading to more maintainable and scalable software designs.

As we conclude our exploration of delegates and events, it is time to turn our attention to another critical aspect of C# programming: exception handling and debugging. In the next chapter, we will learn how to handle runtime errors gracefully, ensuring that our applications remain stable and user-friendly even when unexpected issues arise. We will also explore debugging techniques to identify and resolve problems efficiently.

Multiple choice questions

1. **What is a delegate in C#?**

   a. A type representing references to methods with a specific parameter list and return type.

   b. A special kind of class used for encapsulating data.

   c. A method that always returns void.

   d. A keyword used for handling exceptions.

2. **Which keyword is used to declare a delegate in C#?**

   a. event

   b. delegate

   c. handler

   d. method

3. **What is the purpose of a multicast delegate?**

   a. To hold a reference to a single method.

   b. To call multiple methods in sequence when invoked.

   c. To declare multiple events simultaneously.

   d. To encapsulate data within a single method.

4. **How do you subscribe a method to an event in C#?**

   a. Using the += operator.

   b. Using the = operator.

   c. Using the -= operator.

   d. Using the == operator.

5. **What does the EventArgs.Empty represent in an event handler?**

   a. An event with no data.

   b. An event that was not raised.

   c. A special type of delegate.

   d. An uninitialized object.

6. **Which of the following is not a valid way to handle an event in C#?**

   a. Using a named method.

   b. Using an anonymous method.

    c.   Using a lambda expression.

    d.   Using a class constructor.

7. **What is the primary difference between delegates and events?**

    a.   Delegates are used to encapsulate method references, while events are used to notify objects of specific actions.

    b.   Events can be directly invoked by any object, while delegates cannot.

    c.   Delegates are always multicast, while events are always single-cast.

    d.   Events are a class type, while delegates are a method.

8. **Which of the following best describes a Lambda expression in C#?**

    a.   A method that returns an integer.

    b.   A shorthand notation for an anonymous method.

    c.   A special delegate that cannot be used with events.

    d.   A keyword used to declare events.

9. **In the following code, what does ProcessCompleted?.Invoke(this, e); do?**

    a.   It ensures the event is raised only if there are subscribers.

    b.   It forces the event to be raised even if there are no subscribers.

    c.   It raises an error if the event is not subscribed.

    d.   It prevents the event from being raised.

10. **Which of the following scenarios is most suitable for using an anonymous method or Lambda expression?**

    a.   Complex logic that will be reused across multiple classes.

    b.   Simple, one-time-use operations tied closely to an event or delegate.

    c.   Creating large, reusable libraries of functions.

    d.   Writing constructor methods for classes.

Answers

1. (a) A type representing references to methods with a specific parameter list and return type.

2. (b) delegate

3. (b) To call multiple methods in sequence when invoked.

4. (a) Using the += operator.

5. (a) An event with no data.

6. (d) Using a class constructor.

7. (a) Delegates are used to encapsulate method references, while events are used to notify objects of specific actions.

8. (b) A shorthand notation for an anonymous method.

9. (a) It ensures the event is raised only if there are subscribers.

10. (b) Simple, one-time-use operations tied closely to an event or delegate.

Practice problems

1. You are developing a simple notification system where multiple methods must be called when a user logs in. Create a multicast delegate that invokes multiple methods when a user logs in.

    a. Declare a delegate named UserLoggedInHandler that takes a string parameter representing the username.

    b. Implement two methods:

        i.   **SendWelcomeEmail(string username)**: Simulates sending a welcome email to the user.

        ii. **LogLoginActivity(string username)**: Simulates logging the user's login activity.

    c. Call both methods when a user logs in using the multicast delegate.

    d. Demonstrate this functionality by invoking the delegate with a sample username.

    Expected output: When invoked, the delegate should first call SendWelcomeEmail and then LogLoginActivity, outputting appropriate messages to the console.

2. You are building a simple e-commerce application that needs to notify customers when their order status changes. To do this, implement an event system using custom event arguments.

    a. Create a class named OrderEventArgs that derives from EventArgs. It should contain the following two properties:

        i.   **OrderID (int)**: The ID of the order.

        ii. **Status (string)**: The current status of the order.

    b. Implement a class OrderProcessor that raises an event OrderStatusChanged using the EventHandler<OrderEventArgs> delegate.

   c. Implement a Customer class that subscribes to the OrderStatusChanged event and handles it by displaying the order ID and status.

   d. In the OrderProcessor class, simulate the change of order status and raise the OrderStatusChanged event with relevant details. Demonstrate this by creating an instance of OrderProcessor, a Customer, and simulating an order status change.

Expected output: When the order status changes, the Customer should be notified with a message displaying the order ID and the updated status.

Join our book's Discord space

Join the book's Discord Workspace for Latest updates, Offers, Tech happenings around the world, New Release and Sessions with the Authors:

https://discord.bpbonline.com

CHAPTER 9

C# Exception Handling and Debugging

Introduction

Managing unexpected code behavior is crucial for ensuring smooth program execution. In C#, exception handling and debugging are essential for creating stable and reliable applications.

In this chapter, we will understand that an exception is an event that disrupts a program's normal flow. In C#, exceptions are objects representing error conditions. When an error occurs, an exception is raised, allowing developers to catch and handle it systematically without crashing the application. Standard exceptions include FileLoadException, DivideByZeroException, and ArgumentOutOfRangeException.

We will also learn that debugging involves identifying, analyzing, and fixing software defects. It requires running the program in a controlled environment to observe its behavior and pinpoint issues. Tools like Visual Studio's debugger, with features such as breakpoints, watch windows, and stepwise execution, help developers examine code and understand its behavior.

Mastering exception handling and debugging is vital for C# developers. Effective exception handling ensures applications recover gracefully from errors, improving user experience and preventing data loss. Conversely, debugging helps identify and resolve issues early, ensuring software quality and reliability. By proactively addressing bugs, developers can avoid minor problems escalating into significant challenges that require additional time and resources.

Structure

This chapter covers the following topics:

- Understanding exceptions in C#
- Basic exception handling
- Creating custom exceptions
- Advanced exception handling
- Best practices for exception handling
- Introduction to debugging

Objectives

By the end of this chapter, you will be able to understand the concept of exceptions and how they disrupt program flow in C#. You will learn to implement basic exception handling using try-catch blocks and create and utilize custom exceptions in C# applications. You will also learn how to debug applications using tools like breakpoints and step-through code execution and apply best practices for efficient exception handling and debugging.

Understanding exceptions in C#

A runtime error that occurs during the execution of a C# program is known as an exception. Unlike compile-time errors, which are detected before the program runs by the compiler, exceptions occur while the program is running. These errors may arise from various problems, such as invalid user data, attempts to retrieve unavailable resources, or logical errors in code. When an exception occurs, it disrupts the usual flow of the program, and if not adequately addressed, it may bring about the sudden termination of the program.

C# provides a rich set of built-in exceptions representing different error conditions. Some of the most common types of exceptions include:

- **NullReferenceException**: Thrown when accessing a member of a type whose value is null.

- **ApplicationException**: This is thrown when accessing an unloaded application domain.

- **OutOfMemoryException**: Thrown when the program has insufficient memory to execute.

- **DivideByZeroException**: Thrown when dividing an integer value by zero.

- **System.IO.IOException**: Thrown while an error occurs when reading from or writing to a file.

Learning these standard exceptions aids in understanding problems and putting solid error handling in place.

Exception hierarchy

Exceptions in C# are arranged in a hierarchy with the '**System.Exception**' class at the top. The base class has properties like '**Message**', '**StackTrace**', and '**InnerException**' that give all the error details. '**System.Exception**' has two branches: '**System.SystemException**' and '**System.ApplicationException**':

- **System.SystemException**: This branch contains all the exceptions thrown by the runtime system, such as '**NullReferenceException**', '**IndexOutOfRangeException**', and '**InvalidOperationException**'.

- **System.ApplicationException**: This branch is intended for application-defined exceptions. However, it is helpful in practical scenarios to derive custom exceptions directly from '**System.Exception**'.

This hierarchy is flexible in error management by allowing developers to catch and handle exceptions at any level of specificity.

Basic exception handling

This section covers the basics of how to catch and handle exceptions using the try-catch block, manage multiple exceptions, and ensure that necessary cleanup actions are taken with the '**finally**' block. The 'try-catch' block is the central feature in C# for handling exceptions. The code that might generate an exception should be written within a '**try**' block, while the corresponding code for error handling should be written in one or more '**catch**' blocks. A simple example is as follows:

```
try
{
    // Code that may throw an exception
    int result = 10 / int.Parse(userInput);
}
catch (FormatException)
{
    // Handle format exception
    Console.WriteLine("Input is not a valid number.");
}
catch (DivideByZeroException)
{
    // Handle divide by zero exception
```

```
    Console.WriteLine("Cannot divide by zero.");
}
```

Here, the code in the 'try' block may have either a 'FormatException' or 'DivideByZeroException' exception. There is a separate 'catch' block for both exception types.

Handling multiple exceptions

Sometimes, a block of code may throw more than one type of exception, each handled differently. C# allows developers to implement multiple 'catch' blocks so that different exceptions may be processed separately. Each 'catch' block should target a specific exception type, and the most particular exceptions should be caught first to ensure proper handling:

```
try
{
    // Code that may throw multiple exceptions
    string[] numbers = { "10", "30", "NaN", "40" };
    foreach (var number in numbers)
    {
        int result = 10 / int.Parse(number);
        Console.WriteLine(result);
    }
}
catch (FormatException ex)
{
    // Handle format exception
    Console.WriteLine("A number format issue occurred: " + ex.Message);
}
catch (DivideByZeroException ex)
{
    // Handle divide by zero exception
    Console.WriteLine("Attempted to divide by zero: " + ex.Message);
}
catch (Exception ex)
{
    // Handle any other exceptions
    Console.WriteLine("Unexpected error has occurred: " + ex.Message);
}
```

Here, different exceptions are handled by different '**catch**' blocks, while a final '**catch**' block is also provided for unexpected exceptions.

Finally block

The block labeled as '**finally**' is a part of the exception handling structure that is not mandatory. The code contained in this block will execute irrespective of any exception caught or thrown. The '**finally**' block is primarily helpful for cleanup activities, like resource releasing, resetting states, or closing files, which must execute even if an error occurs:

```
FileStream file = null;
try
{
    // Code that may throw an exception
    file = File.Open("data.txt", FileMode.Open);
    // Operations on the file
}
catch (IOException ex)
{
    // Handle I/O exception
    Console.WriteLine("An I/O error occurred: " + ex.Message);
}
finally
{
    // Code to clean up resources
    if (file != null)
        file.Close();

    Console.WriteLine("File closed.");
}
```

In this scenario, the '**finally**' block ensures that the file closes regardless of the presence of an exception. Resource release is ensured in a way that assures the program's safety.

Creating custom exceptions

While C# has a wide range of built-in exceptions, there might be scenarios where your exceptions should be defined to depict conditions peculiar to your application. Henceforth, this section will teach you how to create and implement custom exceptions effectively.

Custom exceptions are created when programmers must provide more specific error information not sufficiently represented by the existing exception types. Consider creating a custom exception when:

- The error condition is unique to your application or domain.
- You need to provide additional context or data about the error.
- You want to distinguish between several forms of application-dependent errors.

As an illustration, if you want to create a library for processing financial transactions, you might make a custom exception called '**InsufficientFundsException**' indicating error conditions when no money remains in an account for executing any transaction undertakings.

Custom exceptions can be created in C# by creating new classes that either derive from '**System.Exception**' or one of its subclasses. The custom exception class should include constructors that call base class constructors and may also have extra methods and properties to provide a detailed explanation of the error. An example of a custom exception is as follows:

```csharp
using System;


public class InsufficientFundsException : Exception
{
    public decimal Balance { get; }
    public decimal Amount { get; }

    public InsufficientFundsException()
    {
    }

    public InsufficientFundsException(string message) : base(message)
    {
    }

    public InsufficientFundsException(string message, Exception inner) :
base(message, inner)
    {
    }

    public InsufficientFundsException(string message, decimal balance,
decimal amount) : base(message)
    {
        Balance = balance;
        Amount = amount;
```

```
    }

    public override string ToString()
    {
        return $"{base.ToString()}, Balance: {Balance}, Amount: {Amount}";
    }
}
```

Here, '**InsufficientFundsException**' comprises the extra properties '**Balance**' and '**Amount**', which provide more details about the error. The '**ToString**' method is overridden by including this additional information in the exception message.

A custom exception, when created, can be thrown using the '**throw**' statement. Following is how to throw '**InsufficientFundsException**':

```
public class BankAccount
{
    public decimal Balance { get; private set; }

    public BankAccount(decimal initialBalance)
    {
        Balance = initialBalance;
    }

    public void Withdraw(decimal amount)
    {
        if (amount > Balance)
        {
            throw new InsufficientFundsException("Attempt to withdraw more
than the available balance.", Balance, amount);
        }

        Balance -= amount;
    }
}
```

In this scenario, when someone takes out more cash that exceeds their account balance, the '**Withdraw**' function defined in the '**BankAccount**' class throws an '**InsufficientFundsException**'. This generates a clear error message, allowing the caller code to catch and handle the problem correctly:

```
try
{

    BankAccount account = new BankAccount(100);
    account.Withdraw(150);
}
catch (InsufficientFundsException ex)
{

    Console.WriteLine($»Error: {ex.Message}»);
    Console.WriteLine($"Balance: {ex.Balance}, Attempted Withdrawal: {ex.
Amount}");
}
```

Here, the calling code catches the '**InsufficientFundsException**' and processes it, providing the user with detailed information about the error.

Advanced exception handling

There may be occasions when you need to catch an exception within a '**try**' block that lies within another '**try**' block. This provides greater sensitivity in error handling since different levels of a program can respond to exceptions in a different manner. An example of nested 'try-catch' blocks is as follows:

```
try
{
    try
    {
        // Code that might throw an exception
        int result = 10 / int.Parse(userInput);
    }
    catch (FormatException ex)
    {
        // Handle format exceptions specifically
        Console.WriteLine("Input is not a valid number.");
        throw; // Optionally rethrow to be handled by the outer block
    }
}
catch (DivideByZeroException ex)
{
    // Handle divide by zero exception
    Console.WriteLine("Cannot divide by zero.");
```

```
}
catch (Exception ex)
{
    // Handle any other exceptions
    Console.WriteLine("Unexpected error has occurred: " + ex.Message);
}
```

Here, the inner 'try-catch' block catches a particular exception ('**FormatException**'), while the outer block manages additional exceptions. The statement '**throw**' shall be utilized in the inner '**catch**' block; the exception will be thrown again so that the outer block may catch it if needed.

Throw statement

This statement is used to throw either a new or an existing exception. This could be useful for several purposes, like propagating errors up the call stack or even rethrowing an exception to be handled at a higher level. Within a '**catch**' block, you can use '**throw**' to rethrow the currently caught exception without losing the original stack trace:

```
catch (Exception ex)
{
    // Log the exception
    Console.WriteLine("An error occurred: " + ex.Message);

    // Rethrow the exception
    throw;
}
```

Using '**throw**' without specifying an exception preserves the original exception details, which is crucial for accurate debugging and logging.

Using exception properties

Exception objects in C# possess many attributes that help to elaborate on the error that happened. Understanding and using these attributes can go a long way in diagnosing and solving various other issues. The '**Message**' property of an exception provides a descriptive string that explains the nature of the error. This property is initialized with a default error message, but you can also supply a custom message when creating an exception. The '**Message**' property helps log errors and display user-friendly error messages.

An example of using the '**Message**' property is as follows:

```
try
{
```

```
    // Code that might throw an exception
    int result = 10 / int.Parse(userInput);
}
catch (Exception ex)
{
    // Log the error message
    Console.WriteLine("Error: " + ex.Message);
}
```

If an exception occurs, the '**Message**' property will display a descriptive error message.

The '**StackTrace**' property gives a string representation of the call stack, at which point the exception was thrown. It helps diagnose the sequence of method calls that lead to the exception. Viewing the stack trace lets you determine where the error occurs in your code and move backward through the method calls.

An example of using the '**StackTrace**' property is as follows:

```
try
{
    // Code that might throw an exception
    int result = 10 / int.Parse(userInput);
}
catch (Exception ex)
{
    // Log the stack trace
    Console.WriteLine("Stack Trace: " + ex.StackTrace);
}
```

In this example, the '**StackTrace**' property outputs detailed call stack information, aiding debugging and error resolution.

The '**InnerException**' property provides additional information about exceptions caught and wrapped inside another exception. This property helps understand the root cause of complex error conditions, where one exception might lead to another. By examining the '**InnerException**', you can trace the error back through multiple layers of exception handling.

The following is an example of using the '**InnerException**' property:

```
try
{
    try
    {
```

```
        // Code that might throw an inner exception
        int result = 10 / int.Parse(userInput);
    }
    catch (FormatException ex)
    {
        // Wrap the inner exception in a new exception
        throw new ApplicationException("An error occurred in the
application.", ex);
    }
}
catch (ApplicationException ex)
{
    // Log the inner exception
    Console.WriteLine("Inner Exception: " + ex.InnerException?.Message);
}
```

In this example, a '**FormatException**' is caught and wrapped into an '**ApplicationException**'. Through its '**InnerException**' property, the '**ApplicationException**' contains details about what led to the original '**FormatException**', giving a more holistic picture of the error.

Best practices for exception handling

When handling exceptions, catch only those exceptions that you can handle well. Picking general exceptions, such as '**Exception**', may hide other problems, thus making debugging challenging. Instead, catch specific exceptions that you expect and know how to handle. This approach allows you to address different error conditions with tailored solutions:

```
try
{
    // Code that might throw specific exceptions
    int result = 10 / int.Parse(userInput);
}
catch (FormatException ex)
{
    // Handle format exceptions specifically
    Console.WriteLine("Input is not a valid number.");
}
catch (DivideByZeroException ex)
{
```

```
    // Handle divide by zero exception
    Console.WriteLine("Cannot divide by zero.");
}
catch (Exception ex)
{
    // Handle any other exceptions
    Console.WriteLine("Unexpected error has occurred: " + ex.Message);
}
```

However, as illustrated in the preceding example, specific exceptions like '**FormatException**' or '**DivideByZeroException**' must be separately caught and handled for precise error handling.

Avoiding exception handling performance pitfalls

Exception handling can impact performance, especially if exceptions are thrown and caught frequently. While exceptions are designed for exceptional conditions and not for regular control flow, there are ways to minimize performance issues:

- **Avoid overusing exceptions**: Use exceptions to handle exceptional conditions, not for routine control flow or validation checks.

- **Minimize exception scope**: Place exception-prone code inside the smallest possible try block to avoid catching exceptions unnecessarily.

- **Use exception filters**: In C# 6.0 and later, you can use exception filters to handle exceptions based on specific conditions, reducing the need for multiple '**catch**' blocks:

  ```
  try
  {
      // Code that might throw an exception
  }
  catch (Exception ex) when (ex is FormatException || ex is
  DivideByZeroException)
  {
      // Handle specific exceptions with a filter
      Console.WriteLine("A specific error occurred: " + ex.Message);
  }
  ```

Using exceptions for control flow

Exceptions should not be used for regular control flow. They are intended to handle unexpected errors and exceptional conditions. Using exceptions like trying to open a file and catching an exception if it does not exist for control flow can lead to inefficient and hard-to-maintain code.

Instead of using exceptions for control flow, use appropriate methods and checks. For instance, before trying to open any file, check whether it exists:

```csharp
if (File.Exists("data.txt"))
{
    // Code to open and process the file
}
else
{
    Console.WriteLine("File not found");
}
```

Using this approach avoids unnecessary exceptions and keeps your code clean and efficient.

Introduction to debugging

A software program should be free of bugs or defects, so debugging is crucial. It involves running the application under controlled conditions, observing its behavior, looking for abnormal activities, and tracking down the root cause of the problem. Thus, debugging helps ensure the software works well and fulfills its intended requirements.

Developers use various techniques to inspect the application's state at different execution stages during debugging, such as checking variable values, going through code line by line, and setting breakpoints. The main objective is to determine why the application does not behave as expected and fix it.

There are several reasons why debugging is essential in software development, which are as follows:

- **Error discovery**: Detecting and fixing errors that might not have been noticed in initial testing helps ensure the software performs as intended.

- **Improving code quality**: Finding and repairing bugs can improve the quality and reliability of a software product.

- **Understanding application behavior**: Debugging gives insights into how the program works; therefore, we can optimize its performance or enhance its functionality.

- **Reducing maintenance costs**: To prevent minor issues from turning into significant issues, productive debugging can minimize permanent maintenance expenses and be more acceptable to users.

Software programs may contain hidden defects without proper debugging, resulting in unexpected behavior, crashes, or security flaws.

Common debugging tools

C# or any other programming language has diverse tools to assist debugging. Some of them include:

- **Integrated development environments (IDEs)**: Visual Studio has strong bug-fixing capabilities, such as breakpoints, step execution, watch windows, and inspecting variables. Thus, it provides a complete debugging experience within the development environment.

- **Breakpoints**: Allow developers to stop the execution of codes at specific points to observe the application's state. A breakpoint can be created by clicking on the margin next to the line of code where the programmer intends to pause execution. When the program runs down to this line, it will stop moving, so the programmer starts checking.

- **Step Over/Into/Out**: This feature enables developers to execute code line by line, step into method calls, or step out of the current method, providing fine-grained control over code execution.

- **Step Over (F10)**: Executes the current line of code and moves to the following line. If the current line contains a method call, the method is executed, but you do not step into it.

- **Step Into (F11)**: Executes the current line and, if it contains a method call, steps into that method to debug it line by line.

- **Step Out (Shift + F11)**: It runs until the end of the current method and then returns to the calling method, pausing at the following code line after it has been called.

- **Watch windows**: Allow developers to monitor the values of variables and expressions as the application runs. Variables can be added to the watch window to show their current values as you move through the codes. Watch windows help track the condition of variables over time and detect when they change unexpectedly. You can add a variable to the watch window by right-clicking on it and choosing 'add to watch'.

The Immediate Window is an interactive IDE console where developers can evaluate expressions, execute statements, and display variable values when debugging. It is an excellent tool for checking small pieces of code and verifying the application's state without changing its source code.

Debugging tools in Visual Studio

VS Debugger is a powerful tool that offers various features for debugging C# applications. These include breakpoints, step-through codes, watch windows, and immediate windows, among many others. It also enables you to stop your program from running midway so that you can check some local variables and even move around the script designed to find errors.

IntelliTrace is an advanced debugging tool within Visual Studio that records a chronological account of your application's execution. This functionality lets you go back in time and assess your application's status at distinct times throughout its running period. IntelliTrace captures events like method calls, exceptions, and system events to give a detailed timeline of how well or poorly your applications performed over time.

Some key benefits of IntelliTrace include:

- **Historical debugging**: Browse your application's prior levels to find how it transformed into its present form.

- **Event Logs**: See significant happening, such as method entry and exit points, thread activities, and exceptions on a time scale.

- **Enhanced debugging**: Combine traditional debugging with IntelliTrace to get a perfect picture of your applications' runtime execution flow.

Using this tool would be beneficial in terms of time as it would enable you to trace back your applications' history and understand what made them malfunction at a given moment.

During debugging sessions, the Diagnostic Tools window under Visual Studio offers live performance insights about your application. It includes diagnostic data, such as CPU and memory usage, threads, and event information. It helps you monitor the app's resource consumption and identify performance bottlenecks or memory leaks.

Key features of the Diagnostic Tools window include:

- **CPU usage**: Monitor how much CPU your app is using so that you can identify what parts are causing it to be slowest.

- **Memory management**: Keep an eye out for memory allocation and usage to detect possible memory leaks or high memory utilization

- **Event Viewer**: This area shows events like breakpoints, exceptions, and garbage collection.

- **Threads**: Analyze the activity of different threads within your application to understand concurrency issues.

Implementing Logging in C#

The introduction of logging into C# involves frameworks for logging that offer structured and efficient ways to capture and regulate log data. Frequently used logging frameworks are NLog, log4net, and Serilog. These frameworks have flexible configuration options, support multiple log destinations, and possess extra features like log filtering, formatting, etc.

The following is a basic example of implementing logging using NLog:

1. **Install**: Add the NLog package to your project using NuGet:
    ```
    Install-Package NLog
    ```

2. **Configure**: Build an '**nlog.config**' file to configure its settings:
    ```xml
    <?xml version="1.0" encoding="utf-8"?>
    <nlog xmlns = "http://www.nlog-project.org/schemas/NLog.xsd"
          xmlns:xsi="http://www.w3.org/2001/XMLSchema-instance">
        <targets>
                <target xsi:type="File" name="file" filename="${basedir}/
    logs/logfile.txt" />
        </targets>
        <rules>
                <logger name="*" minlevel="Info" writeTo="file" />
        </rules>
    </nlog>
    ```

3. **Use NLog in your code**: Add logging statements to your application:
    ```csharp
    using NLog;

    class NLogExample
    {
        private static readonly Logger Logger = LogManager.
    GetCurrentClassLogger ();

        static void Main (string [] args )
        {
            Logger.Info ("Application started.");
            try
            {
                int x = 5;
                int y = 0;
                int result = x / y; // This will throw an exception
            }
            catch (Exception ex)
            {
                    Logger.Error (ex, "An error occurred while dividing by
    zero.");
    ```

```
        }
        Logger.Info ("Application ended.");
    }
}
```

In this example, **NLog** is set to write log messages to a text file. The '**Logger**' object records informational messages and error details.

Tools for monitoring and diagnostics

In addition to logging frameworks, several tools are available to help monitor and diagnose issues in your application:

- **Application insights**: A robust monitoring service provided by Microsoft Azure. This contains important information about application performance, user behavior, and errors. Also, application insights could identify the problems in your app, diagnose them, and provide instant alerts and elaborate reports for you.

- **Elasticsearch, Logstash, Kibana (ELK) Stack**: The ELK stack is an incredibly famous open-source log management tool that collects, indexes, and analyzes logs quickly and readily. This means they have a single platform on which all their apps are built without worrying about different tools.

- **Sentry**: Sentry is an error-tracking and monitoring tool that sends notifications when something goes wrong in your application. With Sentry, you can identify errors quickly, prioritize them according to severity level, and fix them efficiently.

- **Seq**: It allows you to collect, search, and visualize structured data using various logging frameworks, such as NLog or Log4Net. Its straightforward interface makes it convenient for querying and analyzing logs over time.

Let us look at some real-life applications.

This section explores common scenarios where exception handling and debugging are applied and provides examples from real-world applications:

- **Common scenarios**: In real-world applications, exception handling and debugging are used in various scenarios to maintain application stability and improve user experience. Some common scenarios include:

    o **Validating the user input**: Ensuring the user input is valid or handled otherwise.

    o **Operations on files**: Managing different operations performed on files, such as read and write, and handling cases where the file is missing or corrupted.

    o Database interactions include managing exceptions during database connections, queries, and transactions.

    o **Network communication**: Network communication defines handling exceptions for network workings; API calls, for instance, face timeouts, broken connections, and other network-related issues.

o   **Resource management**: This means ensuring that resources (like memory or file handles) are appropriately allocated and released while handling exceptions during resource management.

Conclusion

In conclusion, mastering exception handling and debugging is essential for any C# developer aiming to build robust, reliable, and maintainable applications. Properly handling exceptions allows your programs to gracefully manage errors without crashing, while debugging ensures that any issues are quickly identified and resolved. You can enhance your software's performance and stability by understanding how to use built-in exceptions, create custom exceptions, and apply best practices in error handling. Additionally, leveraging debugging tools such as breakpoints, watch windows, and logging frameworks will help streamline identifying and correcting issues. Implementing these techniques will lead to developing more efficient, user-friendly applications.

The next chapter will explore C# File and Stream I/O, a crucial topic for managing data input and output in your applications. Understanding how to work with files and streams will allow you to efficiently read, write, and manipulate data stored in external files. We will cover the different classes and methods provided by the .NET Framework to perform file operations, including file creation, reading, writing, appending, and handling streams for more complex data-handling scenarios. This knowledge will enable you to manage data storage and retrieval, essential in building applications that interact with the filesystem or external data sources.

Multiple choice questions

1.   **What is an exception in C#?**

   a.   A syntax error detected by the compiler.

   b.   A runtime error that disrupts the normal flow of a program.

   c.   A method that fixes code bugs automatically.

   d.   A type of loop in C#

2.   **What is not a common built-in exception type in C#?**

   a.   DivideByZeroException

   b.   NullReferenceException

   c.   FileLoadException

   d.   MemoryFullException

3. **What is the primary purpose of the 'try-catch' block in C#?**

   a. To execute code without any errors.

   b. To handle and manage exceptions gracefully.

   c. To optimize the performance of the application.

   d. To prevent syntax errors from occurring.

4. **Which part of the exception handling structure ensures that code is executed regardless of an exception?**

   a. catch

   b. finally

   c. try

   d. throw

5. **What is the correct syntax for creating a custom exception in C#?**

   a. public class MyException : Exception {}

   b. public class MyException : CustomError {}

   c. public class MyException : SystemError {}

   d. public class MyException : FormatException {}

6. **Which of the following statements about multiple 'catch' blocks is true?**

   a. You can only catch one type of exception in a try-catch block.

   b. Each catch block handles a different type of exception.

   c. Multiple catch blocks will handle the same exception.

   d. Multiple catch blocks are not allowed in C#.

7. **What does the throw keyword do in C# exception handling?**

   a. It prevents the program from terminating.

   b. It rethrows the caught exception to be handled elsewhere.

   c. It catches the exception.

   d. It fixes the error automatically.

8. **What is the purpose of the StackTrace property in an exception object?**

   a. To get the error message.

   b. To give a string representation of the call stack at the point where the exception was thrown.

  c. To provide user-friendly error messages.

  d. To stop the program execution.

9. **What is the best practice for exception handling in C#?**

  a. Catch only general exceptions like exceptions.

  b. Use exceptions for regular control flow.

  c. Catch specific exceptions that you can handle properly.

  d. Avoid using exceptions to save performance.

10. **What is the role of debugging tools like breakpoints in Visual Studio?**

  a. To automatically fix all the bugs in the code.

  b. To allow developers to pause execution and inspect variable states.

  c. To compile code faster.

  d. To prevent exceptions from occurring.

Answers

1. (b) A runtime error that disrupts the normal flow of a program

2. (d) MemoryFullException

3. (b) To handle and manage exceptions gracefully

4. (b) finally

5. (a) public class MyException : Exception {}

6. (b)Each catch block handles a different exception type.

7. (b) It rethrows the caught exception to be handled elsewhere.

8. (b) To give a string representation of the call stack at the point the exception was thrown

9. (c) Catch specific exceptions that you can handle properly

10. (b) To allow developers to pause execution and inspect variable states

Practice problems

1. You are tasked with developing a small application that asks users to input two integers. The program should divide the first integer by the second integer and display the result. However, it would be best if you handled potential exceptions that might occur, such as:

    a.   The user enters invalid (non-numeric) input.

    b.   The user enters zero as the second integer (which will cause a divide-by-zero error).

    c.   Any other unforeseen exceptions.

Requirements:

    a.   Prompt the user for two inputs: the numerator and the denominator.

    b.   Implement exception handling using try-catch blocks to manage the following exceptions:

        i.   FormatException for invalid numeric input.

        ii.   DivideByZeroException for division by zero.

        iii. A general Exception block to catch any other unexpected errors.

    c.   Ensure the program displays appropriate error messages for each exception type.

    d.   Use a finally block to display a message that indicates the program has completed the process, regardless of whether an exception was caught.

Example output:

```
If the user inputs "10" and "0", the output should be:
It cannot be divided by zero.
Process completed.
If the user inputs "10" and "abc", the output should be:
Input is not a valid number.
Process completed.
If the user inputs "10" and "2", the output should be:
Result: 5
Process completed.
```

Hint: Use int.Parse() to convert the input strings to integers and structure your try-catch blocks so that each exception type is handled separately.

2.   You are tasked with developing a program that calculates the average of an array of numbers the user enters. The program compiles successfully but produces incorrect results. Your task is to debug the program and fix the logical error using Visual Studio's debugging tools, such as breakpoints, step over, and watch windows to inspect variable values.

Requirements:

    a.   Write a function CalculateAverage(int[] numbers) that accepts an array of integers and returns their average.

b. Prompt the user to input the number of elements they want to enter, followed by the values of those elements.

c. Display the calculated average.

d. Debug the program using breakpoints and the watch window to identify why the result is incorrect.

Buggy code example:

```csharp
using System;
class Program
{
    static void Main()
    {
        Console.WriteLine("How many numbers do you want to input?");
        int count = int.Parse(Console.ReadLine());

        int[] numbers = new int[count];

        for (int i = 0; i < count; i++)
        {
            Console.WriteLine($"Enter number {i + 1}:");
            numbers[i] = int.Parse(Console.ReadLine());
        }

        double average = CalculateAverage(numbers);
        Console.WriteLine($"The average of the numbers is:
{average}");
    }

    static double CalculateAverage(int[] numbers)
    {
        int sum = 0;
        for (int i = 0; i <= numbers.Length; i++)
        {
            sum += numbers[i];
        }

        return sum / numbers.Length;
    }
}
```

Steps for debugging:

a. **Set a breakpoint** inside the CalculateAverage function, particularly at the line where the sum is calculated (sum += numbers[i];).

b. **Use the watch window** to inspect the values of sum and i during each iteration of the loop.

c. Step through the code using **Step Over (F10)** to observe the program's behavior and how the sum is calculated.

d. **Inspect the loop condition** and identify any off-by-one errors that might be causing the program to fail.

e. Correct the issue and ensure the program returns the correct average.

Questions to consider:

a. Does the loop iterate the correct number of times based on the input?

b. What values do i and sum hold at each iteration?

c. How is the average calculated, and is the division happening as expected?

Expected output after fixing the bug:

```
For an input of 3 numbers, 10, 20, and 30, the output should be:
The average of the numbers is: 20
```

Hint: Focus on the loop condition and how it affects array access. During iteration, make sure you do not exceed the array's bounds.

Join our book's Discord space

Join the book's Discord Workspace for Latest updates, Offers, Tech happenings around the world, New Release and Sessions with the Authors:

https://discord.bpbonline.com

CHAPTER 10
C# File and Stream Input/Output

Introduction

File and stream **input/output (I/O)** operations are fundamental components of many C# applications. These operations allow programs to manage data beyond their lifespan, enabling the persistent storage and retrieval of information. In this chapter, we will explore how C# handles file and stream I/O through the System.IO namespace, which offers a range of classes a nd methods for creating, reading, writing, and managing files and directories.

Understanding file and stream operations is crucial for saving user information, managing configuration files, processing large datasets, and handling communication between different parts of an application. Whether reading from a text file, writing binary data, or transferring files over a network, C# provides tools to perform these tasks efficiently and effectively.

This chapter will guide you through the basics of file and stream I/O, including working with text and binary files, handling directories, and leveraging streams to process data sequentially. By the end of this chapter, you will have a solid understanding of integrating file and stream operations into your C# projects, enhancing their functionality and reliability.

Structure

This chapter covers the following topics:

- Introduction to file and stream
- File handling in C#
- Streams in C#

Objectives

By the end of this chapter, you will understand the basic concepts of file and stream I/O operations in C#, including creating, reading, writing, and deleting files using the **File** and **FileInfo** classes. You will also learn to work with directories by creating, deleting, and enumerating files and folders using **Directory** and **DirectoryInfo**. Additionally, you will gain proficiency in reading from and writing to text and binary files using **StreamReader**, **StreamWriter**, and **FileStream**. Furthermore, you will explore advanced stream types such as **BufferedStream**, **MemoryStream**, and **NetworkStream**, enabling you to optimize the performance of file and data operations effectively.

Introduction to file and stream

Files and streams I/O are two of the most fundamental programming components in C#. It empowers applications to read and write files and manage streams of data. This functionality is essential in various tasks like storing data, managing configurations, and communicating between different software program parts.

File I/O describes the activity of reading information from files and writing information back into them again. File I/O operations in C# are performed using classes in the '**System. IO**' namespace. Such classes come with several methods for creating, opening, reading, writing, and closing files, making it relatively simple to handle any information related to files using an organized approach.

File and stream I/O are critical for many C# applications. They allow programs to save data beyond their lifespan, thus allowing long-term storage and recall. This is especially true for applications that require maintaining user information, such as log file contents, throughout their lifespan or any other kind of persistent memory objects. Besides, stream I/O allows efficient processing by manipulating data during transfer from one point to another, making it necessary for activities such as transferring files over the internet network communication and real-time information processing.

File handling in C#

File handling is one of the most important skills for a C# developer. It requires developing the ability to create, read, and manipulate files and their directories, which is critical to data storage, configuration, and many other tasks. Within the '**System.IO**' namespace, C# has a comprehensive set of tools to provide all these operations.

The '**System.IO**' namespace includes classes and methods that help with I/O operations on files and streams. The main courses are:

- **File**: It has static functions for handling files, such as creating, copying, deleting, moving, and opening them.

- **FileInfo**: This class has instance methods that perform the same tasks as the '**File**' class but provide more room for complex scenarios where methods can operate on particular instances of files.

- **Directory**: Provides static methods for creating, moving, and enumerating through directories and subdirectories.

- **DirectoryInfo**: Provides instance methods for the same operations as the '**Directory**' class.

- **Stream**: This is the abstract base class for all streams, providing a generic view of a sequence of bytes.

- **FileStream**: This class provides a stream for file operations.

- **StreamReader and StreamWriter**: These classes allow reading from and writing to streams, respectively.

Basic file operations

In C#, multiple ways exist to create files depending on the application's needs. Two common approaches involve using the **File** class and the **FileInfo** class from the **System.IO** namespace. Both provide the ability to create new files but differ slightly in their use. The **File** class provides static methods for handling files, while the **FileInfo** class provides instance-based methods, offering more control when working with file objects over multiple operations. The following method is how you can use both methods to create a new file:

```
// Using File class
var fileStream = File.Create("example.txt");
fileStream.Close();
// Using FileInfo class
var fileInfo = new FileInfo("example1.txt");
var fileStream2 = fileInfo.Create();
fileStream2.Close();
```

Both approaches will create a new file named **"example.txt"** in the specified directory, if it does not exist.

In C#, data can be read from a file using various methods depending on the operation requirements. For simple use cases, you can utilize **File.ReadAllText** or **File. ReadAllLines**, which quickly reads the entire file as a string or an array of lines. For more control over how the data is read, such as reading chunks or handling large files, you can use the **FileStream** class with a **StreamReader** to process the file line by line or in segments. Here are examples of both approaches:

```
// Using File class
string content = File.ReadAllText("example.txt");
// Using FileStream
using (var streamReader = new StreamReader("example.txt"))
{
    string content2 = streamReader.ReadToEnd();
}
```

The **File.ReadAllText** method reads the entire file content into a single string. At the same time, the **StreamReader** gives you more flexibility in reading the file, such as reading it line by line or until a specific condition is met. Both methods are efficient and valuable depending on the size and structure of the file you are working with.

Writing data to a file can be done using various approaches, depending on the complexity of the task. For straightforward operations, **WriteAllText** or **WriteAllLines** from the **File** class allows text writing to be accessible to a file. When more control is needed over the writing process, **FileStream** combined with **StreamWriter** provides flexibility for handling more extensive or complex data writes. Here are examples of both methods for writing data to a file:

```
// Using File class
File.WriteAllText("example.txt", "Hello, World!");
// Using FileStream
using (var streamWriter = new StreamWriter("example.txt"))
{
    streamWriter.Write("Hello, World!");
}
```

The **File.WriteAllText** method writes the entire string to a file in one step, overwriting the file if it exists. For more granular control, **StreamWriter** allows for writing text incrementally, offering flexibility in how data is processed and written to the file. Both methods are helpful depending on the task at hand.

Both **File.Delete** and **FileInfo.Delete** methods are used to remove files from the filesystem. The **File.Delete** method provides a quick, static way to delete a file, while **FileInfo.Delete** offers an instance-based approach that is useful when managing multiple operations on a file. Here are examples of both methods for deleting a file:

```
// Using File class
File.Delete("example.txt");
// Using FileInfo class
var fileInfo = new FileInfo("example.txt");
fileInfo.Delete();
```

The **File.Delete** method allows you to delete the specified file directly. In contrast, **FileInfo.Delete** is useful when working with a file object, especially when other file-related operations might be needed before deletion. Both methods will effectively remove the file from the system.

Working with FileInfo and DirectoryInfo classes

The **FileInfo** and **DirectoryInfo** classes provide more granular control over file and directory operations compared to their static counterparts (**File** and **Directory**). These classes allow you to perform multiple operations on a single file or directory instance, making them ideal for scenarios where repeated or detailed actions on files and directories are required.

The **FileInfo** class enables instance-based file operations, such as creating, modifying, or deleting a file, while also providing access to file metadata, such as size:

```
var fileInfo = new FileInfo("example.txt");
fileInfo.Create().Close();
Console.WriteLine(fileInfo.Length);
fileInfo.Delete();
```

Similarly, **DirectoryInfo** allows instance-based operations for managing directories, such as creating, accessing directory details, or deleting a directory and its contents:

```
var directoryInfo = new DirectoryInfo("exampleDirectory");
directoryInfo.Create();
Console.WriteLine(directoryInfo.FullName);
directoryInfo.Delete(true);
```

Both **FileInfo** and **DirectoryInfo** offer greater flexibility and control, especially when working with multiple operations on the same file or directory, making them essential tools in file and directory management.

Reading from files

When working with files, reading data is crucial for many applications, such as loading configurations, processing data files, or handling resources. C# offers several classes and methods to efficiently read data from text and binary files. One of the most commonly used classes for reading text files is **StreamReader**, which provides a simple way to read characters from a file using a specified encoding. Here is an example of using **StreamReader** to read the contents of a text file line by line:

```
using (StreamReader reader = new StreamReader("example2.txt"))
{
    string line;
    while ((line = reader.ReadLine()) != null)
    {
        Console.WriteLine(line);
    }
}
```

C# provides the **FileStream** class to handle binary data, which allows reading bytes directly from a file. This is useful when dealing with non-text files, such as images, executable files, or any other binary format. Using **FileStream**, you can open a file, read its raw byte data, and process it accordingly. Here is an example of using **FileStream** to read a binary file:

```
using (FileStream fs = new FileStream("example.bin", FileMode.Open,
FileAccess.Read))
{
    byte[] buffer = new byte[fs.Length];
    int bytesRead = fs.Read(buffer, 0, buffer.Length);

    Console.WriteLine("Bytes read: " + bytesRead);
    // Process the binary data as needed
}
```

The **ReadAllText** and **ReadAllLines** functions belong to the 'File' class and are used to read the whole file simultaneously. **ReadAllText** reads all the text from a file and returns it as a single string, as shown in the following example:

```
content = File.ReadAllText("example2.txt");
Console.WriteLine(content);
```

ReadAllLines reads all the lines from a file and returns them as an array of strings. The following example demonstrates how to use **ReadAllLines** to read every line from a text file and display each line to the console, offering a simple way to handle line-by-line file input:

```
string[] lines = File.ReadAllLines("example2.txt");
foreach (string line in lines)
{
    Console.WriteLine(line);
}
```

Writing to files

Writing files is another essential task in many applications. It allows you to save data, create logs, and manage file-based storage. C# provides several methods and classes to facilitate writing to both text and binary files. The '**StreamWriter**' class is ideal for writing characters to a stream in a particular encoding. An example of how to use **StreamWriter** is as follows:

```
using (StreamWriter writer = new StreamWriter("example3.txt"))
{
    writer.WriteLine("Hello, World!");
    writer.WriteLine("Writing to a text file using StreamWriter");
}
```

The **FileStream** class provides a way to write binary data directly to a file by working with an output stream, which allows byte-level file operations. In the following example, we create a new binary file and write a sequence of bytes to it, ensuring efficient file handling using a statement for automatic resource management:

```
byte[] data = { 0x0, 0x1, 0x2, 0x3, 0x4 };
using (FileStream fs = new FileStream("example2.bin", FileMode.Create,
FileAccess.Write))
{
    fs.Write(data, 0, data.Length);
}
```

The **WriteAllText** and **WriteAllLines** methods of the **File** class offer simple ways to write text-based content to files. **WriteAllText** writes a specified string to a file, creating the file if it does not already exist. The following example demonstrates how to use **WriteAllText** to write a message to a text file in a single operation, ensuring file creation if necessary:

```
string content = "Hello, World!\nWriting to a file using File.WriteAllText";
File.WriteAllText("example4.txt", content);      }
```

WriteAllLines writes an array of strings to a file, creating it if it does not already exist. The following example shows how to use **WriteAllLines** to write multiple lines of text to a file, ensuring the file is created if it does not already exist:

```
string[] lines1 = { "Hello, World!", "Writing to a file using File.
WriteAllLines" };
File.WriteAllLines("example5.txt", lines1);
```

Working with directories

C# provides strong support for file and directory management through the directory and **DirectoryInfo** classes, which enable the creation, deleting, and enumerating of directories. The following example demonstrates how to create a directory, using both the static and instance-based **DirectoryInfo** classes, offering flexibility depending on your needs:

```
// Using Directory class
Directory.CreateDirectory("exampleDirectory");


// Using DirectoryInfo class
DirectoryInfo dirInfo = new DirectoryInfo("exampleDirectoryInfo");
dirInfo.Create();
```

C# makes it easy to delete directories using the directory and **DirectoryInfo** classes. The following example shows how to delete a directory, including its contents, using the static directory class and the instance-based **DirectoryInfo** class, which provide different approaches to directory management:

```
// Using DirectoryInfo class
DirectoryInfo dirInfo1 = new DirectoryInfo("exampleDirectoryInfo");
dirInfo1.Delete(true);
```

C# provides a straightforward way to enumerate files within a directory using the directory class. The following example demonstrates retrieving and listing all the files in a specified directory using the **Directory.GetFiles** method, that returns an array of file paths that can be iterated over and displayed:

```
// Using DirectoryInfo class
DirectoryInfo dirInfo2 = new DirectoryInfo("exampleDirectory");
dirInfo2.Create();
string[] files = Directory.GetFiles("exampleDirectory");
foreach (string file in files)
{
    Console.WriteLine(file);
}
```

C# offers an efficient method for enumerating directories within a parent directory using the **Directory** class. The following example demonstrates retrieving and listing all subdirectories utilizing the **Directory.GetDirectories** method returns an array of directory paths that can be looped through and displayed:

```
string[] directories = Directory.GetDirectories("exampleDirectory");
foreach (string directory in directories)
{
    Console.WriteLine(directory);
}
```

Streams in C#

Streams are abstract representations of a series of bytes that may either be read into or written from; it is possible to have several kinds of data sources with streams. This allows the processing of data in a sequential and efficient way.

The Importance of Streams is as follows:

- **Unified interface**: Streams offer an integrated interface when reading or writing data, irrespective of the data sources.

- **Buffering**: Streams mainly utilize buffering to high-performance levels with fewer I/O operations being involved.

- **Flexibility**: It supports synchronous and asynchronous operations, allowing for efficient I/O handling.

Types of Streams

FileStream offers more granular control over file reading and writing operations than higher-level classes like File. The following example demonstrates the use of **FileStream** to open or create a file, read its content into a byte array, and then convert and display it as a string using UTF-8 encoding:

```
using (FileStream fs = new FileStream("example2.txt", FileMode.OpenOrCreate))
{
    byte[] data1 = new byte[fs.Length];
    fs.Read(data1, 0, data1.Length);
    Console.WriteLine(System.Text.Encoding.UTF8.GetString(data1));
}
```

MemoryStream represents a valuable in-memory data stream for temporarily storing or manipulating data before writing it down to a more permanent location. The following example demonstrates how to use **MemoryStream** to write data into memory, reset the stream position, and then read the data back for display, showcasing its role in handling data without immediately involving disk operations:

```
using (MemoryStream ms = new MemoryStream())
{
    byte[] data2 = System.Text.Encoding.UTF8.GetBytes("Hello, MemoryStream!");
    ms.Write(data2, 0, data2.Length);

    // Reset the position to the beginning of the stream
    ms.Position = 0;
```

```
    byte[] buffer = new byte[ms.Length];
    ms.Read(buffer, 0, buffer.Length);
    Console.WriteLine(System.Text.Encoding.UTF8.GetString(buffer));
}
```

NetworkStream is a specialized stream used for transmitting data over a network, typically in conjunction with sockets, to facilitate communication between networked devices. The following example demonstrates how to use **NetworkStream** with a **TcpClient** to send a basic HTTP GET request to a server and read the response, illustrating how data can be transmitted and received over a network connection:

```
TcpClient client = new TcpClient("example.com", 80);
using (NetworkStream ns = client.GetStream())
{
    byte[] request = System.Text.Encoding.ASCII.GetBytes("GET / HTTP/1.1\r\
nHost: example.com\r\n\r\n");
    ns.Write(request, 0, request.Length);

    byte[] response = new byte[1024];
    int bytesRead = ns.Read(response, 0, response.Length);
        Console.WriteLine(System.Text.Encoding.ASCII.GetString(response,  0,
bytesRead));
}
```

Stream readers and writers

Stream readers and writers provide an easier way to work with streams when dealing with text data. They handle character encoding and provide convenient methods for reading and writing strings.

StreamReader is designed to read characters from a byte stream using a specified encoding, making it ideal for reading text files. The following example demonstrates how to use **StreamReader** to read the entire content of a text file and display it, providing a simple way to handle character-based file input:

```
using (StreamReader reader = new StreamReader("example2.txt"))
{
    string content1 = reader.ReadToEnd();
    Console.WriteLine(content1);
}
```

StreamWriter writes characters to a stream with a specified encoding, making it suitable for writing text to files. The following example demonstrates how to use **StreamWriter** to write a line of text to a file, showcasing a straightforward way to perform character-based file output operations:

```
using (StreamWriter writer = new StreamWriter("example6.txt"))
{
    writer.WriteLine("Hello, StreamWriter!");
}
```

Buffered input/output

Buffered I/O is a technique that increases the effectiveness of input and output operations by diminishing the occurrences of direct transactions with either data source or sink. Hence, rather than utilizing smaller reads and writes, data is kept temporarily in a buffer for larger, more efficient read and write operations.

Buffered streams wrap up other streams to provide buffering capabilities. This implies that information is read into or fetched from a temporary cache located in memory before being transferred to or received from the actual data source. It reduces the number of I/O operations to improve performance effectively.

Let us now look at how buffered streams work:

- **Reading**: When data is read from a buffered stream, a chunk of data is first loaded into a memory buffer. Subsequent read operations can be served from this buffer, reducing the need for multiple, potentially slow, reads from the underlying source.

- **Writing**: When data is sent to a buffered stream, it is initially put inside a memory cache. After it is filled with enough information, all the contents of the buffer are flushed out at once into an original data store, hence minimizing the write operations.

The **BufferedStream** class wraps around other streams like **FileStream** and **NetworkStream** to provide efficient buffering. It enhances performance by reducing the number of read/write operations made to the underlying stream. The following example demonstrates how to use **BufferedStream** for writing and reading large amounts of data, showcasing how buffering improves the efficiency of these operations:

```
string filePath = "example7.txt";
byte[] dataToWrite = new byte[10000]; // Example data
new Random().NextBytes(dataToWrite); // Fill with random bytes


// Writing with BufferedStream
using (FileStream fs = new FileStream(filePath, FileMode.Create, FileAccess.Write))
using (BufferedStream bs = new BufferedStream(fs))
{
    bs.Write(dataToWrite, 0, dataToWrite.Length);
    Console.WriteLine("Data written with BufferedStream.");
```

```
}

// Reading with BufferedStream
byte[] dataRead = new byte[10000];
using (FileStream fs = new FileStream(filePath, FileMode.Open, FileAccess.
Read))
using (BufferedStream bs = new BufferedStream(fs))
{
    int bytesRead = bs.Read(dataRead, 0, dataRead.Length);
    Console.WriteLine($"Data read with BufferedStream: {bytesRead}
bytes.");
}
```

Some advantages of buffered IO include the following:

- **Improved performance**: Since the number of I/O operations is reduced, buffered I/O enhances performance remarkably, especially if there is a lot of information involved or when sources are pretty slow (for example, networks or disks).

- **Decreased delay**: Buffered actions may help reduce latency since they can lower the rate of expensive I/O performances to make applications more responsive.

- **Cost-effective resource use**: By grouping read/write operations, buffered I/O can better use system resources, which may eventually lead to improved system performance.

- **Continuous data stream**: Buffering helps maintain a steady data stream, especially useful in real-time data processing and network communication contexts.

Conclusion

In this chapter, you explored the fundamental concepts of file and stream I/O in C#, gaining practical experience with reading, writing, and managing files and directories. You also learned how to optimize I/O operations using streams and buffering techniques essential for building efficient and reliable applications. Understanding file and stream handling is crucial for creating programs that persist data and manage resources effectively.

The next chapter will build on these concepts as we move forward by introducing **C# asynchronous programming**. In modern applications, it is often necessary to perform file and network operations without blocking the main thread, ensuring that the user interface remains responsive and resources are used efficiently. Asynchronous programming provides the tools to handle such tasks gracefully, allowing for smoother performance and better user experiences. Get ready to dive into how C# enables asynchronous operations, from file handling to complex network communication!

Multiple choice questions

1. **Which namespace contains the classes used for file and stream I/O in C#?**

   a. System.IO

   b. System.Threading

   c. System.Net

   d. System.Text

2. **Which class creates a new file in C#?**

   a. FileWriter

   b. FileStream

   c. FileInfo

   d. File.Create

3. **What method would you use to read all text from a file simultaneously?**

   a. File.ReadLine()

   b. File.ReadText()

   c. File.ReadAllText()

   d. StreamReader.ReadAll()

4. **Which class provides instance-based operations for managing directories in C#?**

   a. DirectoryInfo

   b. DirectoryStream

   c. DirectoryManager

   d. DirectoryHelper

5. **What is the purpose of BufferedStream in C#?**

   a. To provide temporary storage for file operations

   b. To convert text to binary

   c. To handle network communication

   d. To improve performance by reducing the number of I/O operations

6. **Which classes are used to read characters from a text file?**

   a. StreamReader

   b. TextReader

  c. FileReader

  d. File.ReadAllText

7. **How would you delete a file in C#?**

  a. FileInfo.Remove()

  b. File.Delete()

  c. FileStream.Delete()

  d. StreamWriter.Remove()

8. **What does the FileMode.Create an option when opening a file using FileStream?**

  a. It opens the file if it exists; otherwise, it throws an error

  b. It creates a new file or overwrites the existing one

  c. It appends data to an existing file

  d. It opens a file in read-only mode

9. **Which stream type is most appropriate for reading and writing data in memory rather than on disk?**

  a. NetworkStream

  b. FileStream

  c. MemoryStream

  d. BufferedStream

10. **What advantage does using asynchronous file operations provide over synchronous operations?**

  a. It reduces the file size

  b. It prevents thread blocking, ensuring smoother performance

  c. It increases the speed of I/O operations

  d. It automatically compresses the data being read or written

Answers

1. (a) System.IO

2. (d) File.Create

3. (c) File.ReadAllText

4. (a) DirectoryInfo

5. (d) To improve performance by reducing the number of I/O operations

6. (a) StreamReader

7. (b) File.Delete

8. (b) It creates a new file or overwrites the existing one

9. (c) MemoryStream

10. (b) It prevents thread blocking, ensuring smoother performance

Practice problems

1. Write a C# program that:

    a. Create a text file named "data.txt" using the File.WriteAllText method.

    b. Write the following two lines into the file:

        i. "Hello, C# File I/O!"

        ii. "Learning to read and write files is important."

    c. Reads the contents of "data.txt" using File.ReadAllLines and print each line on the console.

    Hint: Use the System.IO namespace for file handling.

2. Write a C# program that:

    a. Create a " SampleDirectory " directory using the Directory—createDirectory method.

    b. Inside this directory, create a binary file named "sample.bin" using FileStream and write an array of 10 random bytes.

    c. Read the contents of "sample.bin" back into a byte array and display the byte values in the console.

    Hint: Use FileStream to write and read the binary file and Random to generate the random bytes.

Join our book's Discord space

Join the book's Discord Workspace for Latest updates, Offers, Tech happenings around the world, New Release and Sessions with the Authors:

https://discord.bpbonline.com

CHAPTER 11

C# Asynchronous Programming

Introduction

As software applications become increasingly complex, responsiveness and efficiency have become crucial factors in delivering a smooth user experience. Asynchronous programming in C# is designed to handle tasks that take significant time, such as file I/O, database access, and network requests, without blocking the main thread. This ensures that the application remains responsive even when performing resource-intensive operations.

In C#, asynchronous programming is primarily achieved using the async and await keywords. These tools allow developers to write asynchronous code that looks and behaves similarly to synchronous code, making it more readable and maintainable. The core idea behind asynchronous programming is to let tasks run in the background while the main thread continues executing other operations. When the background task is completed, it informs the program, and the result is processed.

This chapter will explore key concepts of asynchronous programming in C#, including implementing asynchronous methods, handling exceptions, managing task cancellations, and using timeouts. You will learn to combine multiple asynchronous methods, manage synchronization contexts, and avoid common pitfalls like deadlocks. You will discover how asynchronous programming can improve performance, scalability, and resource management in your applications through examples and explanations.

By the end of this chapter, you will be equipped with the knowledge to effectively use asynchronous programming in your C# applications, ensuring that they remain responsive and efficient under various workloads.

Structure

This chapter covers the following topics:

- Introduction to asynchronous programming
- Synchronous versus asynchronous programming
- Combining multiple async methods
- Tasks and the Task Parallel Library
- Understanding the synchronization context
- Avoiding deadlocks and ensuring thread safety
- Setting timeouts for asynchronous operations
- Exception handling in asynchronous programming

Objectives

In this chapter, we will explore the key concepts and techniques of asynchronous programming in C#. You will learn how the **async** and **await** keywords enable the creation of responsive and efficient code. We will discuss when and why to prefer asynchronous programming over traditional synchronous methods, particularly in scenarios where improved performance and scalability are critical. The chapter will also cover strategies for combining multiple asynchronous methods, whether executed sequentially or concurrently, to achieve desired outcomes. Additionally, you will learn how to use the **CancellationToken** class to manage task cancellations and implement timeouts for long-running operations. Finally, we will delve into best practices for handling exceptions in asynchronous methods, including the use of *try-catch* blocks and the **Task.Exception** property to build resilient and error-handling-capable applications.

Introduction to asynchronous programming

In the context of an introductory C# book, asynchronous programming is an essential concept for managing tasks that take significant time, such as reading from a file or making a web request, without freezing or slowing down your application's main thread. In C#, this is done using the async and await keywords. When you write a method that performs a long-running operation (like accessing a database or calling an API), you can mark it with the async keyword. Inside that method, you use the await keyword before the long-running task. This allows the program to start the task without waiting for it to finish. Instead, the rest of the code continues to execute. Once the task is done, the program *comes back* to the awaited task and processes the result.

This approach improves performance and user experience, especially in applications with a **graphical user interface** (**GUI**), where responsiveness is crucial. One of the parallel programming techniques without blocking the main thread is asynchronous programming. With this approach, a program can start a long-running, potentially blocking operation, such as file I/O or network operations, and then continue further execution. The program gets notified when the first task finishes and then deals with the result.

In today's software creation, responsiveness and efficiency are essential to note with utmost attention. In achieving these objectives, asynchronous programming is vital for the following reasons:

- **Improved responsiveness**: In GUI applications, this helps prevent user interface freezing during background operations. For example, a long database query or downloading a file could be done asynchronously, so that even if the application freezes momentarily, the user will not have to stop using it.

- **Better use of resources**: Asynchronous programming effectively utilizes more system resources. When applications do not block threads during input/output operations, they can proceed with other tasks simultaneously, thus increasing performance and throughput.

- **Scalability**: Asynchronous programming in server-side applications helps manage multiple simultaneous requests without necessitating many threads. This behavior reduces the cost of managing threads and thus promotes scalability in the application.

- **Energy-efficient**: For mobile and embedded applications, energy efficiency is enhanced by allowing the CPU to sleep or perform low-power functions while waiting for I/O operations to finish within the framework of asynchronous programming.

Synchronous versus asynchronous programming

In synchronous programming, tasks are performed sequentially. When a task is initiated, the program pauses (or "blocks") and waits for that task to complete before moving on to the next one. This approach can lead to inefficiencies, especially with **input/output** (**I/O**) bound tasks like reading from a file or making a network request. During the wait time, the CPU remains idle, wasting valuable processing resources.

Here is an example of synchronous code that reads a file and prints its content:

```
void ReadFile()
{
    var content = File.ReadAllText("file.txt");
    Console.WriteLine(content);
}
```

In this example, the **ReadFile** method reads the entire content of **file.txt**. However, while the file is being read, the program does nothing else, and the main thread is blocked until the reading operation is completed. This can negatively impact performance, especially in applications that require high responsiveness.

Asynchronous programming allows tasks to be initiated without blocking the program's execution of subsequent tasks. Instead of waiting for each task to finish, the program continues running, improving efficiency and responsiveness. Once the initiated asynchronous tasks are completed, a callback or continuation part is executed to handle their results. This non-blocking approach ensures better use of system resources and keeps the application responsive, especially for I/O-bound or long-running operations. Here is an example of asynchronous code in C# that reads a file without blocking the main thread:

```
async Task ReadFileAsync()
{
    var content = await File.ReadAllTextAsync(«file.txt»);
    Console.WriteLine(content);
}
```

In this example, the **ReadFileAsync** method reads the file in the background using the await keyword. While the file is being read, the program can continue executing other code. Once the file is read, it prints the content to the console. This approach ensures that the main thread remains free to handle different tasks, making the application more efficient and responsive.

Basics of async and await

In C#, the async and await keywords are essential tools for writing asynchronous code that looks and behaves similarly to synchronous code, making it more readable and maintainable:

- **The async keyword**: It marks a method as asynchronous. An async method can contain one or more await expressions but must return **Task**, **Task<T>**, or void. It signals that the process will run asynchronously.

- **The await keyword**: This pauses the execution of the async method until the awaited task is complete. While the technique is paused, control is returned to the caller, allowing other code to run without blocking the main thread.

When an async method is called, it executes synchronously until it encounters an await expression. At that point, execution pauses, and control returns to the caller. Once the awaited task is complete, the method resumes from where it left off.

Here is an example:

```
async Task ProcessDataAsync()
{
```

```csharp
    Console.WriteLine("Starting data processing...");

    // Simulate a long-running operation
    await Task.Delay(2000);

    Console.WriteLine("Data processing completed.");
}

async Task MainMethodAsync()
{
    await ProcessDataAsync();
    Console.WriteLine("Main method execution continues.");
}
```

Output:

Starting data processing.

Data processing completed.

Main method execution continues.

The **ProcessDataAsync** method is asynchronous and simulates a data processing task by adding a two-second delay. The **MainMethodAsync** method calls **ProcessDataAsync** and uses the await keyword to pause its execution until the data processing is complete. Once the task finishes, the main method resumes, illustrating how async code allows for non-blocking execution. By leveraging async and await, developers can manage long-running operations more efficiently, ensuring that the main thread remains accessible and improving the application's responsiveness.

Combining multiple async methods

In many situations, you will need to call multiple asynchronous methods within another async method. Depending on your requirements, you can combine these methods sequentially or concurrently.

Each asynchronous method is in order in a sequential combination, particularly when there is a dependency between them. For example, if one async method relies on the result of another, you would wait for the first to complete before calling the next. Consider the following code:

```csharp
async Task<int> CalculateTotalAsync(int value1, int value2)
{
    int sum = await AddAsync(value1, value2);
    int square = await SquareAsync(sum);
```

```
        return square;
}


async Task<int> AddAsync(int a, int b)
{
        return await Task.Run(() => a + b);
}


async Task<int> SquareAsync(int number)
{
        return await Task.Run(() => number * number);
}
```

Here, **CalculateTotalAsync** waits for **AddAsync** to complete and return a sum, then passes that sum to **SquareAsync**. This sequential process ensures that each step relies on the result of the previous one.

On the other hand, in a concurrent combination, async methods that do not depend on each other can be run simultaneously. This improves performance by allowing tasks to be executed in parallel. You can start multiple tasks concurrently and then await them together using **Task.WhenAll**. Here is an example:

```
async Task ProcessMultipleTasksAsync()
{
        Task<int> task1 = CalculateAsync(10);
        Task<int> task2 = CalculateAsync(20);

        int[] results = await Task.WhenAll(task1, task2);

        Console.WriteLine($"The results are {results[0]}, {results[1]}");
}


async Task<int> CalculateAsync(int value)
{
        return await Task.Run(() => value * 2);
}
```

In this example, **ProcessMultipleTasksAsync** concurrently initiates two independent tasks, **task1** and **task2**, using **Task.WhenAll** waits for both tasks to complete before continuing execution. This concurrent approach can significantly improve performance when no dependencies exist between the functions.

Benefits of using async and await

The benefits of using 'async' and 'await' include the following:

- **Better comprehension and maintenance**: Asynchronous code mostly looks like synchronous code, which makes it easier to read and maintain.

- **Non-blocking operations**: This is because it does not block the main thread but allows for longest-running operations to be done at the same time while keeping the program responsive.

- **Better exception handling**: Asynchronous methods can utilize standard try-catch blocks for exception handling, thus providing a usual error handler.

- **Scalability**: In server applications, asynchronous programming allows concurrent requests to be handled efficiently without the need for many threads, leading to improved scalability and efficiency.

Tasks and the Task Parallel Library

In C#, an asynchronous task designates an operation that might execute concurrently with other tasks and is represented by a 'Task'. TPL provides efficient parallel and asynchronous programming tools through its central component called the 'Task' class and its generic counterpart 'Task<T>'. The key difference between them is that Task represents an operation that does not return a result, while **Task<T>** represents an operation that returns a value of type T. Tasks are ideal for representing and managing background operations, such as performing calculations, accessing a database, or making network requests. They offer greater control over asynchronous execution, allowing developers to monitor, wait for, and manage the results of these operations.

To initialize a specific task, use the 'Task.Run' method or create an instance of the 'Task' class and invoke its 'Start' function. However, most people prefer starting their tasks through the 'Task.Run' command due to its automatic queuing ability, which sends it off to return to some thread pool thread.

Here is an example of how to use **Task.Run** to start a task:

```
void PerformTask()
{
    Task task = Task.Run(() =>
    {
        Console.WriteLine("Task started...");
        Thread.Sleep(2000); // Simulate a time-consuming operation
        Console.WriteLine("Task completed.");
    });
}
```

This example creates a task using '**Task.Run**'. The task simulates a time-consuming operation by sleeping for two seconds. When you start a task, you will see a print message, **"Task started …"** and, after two seconds, **"Task completed"** will be displayed.

Tasks in C# can also return a value by using **Task<T>**, making handling results from asynchronous operations straightforward. This allows you to execute an operation in the background and retrieve its result once the task is completed. For example:

```
async Task<int> CalculateSquareAsync(int number)
{
    return await Task.Run(() =>
    {
        return number * number;
    });
}
```

In this example, the **CalculateSquareAsync** method is an asynchronous method that calculates the square of a number using **Task<T>**. The result of the operation is returned asynchronously. **Task<int>** allows the process to perform its calculation in the background without blocking the main thread, ensuring the result is returned once the task is completed. This pattern is highly effective for handling operations that involve computations or any other background tasks that need to return a result.

Task-based Asynchronous Pattern

Task-based Asynchronous Pattern (TAP) was introduced as a design standard to unify how asynchronous operations are conducted using tasks. Using '**Task**' and '**Task <T>**' for delayed execution defines it; additionally, it operates perfectly with '**async**' and '**await**' keywords.

Some key features of TAP include the following:

- **Consistency**: TAP provides a consistent programming model for asynchronous operations, making it easier for developers to understand and implement asynchronous methods.

- **Interoperability**: TAP-based methods can be composed and chained together using tasks, allowing for complex asynchronous workflows.

- **Cancellation and progress reporting**: TAP supports cancellation through '**CancellationToken**', enabling tasks to be canceled before completion. It also supports progress reporting, allowing for updates on long-running tasks.

Here is an example of a TAP-compliant method:

```
async Task DownloadFileAsync(string url, string destinationPath,
CancellationToken cancellationToken)
```

```
{
    using (HttpClient client = new HttpClient())
    {
        HttpResponseMessage response = await client.GetAsync(url,
cancellationToken);
        response.EnsureSuccessStatusCode();

        using (FileStream fs = new FileStream(destinationPath, FileMode.
Create, FileAccess.Write, FileShare.None))
        {
            await response.Content.CopyToAsync(fs, cancellationToken);
        }
    }
}
```

In this example, **DownloadFileAsync** demonstrates downloading a file asynchronously following TAP principles. The method supports cancellation by accepting a **CancellationToken**, which allows the operation to be canceled before completion. The use of await ensures that the task is executed asynchronously without blocking the main thread, and the **CancellationToken** provides a mechanism for halting the download gracefully.

Asynchronous methods

An asynchronous method is marked with the keyword '**async**'. The keyword '**await**' is also utilized to perform asynchronous operations. An asynchronous method may return '**Task**', '**Task <T>**', or '**void**':

- **'Task'**: Used when the method does not return a value.
- **'Task<T>'**: Used when the method returns a type '**T**' value.
- **'void'**: Rarely used, typically for event handlers.

The main aim of an asynchronous method is non-blocking operations so that the program remains responsive during operation. Here is an example:

```
async Task SaveDataAsync(string data)
{
    await Task.Run(() =>
    {
        // Simulate saving data to a database
        Thread.Sleep(2000);
        Console.WriteLine("Data saved successfully.");
    });
}
```

In this example, **SaveDataAsync** is an asynchronous method that simulates saving data to a database. The **async** keyword marks it as asynchronous, while the await keyword ensures that the operation runs in the background without blocking the main thread, keeping the application responsive. The task simulates a time-consuming operation, such as saving data, by using **Thread.Sleep** to pause execution for two seconds.

When defining asynchronous methods, returning a '**Task**' or '**Task<T>**' is essential for enabling the caller to await the method's completion and handle its result. This return type also allows the chaining of asynchronous methods, enabling more complex workflows.

In the following example:

```
async Task<int> FetchDataAndProcessAsync()
{
    int result = await Task.Run(() =>
    {
        // Simulate fetching and processing data
        Thread.Sleep(3000);
        return 42; // Example result
    });
    return result;
}
```

The method **FetchDataAndProcessAsync** returns an integer type after asynchronously fetching and processing data. The await keyword ensures that the technique pauses and waits for the task to complete before proceeding with the following line of code.

Similarly, you can define methods that return only a Task when no result is needed. This is useful for procedures that perform operations without returning data. An example of this is as follows:

```
async Task LogMessageAsync(string message)
{
    await Task.Run(() =>
    {
        // Simulate logging a message
        Thread.Sleep(1000);
        Console.WriteLine($"Logged: {message}");
    });
}
```

In this example, **LogMessageAsync** logs a message asynchronously. It returns a Task to indicate when the logging operation is complete, though it does not return any result data. This pattern is helpful for fire-and-forget operations where only the completion of the task matters, such as logging or sending notifications.

Asynchronous method exceptions

Exception handling in '**async**' methods follows the same pattern as synchronous ones. You can catch exceptions happening there through try-catch blocks. However, exceptions in asynchronous methods are thrown when the task is awaited.

Here is an example:

```
async Task<int> DivideAsync(int dividend, int divisor)
{
    try
    {
        return await Task.Run(() =>
        {
            if (divisor == 0)
                throw new DivideByZeroException("Divisor cannot be zero.");
            return dividend/divisor;
        });
    }
    catch (DivideByZeroException ex)
    {
        Console.WriteLine($»Error: {ex.Message}»);
        return -1; // Return an error code
    }
}
```

In this example, the **DivideAsync** method divides two numbers asynchronously. If the divisor is zero, a **DivideByZeroException** is thrown and caught within the try-catch block. The process then handles the exception by logging the error message and returning an error code instead of the division result.

It is important to understand that when working with asynchronous methods, any unhandled exception within an async method propagates to the caller when that method is awaited. However, if the technique is not awaited, the exception can go unobserved, leading to potential bugs that are hard to track down.

Here is an additional example:

```
async Task PerformOperationAsync()
{
    throw new InvalidOperationException("Something went wrong.");
}
```

```
async Task MainMethodAsync()
{
    try
    {
        await PerformOperationAsync();
    }
    catch (InvalidOperationException ex)
    {
        Console.WriteLine($"Caught exception: {ex.Message}");
    }
}
```

In this example, **PerformOperationAsync** throws an **InvalidOperationException**. Since **MainMethodAsync** awaits **PerformOperationAsync**, the exception is propagated to the caller and correctly handled in the try-catch block, ensuring the application remains stable and the error is logged.

To avoid exceptions going unnoticed, it is essential always to await async methods or handle any tasks created that may potentially throw exceptions.

Understanding the synchronization context

A synchronization context is a component that coordinates code execution across different threads, making sure that it runs in the right thread or context. One way to protect against this is by transferring code execution between threads, which can be highly beneficial when operating in single-threaded **user interfaces** (**UI**) such as Windows Forms or WPF software.

The synchronization context captures and manages the thread used to execute code when it is awaited. This context helps maintain thread affinity, ensuring code runs on the appropriate thread, such as updating UI elements on the main thread.

In .NET, '**SynchronizationContext**' is an abstract class with various implementations depending on the application type. For instance, '**SynchronizationContext**' marshals updates for Windows Forms or WPF applications' user interface thread.

The synchronization context is crucial within asynchronous programming as it dictates how asynchronous operations are related to their original threads. When an '**await**' clause appears, the existing synchronization context is stored away; later, when the awaited task returns, control is handed back to the same context where everything started.

Such behavior ensures that the code that needs to execute at a specific thread (e.g., UI update) runs on that thread after the asynchronous operation completes. Here is an example:

```
async Task UpdateLabelAsync (Label label)
{
    // Simulate a delay
    await Task.Delay (2000);

    // This code runs on the original SynchronizationContext
    label.Text = "Update complete";
}
```

In this example, '**UpdateLabelAsync**' updates a UI label after a delay. The '**await**' ensures that after the delay, the code that updates the label is returned to the UI thread, where the '**label.Text**' property can be safely updated.

Avoiding deadlocks and ensuring thread safety

Deadlocks and thread safety issues can arise in asynchronous programming if not managed correctly. Understanding the synchronization context helps avoid common pitfalls, such as deadlocks, which can occur when synchronous waits are used with asynchronous code.

A common deadlock scenario happens when a synchronous method waits on an asynchronous process that attempts to post back to the original synchronization context. A deadlock occurs if the original thread is blocked while waiting for the async method to complete and the async method is trying to post back to that thread.

To avoid deadlocks, avoid synchronous waits ('**Task.Wait()**' or '**Task.Result**') on asynchronous tasks. Instead, use '**await**' to allow the **async** method to complete naturally.

Example of a potential deadlock:

```
void CallAsyncMethod ()
{
    // Potential deadlock
    var result = GetDataAsync ().Result;
}

async Task<string> GetDataAsync ()
{
    await Task.Delay (1000);
    return "Data";
}
```

Here, synchronously waiting for "**GetDataAsync**" using "**.Result**" could raise an exception if it is executed in a blocked synchronization context because of deadlocks.

Ensuring thread safety: Ensure shared resources are consistently accessed across threads when working with asynchronous code segments. When accessing shared states, use synchronization primitives like '**lock**', '**Mutex**', or '**Semaphore**'. Here is an example:

```
object _lock = new object ();
int _counter;

async Task IncrementCounterAsync ()
{
    await Task.Run (() =>
    {
        lock (_lock)
        {
            _counter++;
        }
    });
}
```

In this example, the '**lock**' statement ensures that '**_counter**' is accessed in a thread-safe manner, preventing race conditions during asynchronous operations.

Cancellations

Asynchronous programming in C# allows the cancellation of ongoing operations before they are complete. This is especially important for long-running tasks that may need to stop due to user input or other conditions. The **CancellationToken** and **CancellationTokenSource** classes are commonly used to handle cancellations. The **CancellationToken** represents a token that signals when to cancel, while the **CancellationTokenSource** triggers the cancellation request.

Here is an example demonstrating cancellation in asynchronous operations:

```
async Task<string> FetchDataAsync(string url, CancellationToken
cancellationToken)
{
    using (HttpClient client = new HttpClient())
    {
        HttpResponseMessage response = await client.GetAsync("https://
example.com/api/data", cancellationToken);
        response.EnsureSuccessStatusCode();
        return await response.Content.ReadAsStringAsync();
    }
```

```
}
async Task RunFetchDataWithCancellationAsync()
{
    var cts = new CancellationTokenSource();
    CancellationToken token = cts.Token;

    Task<string> fetchDataTask = FetchDataAsync("https://example.com/api/
data", token);

    // Simulate the user canceling the operation
    cts.CancelAfter(5000); // Cancel after 5 seconds

    try
    {
        string data = await fetchDataTask;
        Console.WriteLine("Data fetched: " + data);
    }
    catch (OperationCanceledException)
    {
        Console.WriteLine("Operation was canceled.");
    }
}
```

In this example, '**RunFetchDataWithCancellationAsync**' demonstrates how to use '**CancellationTokenSource**' to issue a cancellation request after a timeout of five seconds. The '**FetchDataAsync**' method checks the token and throws an '**OperationCanceledException**' if cancellation is requested.

Handling task cancellations in asynchronous programming involves catching the **OperationCanceledException**, which is thrown when a task is canceled. This exception allows you to perform any necessary cleanup or state management when the operation is interrupted.

Here is an example demonstrating how to handle task cancellation:

```
async Task ProcessDataAsync(CancellationToken cancellationToken)
{
    try
    {
        await Task.Run(() =>
        {
```

```
        for (int i = 0; i < 100; i++)
        {
            // Check for cancellation at each step
            cancellationToken.ThrowIfCancellationRequested();
            Thread.Sleep(100); // Simulate work
            Console.WriteLine($"Processing {i}%");
        }
    }, cancellationToken);
}
catch (OperationCanceledException)
{
    Console.WriteLine("Data processing was canceled.");
}
}
```

ProcessDataAsync simulates a long-running task in this example, processing data in a loop. Each iteration checks if a cancellation has been requested by calling **cancellationToken.ThrowIfCancellationRequested()**. If the task is canceled, an **OperationCanceledException** is thrown, and the exception is caught in the **catch** block. This allows you to handle the cancellation gracefully by displaying a message or performing any necessary cleanup.

This approach ensures that cancellations are handled efficiently and that the application remains responsive when a task is interrupted.

Setting timeouts for asynchronous operations

In asynchronous operations, timeouts can be implemented to define the maximum time a task can take. If the task is not finished within this time frame, it can be canceled, as it is no longer relevant. This is particularly useful for operations where waiting indefinitely is undesirable.

Here is an example demonstrating how to implement a timeout for an asynchronous operation:

```
async Task<string> FetchDataWithTimeoutAsync()
{
    using (var cts = new CancellationTokenSource())
    {
        Task<string> fetchDataTask = FetchDataAsync("https://example.com/
api/data", cts.Token);
```

```
        Task timeoutTask = Task.Delay(10000); // 10 seconds timeout

        Task completedTask = await Task.WhenAny(fetchDataTask,
timeoutTask);

        if (completedTask == timeoutTask)
        {
            cts.Cancel(); // Cancel the fetchDataTask if timeout occurs
            throw new TimeoutException("The operation timed out.");
        }

        return await fetchDataTask; // If fetchDataTask completes first,
return its result
    }
}
```

In this example, '**FetchDataWithTimeoutAsync**' demonstrates setting a timeout for an asynchronous operation. It creates a '**Task.Delay**' for the timeout period and uses '**Task. WhenAny**' to wait for the fetch or timeout tasks to complete. If the timeout task is completed first, the '**CancellationTokenSource**' cancels the fetch task, and a '**TimeoutException**' is thrown.

Exception handling in asynchronous programming

Exception handling works similarly to synchronous methods but requires special attention to how exceptions are propagated in asynchronous methods. Exceptions thrown by an asynchronous method are captured and thrown when the task is awaited, allowing you to use try-catch blocks to manage these exceptions.

Here is an example of handling exceptions in an asynchronous method:

```
async Task<string> FetchDataAsync(string url)
{
    using (HttpClient client = new HttpClient())
    {
        try
        {
            string data = await client.GetStringAsync(url);
            return data;
```

```
        }
        catch (HttpRequestException ex)
        {
            Console.WriteLine($"Error fetching data: {ex.Message}");
            throw; // Optionally rethrow to let the caller handle it
        }
    }
}
```

In this example, **FetchDataAsync** makes an HTTP request and handles any **HttpRequestException** that occurs during the request. The exception is caught, the error message is logged, and the exception can be rethrown if necessary to let the caller handle it further.

In addition to using try-catch, you can inspect exceptions after a task has been completed by checking the **Exception** property of the **Task** object. This property is available on tasks completed with exceptions and details the exception(s) that occurred.

Here is an example of using the **Task.Exception** property:

```
async Task ProcessDataAsync2()
{
    Task<string> dataTask = FetchDataAsync("https://example.com/api/data",
new CancellationToken());

    try
    {
        string result = await dataTask;
        Console.WriteLine($"Data: {result}");
    }
    catch (Exception ex)
    {
        Console.WriteLine($"Caught exception: {ex.Message}");
    }

    if (dataTask.IsFaulted)
    {
        Exception ex = dataTask.Exception;
        Console.WriteLine($"Task exception: {ex.InnerException?.Message}");
    }
}
```

In this example, **ProcessDataAsync** calls **FetchDataAsync** and uses a try-catch block to handle any exceptions the await throws. Additionally, it checks whether the task was faulted (i.e., completed with an exception) by inspecting the **IsFaulted** property. If the task fails, the **Exception** property is used to access details about the exception, including the **InnerException**, which provides more specific information about the cause.

This approach allows you to handle exceptions both during the task execution and after the task is completed, giving you flexibility in managing errors in asynchronous workflows.

In this example, '**ProcessDataAsync**' handles exceptions thrown by '**FetchDataAsync**' and checks the '**Exception**' property of the task to access details about any exceptions that occurred.

Conclusion

This chapter has equipped you with a solid understanding of asynchronous programming in C# and how to use the async effectively and await keywords to write efficient and responsive code. You now have the tools to identify when asynchronous methods provide a performance advantage over synchronous approaches and how to combine multiple asynchronous operations to achieve desired outcomes. Additionally, you learned the importance of using CancellationToken to manage task cancellations and set operation timeouts, ensuring greater control over your applications. Finally, the strategies for handling exceptions in asynchronous methods will help you build robust and reliable code. With these skills, you can leverage asynchronous programming to create scalable, high-performance applications.

With a solid understanding of asynchronous programming, you are now ready to explore another advanced feature of C#: **Reflection and Attributes**. In the next chapter, we will delve into how C# allows you to inspect metadata and interact with types dynamically at runtime using reflection and how attributes provide a powerful way to add declarative information to your code. These tools open up new possibilities for dynamic behavior and enhanced application flexibility.

Multiple choice questions

1. **What is the primary purpose of asynchronous programming in C#?**

   a. To write less code.

   b. Allow operations to run in the background without blocking the main thread.

   c. To speed up every task execution.

   d. To reduce memory usage in applications.

2. **Which keywords are essential for implementing asynchronous programming in C#?**

   a. try and catch

   b. run and wait

   c. async and await

   d. sync and block

3. **What is the main difference between synchronous and asynchronous programming?**

   a. Asynchronous programming always runs faster than synchronous programming.

   b. Asynchronous programming allows tasks to run concurrently without blocking.

   c. Synchronous programming uses more memory than asynchronous programming.

   d. Synchronous programming cannot be used in web applications.

4. **How do you handle a task cancellation in C#?**

   a. By throwing a TimeoutException

   b. By using a CancellationToken and CancellationTokenSource

   c. By using a Task.Run method

   d. By using a Task.Delay method

5. **What happens if an asynchronous method throws an exception?**

   a. The exception is ignored.

   b. The exception is thrown immediately.

   c. The exception is thrown when the task is awaited.

   d. The task is automatically canceled.

6. **Which of the following is a benefit of using asynchronous programming?**

   a. Better performance for short, CPU-bound operations.

   b. Improved responsiveness in long-running I/O-bound tasks.

   c. Reduced memory consumption.

   d. Simplified debugging process.

7. **Which method allows you to wait for multiple asynchronous tasks to complete?**
   a. Task.Wait()
   b. Task.WhenAll()
   c. Task.WhenAny()
   d. Task.Run()

8. **Which types can be returned by an asynchronous method?**
   a. Task, Task<T>, or void
   b. Task, string, or void
   c. Task, object, or Task<T>
   d. void, Task<int>, or Task<char>

9. **How can you avoid deadlocks in asynchronous programming?**
   a. By using synchronous methods instead of asynchronous ones.
   b. By never using the await keyword.
   c. By avoiding the use of synchronous waits like Task.Wait() or Task.Result.
   d. By always running tasks in parallel.

10. **What is the purpose of the Task.Exception property?**
   a. To stop a task that is running too long.
   b. To log the start time of a task.
   c. To access details of any exceptions during the task's execution.
   d. To check if a task has finished successfully.

Answers

1. (b) To allow operations to run in the background without blocking the main thread.
2. (c) async and await
3. (b) Asynchronous programming allows tasks to run concurrently without blocking.
4. (b) By using a CancellationToken and CancellationTokenSource
5. (c) The exception is thrown when the task is awaited.
6. (b) Improved responsiveness in long-running I/O-bound tasks.
7. (b) Task.WhenAll()
8. (a) Task, Task<T>, or void
9. (c) By avoiding the use of synchronous waits like Task.Wait() or Task.Result.
10. (c) To access details of any exceptions that occurred during the task's execution.

Practice problems

1. You are tasked with building a simple C# console application that simulates a long-running data processing operation. The program should fetch data from an external source (simulated by a delay), process it, and log the results asynchronously. The program should also handle the following:

    a. **Time out handling**: If the data fetch takes longer than 5 seconds, the operation should be canceled, and a message should be logged.

    b. **Exception handling**: If an exception occurs (for example, if the data is invalid), it should be caught and logged appropriately.

    c. **Combining async methods**: The program should first fetch the data, then process the data asynchronously, and finally log the results in sequence.

    d. **Cancellation token**: Allow the user to cancel the data processing at any time manually.

   Requirements:

    a. Create a method FetchDataAsync() that simulates fetching data with a 3-second delay. The task should be canceled if the user cancels the operation or it times out (after five seconds).

    b. Create a method ProcessDataAsync() that takes the fetched data and performs a simple transformation (e.g., converts a string to uppercase), simulating a two-second processing delay.

    c. Create a method LogDataAsync() that logs the processed data asynchronously.

    d. Use CancellationTokenSource to enable the user to cancel the operation.

    e. Ensure proper exception handling is in place for potential issues (such as division by zero, null data, or a timeout).

   Example output:

   ```
   Fetching data...
   Processing data...
   Data: HELLO WORLD
   Data processing completed.


   If canceled or timed out:
   Fetching data...
   The operation was canceled.
   ```

Instructions:

a. Implement the methods FetchDataAsync, ProcessDataAsync, and LogDataAsync using the async and await keywords.

b. Use CancellationTokenSource to handle task cancellations.

c. Implement exception handling using try-catch blocks to ensure errors are logged and managed gracefully.

2. You are tasked with creating a C# console application that simulates reading data from multiple files, processing the contents asynchronously, and saving the results to a new file. Your program should incorporate the following concepts:

a. **Concurrency**: The program should read two files concurrently without blocking the main thread.

b. **Cancellation handling**: Allow the user to cancel the operation at any point and ensure that partial results are cleaned up when cancellation occurs.

c. **Exception handling**: If any error occurs (e.g., file not found or invalid content), it should be caught and logged.

d. **Combining async methods**: Once both files are read asynchronously, process and merge the contents into a new file.

Requirements:

a. **ReadFileAsync()**: Create a method to read the contents of a file asynchronously, simulating a delay of two seconds for each file read. Handle the possibility of errors in the file that are not found.

b. **ProcessFileDataAsync()**: Create a method that takes and processes the file contents (e.g., sorts the data or transforms it somehow). Simulate a one-second processing delay.

c. **SaveFileAsync()**: Asynchronously save the processed data into a new file. Log a message when the file is saved successfully.

d. **CancellationToken**: Allow the user to cancel the file processing and clean up any resources if the operation is canceled midway.

Example output:

```
Reading file1.txt...
Reading file2.txt...
Processing data...
Saving merged data to output.txt...
Data saved successfully.
```

```
If canceled:
Reading file1.txt...
Reading file2.txt...
The operation was canceled.

If an error occurs:
Error: File not found (file1.txt)
```

Instructions:

a. Use the async and await keywords to Implement the methods ReadFileAsync, ProcessFileDataAsync, and SaveFileAsync methods.

b. Read two files concurrently using Task.WhenAll to handle both files reads in parallel.

c. Use CancellationTokenSource to handle task cancellations, ensuring that partial data is discarded or cleaned up.

d. Use try-catch blocks for exception handling to manage file access errors or invalid content.

Join our book's Discord space

Join the book's Discord Workspace for Latest updates, Offers, Tech happenings around the world, New Release and Sessions with the Authors:

https://discord.bpbonline.com

CHAPTER 12

C# Reflection and Attributes

Introduction

In modern C# programming, reflection and Attributes play a critical role in enhancing the flexibility and dynamic capabilities of your applications. Reflection allows a program to inspect its own structure or the structure of another program during runtime, making it possible to access and manipulate types, methods, and properties dynamically. This is particularly useful in scenarios where you need to work with objects or assemblies that may not be known at compile time.

Attributes, on the other hand, provide a way to associate metadata with your code. They can be used by both developers and compilers to alter program behavior or enforce certain rules. For example, Attributes can mark certain methods as obsolete or specify how classes should be serialized. Together, reflection and Attributes give developers the tools to create more flexible and maintainable code.

In this chapter, we will explore the essential concepts of reflection and Attributes in C#, and how they can be used to inspect and modify code at runtime, providing deeper control and dynamic capabilities within your applications.

Structure

This chapter covers the following topics:

- Understanding reflection

- System.Reflection namespace
- Reflection and assemblies
- Performance impacts of using reflection
- Working with Attributes

Objectives

By the end of this chapter, you will have a thorough understanding of the concept and application of C# Reflection and Attributes. You will learn how to use Reflection to access and manipulate type information, enabling dynamic interaction with objects at runtime. Additionally, you will explore how to apply Reflection for dynamic method invocation and instance creation, enhancing the flexibility of your code. The chapter will also delve into the purpose and function of Attributes in C#, demonstrating their role in adding metadata to your code. Finally, you will gain the skills to retrieve and process Attributes dynamically using Reflection, unlocking powerful capabilities for creating versatile and adaptive applications.

Understanding reflection

Reflection allows a program to inspect its own structure or the structure of another program at runtime. This is particularly useful when you want to access class members like methods or properties without hardcoding their names. The following code demonstrates how to use reflection to retrieve and display all the methods within a class during runtime:

```csharp
using System;
using System.Reflection;
public class Example
{
    public void Method1() { }
    public void Method2() { }
}
class Program
{
    static void Main()
    {
        // Retrieve type information of the 'Example' class.
        Type type = typeof(Example);

        // Get all methods from the 'Example' class using reflection.
        MethodInfo[] methods = type.GetMethods();
```

```
    // Loop through the methods and print their names.
    foreach (var method in methods)
    {
        Console.WriteLine(method.Name);
    }
  }
}
```

In the previous code, reflection is used to dynamically retrieve and display the methods of the **Example** class at runtime. First, the **Type** object is used to capture the structure of the **Example** class, allowing the program to inspect its metadata. The **GetMethods()** function then retrieves an array of **MethodInfo** objects, each representing a method in the class. This allows the program to access details like the method names without having to hardcode them. The foreach loop iterates over the retrieved methods using **method. Name** to print the names of each method to the console. This demonstrates the power of reflection in C#, enabling developers to work with class members dynamically, even when they are not known until runtime.

Attributes

Attributes in C# are a way to add metadata to your code. This metadata can then be accessed at runtime through reflection or used by the compiler for various purposes. Attributes are placed above classes, methods, properties, or other code elements, and they provide additional information that can influence the behavior of these elements.

For instance, you might use the '**[Obsolete]**' attribute to mark a method as outdated as shown in the following code:

```
[Obsolete("Use NewMethod instead")]
void OldMethod()
{
    // Old implementation
}
```

In this example, the '**[Obsolete]**' attribute explains that '**OldMethod**' has been phased out and must be replaced by '**NewMethod**'. This type of metadata conveys crucial information both for the developer and for the compiler.

Reflection and Attributes are essential tools in C#. They enable developers to write more dynamic, flexible, and maintainable code. Reflection provides run-time discovery of datatype, which is especially beneficial whilst building frameworks, custom serializers, or applying dependency injection. Attributes, on the other hand, allow you to add metadata that can be exploited by different tools or frameworks so that they may alter behavior or enforce rules.

For example, in testing frameworks, reflection is often used to discover test methods marked with specific attributes. Thus, it allows one to write generic codes that automatically detect and execute test cases without understanding the content of every individual test case beforehand.

In C# applications, mastering Reflection and Attributes gives you greater access and flexibility, thus better resilience against changing requirements.

System.Reflection namespace

The '**System.Reflection**' namespace in C# is the core of reflection functionality. Accessing metadata associated with one's code is made possible through classes and methods found therein. Some of these include '**Assembly**', '**Type**', '**MethodInfo**', '**PropertyInfo**', and '**FieldInfo**', which provide special functions for examining or altering how assemblies are structured or what they contain. For instance, developers can make use of the '**Assembly**' class to load an assembly then later employ the '**Type**' class in order to examine its types as shown in the following code:

```
using System;
using System.Reflection;

Assembly assembly = Assembly.Load("mscorlib");
Type[] types = assembly.GetTypes();

foreach (Type type in types)
{
    Console.WriteLine(type.FullName);
}
```

In this code, we load the '**mscorlib**' assembly using the method '**Assembly.Load**' which is a core library within the .NET Framework. All types defined in that assembly are retrieved via the '**GetTypes()**' method, and their full names are printed by iterating through them. Thus, it brings out how reflection can be utilized for a thorough exploration of the whole assembly.

Inspecting metadata with reflection

Reflection allows querying metadata information much more flexibly than through traditional programming means, such as explicit calls on particular methods or member variables, among others. This means that you can look at objects during program execution to see what they look like and what they can do without knowing their types at compile time. Hence, for example, we can utilize reflection to retrieve Attributes assigned to a class or method:

```csharp
using System;
using System.Reflection;
[Obsolete ("This class is obsolete")]
public class MyClass
{
    public void MyMethod() { }
}

class Program
{
    static void Main()
    {
        Type type = typeof(MyClass);
        object[] attributes = type.GetCustomAttributes(false);

        foreach (var attribute in attributes)
        {
            Console.WriteLine(attribute);
        }
    }
}
```

Output:

...\Program.cs(13,28): warning CS0618: 'MyClass' is obsolete: 'This class is obsolete'

System.ObsoleteAttribute

In this example, we retrieve and display Attributes assigned to the class using reflection by accessing its '**MyClass**'. With these Attributes tightly coupled with it through '**GetCustomAttributes**' method, we analyze the metadata that influences its behavior during execution time.

Accessing types and members at runtime

One of the most potent features of reflection is the ability to access various types and their members (for example, methods, properties, and fields) during run time. This means that it is possible to invoke methods on the fly, set or get the values of properties, and even create instances of types that only exist once the program has started. Consider the following example where we dynamically invoke a method:

```csharp
using System;
using System.Reflection;
public class Calculator
{
    public int Add(int a, int b)
    {
        return a + b;
    }
}

class Program
{
    static void Main()
    {
        Type? type = typeof(Calculator);
        object instance = Activator.CreateInstance(type);
        MethodInfo method = type.GetMethod("Add");

        int? result = (int)method.Invoke(instance, new object[] { 5, 10 });
        Console.WriteLine($"Result: {result}");
    }
}
```

Output:

Result: 15

Here, we use reflection to dynamically create an instance of the '**Calculator**' class and invoke the '**Add**' method with specific arguments. The '**Activator.CreateInstance**' method creates an object of the '**Calculator**' type, and '**GetMethod**' retrieves the '**Add**' method. Finally, '**method.Invoke**' calls the method with the provided arguments, demonstrating how reflection can be used to interact with objects at runtime without knowing their specifics at compile time.

Examining and manipulating types enables developers to write generic code that can process various cases without hardcoding specific implementations. Reflection provides the means for peering into the details of a '**type**', including its methods, properties, fields, and events, even to create instances of those types dynamically.

The '**Type**' class is central to working with type information in C#. It represents the metadata of a type; it gives access to classes, interfaces, structs, etc. '**Type**' classes are used when a type needs to be examined for its characteristics, such as methods, properties fields, or events, as well as base type interface and Attributes. Following is a simple example concerning how to obtain the '**Type**' class and its usage:

```
using System;
public class MyClass
{
    public void MyMethod() { }
}

class Program
{
    static void Main()
    {
        Type type = typeof(MyClass);
        Console.WriteLine($"Type Name: {type.Name}");
        Console.WriteLine($"Namespace: {type.Namespace}");
        Console.WriteLine($"Is Class: {type.IsClass}");
    }
}
```

Output:

Type Name: MyClass

Namespace:

Is Class: True

This code uses the type of '**MyClass**' to obtain the '**Type**' object that represents '**MyClass**'. The basic information about this type can then be accessed by using properties of the '**Type**' class, for example, '**Name**', '**Namespace**', and '**IsClass**'.

Retrieving type information

The reflection mechanism allows you to retrieve detailed information about the members of a type, including methods, properties, fields, and events. This information is important in situations where you need to do things dynamically with objects, such as in frameworks, libraries, or utilities that operate on different types without prior knowledge of their structures. The following is an example of retrieving different members of a type:

```
using System;
using System.Reflection;
public class MyClass
{
    public int MyProperty { get; set; }
    public event EventHandler MyEvent;
    public void MyMethod() { }
```

```csharp
}

class Program
{
    static void Main()
    {
        Type type = typeof(MyClass);

        Console.WriteLine("Methods:");
        foreach (var method in type.GetMethods())
        {
            Console.WriteLine(method.Name);
        }

        Console.WriteLine("\nProperties:");
        foreach (var property in type.GetProperties ())
        {
            Console.WriteLine(property.Name);
        }

        Console.WriteLine("\nFields:");
        foreach (var field in type.GetFields (BindingFlags.Instance |
BindingFlags.NonPublic | BindingFlags.Public))
        {
            Console.WriteLine(field.Name);
        }

        Console.WriteLine("\nEvents:");
        foreach (var ev in type.GetEvents())
        {
            Console.WriteLine(ev.Name);
        }
    }
}
```

Output:

Methods:

get_MyProperty

```
set_MyProperty
add_MyEvent
remove_MyEvent
MyMethod
GetType
ToString
Equals
GetHashCode

Properties:
MyProperty

Fields:
<MyProperty>k__BackingField
MyEvent

Events:
MyEvent
```

The preceding code uses reflection to retrieve and show the methods, properties, fields, and events of the type "**MyClass**". The respective members are retrieved using **GetMethods()**, **GetProperties()**, **GetFields()**, and **GetEvents()** thus demonstrating how different aspects of a particular type can be explored and used dynamically.

Instantiating objects dynamically

Among the powerful features of reflection is creating instances of types at runtime, even when a specific type is not known until execution time itself. This is particularly useful in scenarios like plugin systems or when building objects based on user input or configuration files. Following is how you can instantiate objects dynamically using reflection:

```
using System;
using System.Reflection;
public class MyClass
{
    public MyClass() { }
    public MyClass(string message)
    {
        Console.WriteLine($"Message: {message}");
    }
}
```

```
}

class Program
{
    static void Main()
    {
        Type type = typeof(MyClass);

        // Default constructor
        object? instance1 = Activator.CreateInstance(type);
        Console.WriteLine($"Instance1 created: {instance1?.GetType().
Name}");

        // Constructor with parameters
        object? instance2 = Activator.CreateInstance(type, new object[] {
"Hello, Reflection!" });
        Console.WriteLine($"Instance2 created: {instance2?.GetType().
Name}");
    }
}
```

Output:

Instance1 created: MyClass

Message: Hello, Reflection!

Instance2 created: MyClass

The preceding code demonstrates how to use the '**Activator.CreateInstance**' method for creating instances of type '**MyClass**' using a no-argument constructor and constructor with string parameters respectively. It shows that it is possible to create and manage objects depending on runtime conditions.

Invoking members with reflection

Reflection in C# not only allows you to inspect the types and their members but also provides the capability to invoke methods, access and modify fields and properties, and work with constructors and events dynamically. This ability is particularly powerful in scenarios where the exact members to be invoked are determined at runtime, offering a high degree of flexibility in application design.

One well-known application of reflection is dynamic method invocation. This enables the developers to call a method from an object without knowing anything about the methods during compilation or when developing the program. Using the '**MethodInfo**' class, one can find out the desired method and run it against given parameters. The following is an example of dynamically invoking a method:

```
using System;
using System.Reflection;
public class Calculator
{
    public int Multiply(int x, int y)
    {
        return x * y;
    }
}

class Program
{
    static void Main()
    {
        Type type = typeof(Calculator);
        object? instance = Activator.CreateInstance(type);
        MethodInfo? method = type.GetMethod("Multiply");

        int? result = (int?)method?.Invoke(instance, new object[] { 6, 7
});
        Console.WriteLine($"Result: {result}");
    }
}
```

Output:

Result: 42

The preceding code depicts using reflection to call the '**Multiply**' method from the '**Calculator**' class dynamically. The method named '**Multiply**' is retrieved by utilizing a function known as '**GetMethod**' while invoking that method enables passing specified variable values. This demonstrates how methods can be executed dynamically, based on runtime information.

Accessing and editing fields and properties

Reflection also offers a way to get and set an object's fields and properties during runtime. This can be very useful in scenarios where there is a need to set an object's state dynamically or interact with its properties per the user's input or according to external data. The following example shows how one can access and change fields and properties with reflection:

```csharp
using System;
using System.Reflection;
public class Person
{
    public string Name { get; set; } = "";
    private int age;

    public int Age
    {
        get { return age; }
        set { age = value; }
    }
}

class Program
{
    static void Main()
    {
        Type type = typeof(Person);
        object? instance = Activator.CreateInstance(type);

        // Set and get property
        PropertyInfo? nameProperty = type.GetProperty("Name");
        nameProperty?.SetValue(instance, "John Doe");
        Console.WriteLine($"Name: {nameProperty?.GetValue(instance)}");

        // Set and get private field
        FieldInfo? ageField = type.GetField("age", BindingFlags.NonPublic |
BindingFlags.Instance);
        ageField?.SetValue(instance, 30);
        Console.WriteLine($"Age: {ageField?.GetValue(instance)}");
    }
}
```

Output:

Name: John Doe

Age: 30

This code reflects both the public property "**Name**" and the private field "**age**" of the '**Person**' class and modifies them. The respective members are retrieved through '**GetProperty**' and '**GetField**', while the values can be accessed for manipulation via '**SetValue**' and '**GetValue**'. It shows how reflection can actually change the state of an object at run-time.

Working with constructors and events

Reflection also provides the ability to interact with constructors and events. Constructors can be invoked to create new instances of a type, while events can be accessed and manipulated dynamically, allowing you to add or remove event handlers at runtime. Reflection gives you a way to invoke constructors; this is especially useful when you want to create instances of classes with specific parameters that are known only at run-time:

```
using System;
using System.Reflection;
public class MyClass
{
    public MyClass(string message)
    {
        Console.WriteLine(message);
    }
}

class Program
{
    static void Main()
    {
        Type type = typeof(MyClass);
        ConstructorInfo? constructor = type.GetConstructor(new Type[] {
typeof(string) });

        object instance = constructor?.Invoke(new object?[] { "Hello from
Reflection!" });
    }
}
```

Output:

`Hello from Reflection!`

In this example, we apply reflection to retrieve and call the constructor of the class '**MyClass**' which takes a parameter of '**string**' data type. '**GetConstructor**' is used to find the constructor, and '**Invoke**' creates an instance of '**MyClass**', passing the specified argument to the constructor.

In addition, adding or removing event handlers becomes possible through reflection. This will come in handy where the event handler is determined during runtime:

```csharp
using System;
using System.Reflection;
public class Publisher
{
    public event EventHandler MyEvent;

    public void RaiseEvent()
    {
        MyEvent?.Invoke(this, EventArgs.Empty);
    }
}

class Program
{
    static void Main()
    {
        Type type = typeof(Publisher);
        object instance = Activator.CreateInstance(type);
        EventInfo eventInfo = type.GetEvent("MyEvent");

        EventHandler handler = new EventHandler((sender, e) =>
        {
            Console.WriteLine("Event raised!");
        });

        eventInfo.AddEventHandler(instance, handler);

        MethodInfo raiseEventMethod = type.GetMethod("RaiseEvent");
        raiseEventMethod.Invoke(instance, null);
    }
}
```

Output:

```
Event raised!
```

In the preceding code, we used reflection to attach an event handler onto the event called '**MyEvent**' belonging to a class named '**Publisher**'. This method called '**RaiseEvent**', raises the event after which it invokes the dynamically added handler. This shows how reflection can be used to work with events, adding flexibility to how and when event handlers are attached or detached. The output is as follows:

Reflection and assemblies

Reflection allows you to work with assemblies dynamically, enabling the loading, exploration, and interaction with these assemblies at runtime. This capability is crucial for scenarios like plugin development, dynamic type discovery, and custom application frameworks.

An assembly is a compiled code library used by applications for deployment, versioning, and security in C#. Common file formats for assemblies are **dynamic link library (.dll)** or .exe (executable). They normally carry with them several namespaces, types as well as resources. They serve as the primary unit of deployment in .NET and can include multiple types like classes, interfaces, enums, and delegates.

Assemblies also have some extra information about the types and members that can be accessed through reflection. This data is necessary for understanding how code is structured, as it allows one to perform many runtime tasks, including invoking methods dynamically or creating instances of types on the fly.

Reflection enables you to load assemblies at runtime, which is particularly useful in applications that need to dynamically load plugins or modules. By loading an assembly, you can inspect its types and members and interact with them without having prior knowledge of their existence at compilation time. The following is an example of how to load an assembly dynamically:

```
// Load assembly from file
// Assembly assembly = Assembly.LoadFrom("SomeAssembly.dll");
// Console.WriteLine($"Loaded Assembly: {assembly.FullName}");


// Load assembly by name
Assembly anotherAssembly = Assembly.Load("mscorlib");
Console.WriteLine($" Loaded Assembly: {anotherAssembly.FullName} ");
```

Output:

```
Loaded Assembly: mscorlib, Version=4.0.0.0, Culture=neutral,
PublicKeyToken=b77a5c561934e089
```

The function '`Assembly.LoadFrom`' is used in this code to load an assembly at runtime from a file while '`Assembly.Load`' loads an assembly by referring to its name. Reflection can then be used to explore the types and members once an assembly has been loaded. This is especially useful in scenarios like plugin architectures, where the application needs to load and execute code that was not available at compilation time.

Exploring types and members within assemblies

After loading an assembly, reflection provides the tools to explore its contents, including the types and their members (methods, properties, fields, etc.). This exploration allows you to discover and interact with the components of an assembly dynamically. The following is how you can explore the types and members within an assembly:

```csharp
using System;
using System.Reflection;
class Program
{
    static void Main()
    {
        // Load an assembly
        Assembly assembly = Assembly.LoadFrom("SomeAssembly.dll");

        // Get all types in the assembly
        Type[] types = assembly.GetTypes();

        foreach (Type type in types)
        {
            Console.WriteLine($"Type: {type.FullName}");

            // Get all methods in the type
            MethodInfo[] methods = type.GetMethods();
            foreach (var method in methods)
            {
                Console.WriteLine($" - Method: {method.Name}");
            }

            // Get all properties in the type
            PropertyInfo[] properties = type.GetProperties();
            foreach (var property in properties)
            {
                Console.WriteLine($" - Property: {property.Name}");
            }

            // Get all fields in the type
            FieldInfo [] fields  = type.GetFields (BindingFlags.Public |
```

```
BindingFlags.NonPublic | BindingFlags.Instance | BindingFlags.Static);
            foreach (var field in fields)
            {
                Console.WriteLine($" - Field: {field.Name}");
            }


            // Get all events in the type
            EventInfo[] events = type.GetEvents();
            foreach (var ev in events)
            {
                Console.WriteLine($" - Event: {ev.Name}");
            }
        }
    }
}
```

In the preceding example, after calling '**Assembly.LoadFrom**' to load an assembly, we use reflection to retrieve all types within it with '**GetTypes()**'. For each type, we will also look into its methods, properties, fields, and events. This approach demonstrates how reflection can be used to dynamically discover and interact with the contents of an assembly, which is especially useful in scenarios where types and members need to be accessed without prior knowledge.

Performance impacts of using reflection

Reflection, by its nature, involves examining metadata and performing operations that are typically resolved at compile time, such as method invocations or type instantiations. Since these operations are resolved at runtime, they can be considerably slower than their non-reflection counterparts.

Key performance impacts of using reflection include the following:

- **Increased overhead**: Reflection adds overhead because it bypasses compile-time optimizations and relies on metadata processing. This means that actions like method invocation or object creation are slower when performed via reflection.

- **Late binding**: Reflection involves late binding, where the method, property, or type to be accessed is determined at runtime. This delay can introduce latency, especially in applications where such operations are frequent.

- **No inlining**: There should be no benefits of inlining for methods called via reflection since it means that the compiler would replace the method call with the actual body of the method itself, reducing time wasted on calls.

- **Security considerations**: Since it bypasses the ordinary security mechanisms of an application, allowing higher levels of access than those allowed by its user interface or its API means that reflection could make such applications more vulnerable to some kinds of attacks if not done right hence precautions must always be taken when working with reflection.

Best practices for optimizing reflection usage

While reflection is inherently slower than direct code execution, there are best practices that can help mitigate its performance impacts:

- **Minimize reflection usage**: Use reflection only when necessary. If the same operation can be accomplished through regular code, prefer that approach over reflection.

- **Cache reflection results**: When using reflection to access metadata or perform operations, cache the results where possible. For example, if you need to repeatedly invoke a method via reflection, cache the '`MethodInfo`' instance rather than retrieving it each time.

- **Use dynamic in moderation**: The '`dynamic`' keyword in C# can be used for dynamic method invocation without reflection syntax, but it still uses reflection under the hood. Use it judiciously, as it has similar performance implications.

- **Limit reflection scope**: If possible, limit the scope of reflection to specific parts of the application. Avoid using reflection in performance-critical paths, such as tight loops or real-time processing code.

- **Combine reflection with compiled expressions**: For certain tasks like dynamic method invocation, using compiled expression trees can provide better performance than raw reflection.

Alternatives to reflection for performance-critical applications

In scenarios where performance is critical and reflection poses too much of a performance penalty, consider the following alternatives:

- **Generics**: Generics are a way of creating flexible and reusable code that does not use reflection. Using generics enables programmers to write type-safe code that works for different types without performance degradation.

- **Dependency injection (DI)**: Management of object creation and dependency resolution can be done through DI. The DI frameworks like ASP.NET Core's built-in DI container can manage object lives and dependencies without using reflection.

- **Source generators**: C# source generators offer a way to produce code at compile time, saving you from using reflection in some cases. Source generators give you APIs to write codes for generating new codes during your build process offering ways for achieving runtime behavior with compiler time safety features as well as performance gains.

- **Precompiled expressions**: For dynamic method invocation, consider using precompiled 'Expression' trees instead of raw reflection. These can be more efficient as they are compiled into delegates, reducing the overhead of runtime method invocation.

Working with attributes

.NET has a set of predefined Attributes that are often used in various applications. These Attributes belong to the .NET Framework and provide ready-made functionality for common circumstances. The following are a few commonly used predefined Attributes:

- **'[Obsolete]'**: Marks a program element as obsolete, generating a compiler warning or error if it is used. This means that a method or class should not be used anymore, and it may even be removed in future versions.

- **'[Serializable]'**: Indicates that a class or struct can be serialized, which means its instances can be sent over the web or saved in other formats and then later reconstructed.

- **'[NonSerialized]'**: Specifies that a field of a serializable class should not be serialized.

- **'[DllImport]'**: Used to import functions from unmanaged code (e.g., DLLs). This is often used for interop scenarios with native libraries.

- **'[DataContract]' and '[DataMember]'**: Both Attributes are used in **Windows Communication Foundation (WCF)**; they define data contracts for serializing and deserializing classes.

Apart from the predefined, you can define your own custom Attributes. Custom Attributes are mechanisms whereby users define their own metadata that can be applied to classes, methods, properties, and so on. This metadata can then be queried and processed using reflection.

To develop your own attribute, start by constructing a class derived from '`System. Attribute`' and then apply it to your code constructs.

Custom Attributes come handy for configuration, documentation, or code analysis purposes, among others, where extra information about these code elements might need to be attached and processed in real-time.

Creating custom attributes

To create a custom attribute, first construct a class that inherits from '**System.Attribute**'. Then, using the '**AttributeUsage**' property, indicate the actual code elements that will have this attribute attached to them. Define the **Attribute** class: Inherit from '**System. Attribute**' and define any properties or methods that your attribute will use. Here is an example:

```
using System;
[AttributeUsage (AttributeTargets.Class | AttributeTargets.Method ,
Inherited = false , AllowMultiple  =  false ) ]
public class DeveloperInfoAttribute : Attribute
{
    public string Name { get; }
    public string Date { get; }

    public DeveloperInfoAttribute(string name, string date)
    {
        Name = name;
        Date = date;
    }
}
```

In the preceding example, '**DeveloperInfoAttribute**' is a custom attribute that includes '**Name**' and '**Date**' properties. The '**AttributeUsage**' attribute specifies that '**DeveloperInfoAttribute**' can be applied to classes and methods but not to properties or fields. The '**Inherited**' property denotes whether such inherited classes will inherit this specific attribute, and '**AllowMultiple**' indicates if more than one instance of such an attribute could be attached.

After defining custom Attributes, they can be applied to classes, methods, or properties. They are applied using square brackets above the code element they annotate. The following is how to apply the custom attribute:

```
using System;
[DeveloperInfo("Alice Smith", "2024-08-14")]
public class SampleClass
{
    [DeveloperInfo("Bob Jones", "2024-08-15")]
    public void SampleMethod() { }
}
```

This example applies '**DeveloperInfoAttribute**' to a class ('**SampleClass**') and a method ('**SampleMethod**'). This annotation is useful for documentation or tracking purposes as it provides metadata about the developer and the date.

Retrieving attribute information with reflection

Reflection allows you to retrieve and process custom attribute information at runtime. By querying the metadata of the code elements, you can access the values of Attributes and use them as needed. Following is how to retrieve attribute information using reflection:

```csharp
using System;
using System.Reflection;
class Program
{
    static void Main()
    {
        // Retrieve custom attributes for a class
        Type type = typeof(SampleClass);
        object[] classAttributes = type.
GetCustomAttributes(typeof(DeveloperInfoAttribute), false);
        foreach (DeveloperInfoAttribute attr in classAttributes)
        {
            Console.WriteLine($"Class Developer: {attr.Name}, Date: {attr.
Date}");
        }


        // Retrieve custom attributes for a method
        MethodInfo method = type.GetMethod("SampleMethod");
        object[] methodAttributes = method.
GetCustomAttributes(typeof(DeveloperInfoAttribute), false);
        foreach (DeveloperInfoAttribute attr in methodAttributes)
        {
            Console.WriteLine($"Method Developer: {attr.Name}, Date: {attr.
Date}");
        }


        // Retrieve custom attributes for a property
        PropertyInfo property = type.GetProperty("SampleProperty");
        object[] propertyAttributes = property.
GetCustomAttributes(typeof(DeveloperInfoAttribute), false);
```

```
        foreach (DeveloperInfoAttribute attr in propertyAttributes)
        {
            Console.WriteLine ($" Property Developer: {attr.Name}, Date:
{attr.Date} ");
        }
    }
}
```

Reflection is used in this case to obtain the '**DeveloperInfoAttribute**' applied on '**SampleClass**' class, its method '**SampleMethod**', and the property '**SampleProperty**'. The '**GetCustomAttributes**' method is used to obtain the Attributes, and their properties are accessed to display the developer information. This demonstrates how to query and use custom attribute data at runtime.

Conclusion

In this chapter, we explored the powerful features of reflection and Attributes in C#, which allow for dynamic inspection and manipulation of code at runtime. You have learned how reflection can be used to access and invoke class members, create instances dynamically, and retrieve important metadata. We also discussed the role of Attributes in providing additional metadata to your code and how to use reflection to process those Attributes. By mastering these concepts, you can create more flexible, dynamic, and maintainable applications.

As we move forward, the next chapter will delve into C# dynamic programming, where we will explore how to write even more flexible code by utilizing the dynamic keyword and other dynamic features. Dynamic programming in C# allows developers to bypass compile-time type checking, providing greater flexibility in scenarios where types and operations are determined at runtime. This approach complements the reflection and attribute concepts learned in this chapter, as both provide tools for creating adaptable and powerful applications.

Multiple choice questions:

1. **What is the main purpose of C# reflection?**
   a. To access data from a database.
   b. To inspect and manipulate program structure at runtime.
   c. To compile the program more efficiently.
   d. To debug the program without external tools.

2. **Which namespace is used for reflection in C#?**

   a. System.Reflection

   b. System.Dynamic

   c. System.IO

   d. System.Runtime

3. **What method is used to retrieve the methods of a class using reflection?**

   a. GetFields()

   b. GetProperties()

   c. GetMethods()

   d. GetConstructors()

4. **What is an attribute in C#?**

   a. A keyword to initialize classes.

   b. A data type that stores metadata about code.

   c. A method for accessing private fields.

   d. A type of interface.

5. **Which of the following is an example of a predefined attribute in C#?**

   a. [Deprecated]

   b. [Serializable]

   c. [Final]

   d. [Override]

6. **Which method is used to create an instance of a class dynamically at runtime?**

   a. Activator.CreateInstance()

   b. MethodInfo.Invoke()

   c. Assembly.Load()

   d. Type.GetType()

7. **What does the [Obsolete] attribute do in C#?**

   a. It indicates that the program will not compile.

   b. It signals that a method or class is outdated and should not be used.

   c. It marks a method as private.

   d. It prevents a method from being serialized.

8. **Which method allows reflection to retrieve custom Attributes assigned to a class?**

   a. GetMethod()

   b. GetCustomAttributes()

   c. GetField()

   d. GetConstructor()

9. **Which of the following is not a key benefit of using reflection?**

   a. Allows dynamic method invocation.

   b. Enables access to metadata.

   c. Improves performance in real-time processing.

   d. Supports runtime object creation.

10. **What is one potential drawback of using reflection in C#?**

    a. It can only be used with static types.

    b. It increases the overall execution speed.

    c. It adds performance overhead compared to compile-time access.

    d. It cannot be used with dynamic types.

Answers

1. (b) To inspect and manipulate program structure at runtime.
2. (a) System.Reflection
3. (c) GetMethods()
4. (b) A data type that stores metadata about code.
5. (b) [Serializable]
6. (a) Activator.CreateInstance()
7. (b) It signals that a method or class is outdated and should not be used.
8. (b) GetCustomAttributes()
9. (c) Improves performance in real-time processing.
10. (c) It adds performance overhead compared to compile-time access.

Practice problems

In this problem, you are tasked with creating a small program that uses C# reflection and Attributes to inspect the structure of a class, dynamically invoke its methods, and retrieve custom Attributes applied to its members.

Steps:

1. Create a class named Person with the following:
   ○ A property Name of type string.
   ○ A method SayHello() that prints "Hello, [Name]!" to the console, where [Name] is the value of the Name property.

2. Create a custom attribute named AuthorAttribute that takes the following two parameters:
   ○ The author's name (string).
   ○ The date of creation (string).

3. Apply the AuthorAttribute to the Person class and the SayHello method.

4. In your main program:
   ○ Use reflection to:
      ▪ Retrieve the list of methods in the Person class.
      ▪ Dynamically invoke the SayHello() method.
   ○ Retrieve and display any custom Attributes applied to the Person class and SayHello method using reflection.

Expected output:

- The program should display the names of the methods in the Person class.
- It should invoke the SayHello() method dynamically.
- It should retrieve and print the AuthorAttribute information from both the class and the method.

Code skeleton:

```
using System;
using System.Reflection;

// Step 1: Create the Person class
[Author("Alice Smith", "2024-09-30")]
public class Person
{
    public string Name { get; set; }

    [Author("Bob Jones", "2024-09-30")]
    public void SayHello()
    {
```

```
                Console.WriteLine($"Hello, {Name}!");
        }
}


// Step 2: Create the custom attribute
[AttributeUsage(AttributeTargets.Class | AttributeTargets.Method)]
public class AuthorAttribute : Attribute
{
    public string Name { get; }
    public string Date { get; }

    public AuthorAttribute(string name, string date)
    {
        Name = name;
        Date = date;
    }
}

class Program
{
    static void Main()
    {
        // Step 4: Use reflection to inspect the class and invoke its
methods

        // Retrieve the type of the Person class
        Type personType = typeof(Person);

        // Retrieve methods from the class
        MethodInfo[] methods = personType.GetMethods();
        Console.WriteLine("Methods in Person class:");
        foreach (var method in methods)
        {
            Console.WriteLine(method.Name);
        }

        // Dynamically create an instance of the Person class and
set Name
        object personInstance = Activator.CreateInstance(personType);
```

```
        PropertyInfo nameProperty = personType.GetProperty("Name");
        nameProperty.SetValue(personInstance, "John Doe");

        // Dynamically invoke the SayHello method
        MethodInfo sayHelloMethod = personType.
GetMethod("SayHello");
        sayHelloMethod.Invoke(personInstance, null);

        // Retrieve and display custom attributes from the class and
method
        Console.WriteLine("\nCustom Attributes:");
        object[] classAttributes = personType.
GetCustomAttributes(false);
        foreach (AuthorAttribute attr in classAttributes)
        {
            Console.WriteLine($"Class Author: {attr.Name}, Date:
{attr.Date}");
        }

        object[] methodAttributes = sayHelloMethod.
GetCustomAttributes(false);
        foreach (AuthorAttribute attr in methodAttributes)
        {
            Console.WriteLine($"Method Author: {attr.Name}, Date:
{attr.Date}");
        }
    }
}
```

Challenge:

- Modify the code to use reflection to list all properties and invoke a constructor dynamically for the Person class.

Join our book's Discord space

Join the book's Discord Workspace for Latest updates, Offers, Tech happenings around the world, New Release and Sessions with the Authors:

https://discord.bpbonline.com

CHAPTER 13
C# Dynamic Programming

Introduction

Dynamic programming in C# is a versatile approach that brings flexibility and adaptability to code, primarily through the use of the dynamic type. This chapter delves into the dynamic features introduced in C# 4.0, including how dynamic typing differs from traditional static typing, and explores the practical applications of this powerful tool. C# developers can bypass compile-time type checking through dynamic programming, allowing runtime type resolution. This is particularly valuable when working with data sources, libraries, or APIs that deliver variable object types, offering enhanced interoperability and streamlined coding practices.

In this chapter, you will learn about the core principles of dynamic typing and how to utilize it effectively and avoid potential pitfalls. You will gain insight into creating more responsive and maintainable applications by understanding the key differences between dynamic and object types and the role of the **dynamic language runtime (DLR)**.

Structure

This chapter covers the following topics:

- Dynamic programming in C#
- Dynamic language runtime

- Dynamic LINQ queries
- Performance considerations with dynamic

Objectives

By the end of this chapter, you will understand the fundamentals of dynamic programming in C# and the differences between static and dynamic typing. You will be able to use the dynamic type to create flexible and adaptable code while implementing effective error handling. Additionally, you will learn best practices for dynamic programming to ensure robust and maintainable applications.

Dynamic programming in C#

C# Dynamic programming is a powerful technique for writing flexible and adaptable code. This method applies to mathematical optimization in general and C#, which refers to using a '**dynamic**' type that allows bypassing compile-time type checking and resolving types at run time. This can be beneficial when the actual object type is unknown during application execution. It is also useful when dealing with libraries and APIs that return variable object types.

The primary focus of dynamic programming in C# is on the '**dynamic**' keyword, first introduced in C# 4.0. Unlike other variable types checked against their type during compile-time, a '**dynamic**' variable has its type set at runtime. This allows for seamless interaction with different kinds of objects; however, it results in a loss of compile-time checking alongside risks of run-time errors. For example:

```
dynamic example = "Hello, Dynamic World!";
Console.WriteLine(example.Length);  // Output: 18
example = 100;
Console.WriteLine(example + 50);  // Output: 150
```

In this code, the variable '**example**' is first assigned a string and later an integer. The code works because the type is resolved dynamically at runtime, allowing the operations to be performed based on the variable's current type.

Differences between static and dynamic typing

In C#, static typing is obligatory because all variable types must be determined when compiled. This action ensures that any mistakes regarding data types are discovered early enough, making code easier to manage regarding robustness and predictability. On the contrary, the '**dynamic**' keyword makes it possible for type checking to occur after program execution has commenced, thus enhancing flexibility at the cost of potential runtime errors. Following is a quick comparison:

- **Static typing:**
  - o Type is known and verified at compile-time.
  - o Code is generally safer and faster due to early error detection.
  - o IDEs provide better IntelliSense and refactoring tools.
- **Dynamic typing:**
  - o Type is determined at runtime, offering more flexibility.
  - o Errors related to type mismatch might only surface during execution.
  - o Useful in scenarios where types are unknown until runtime, such as interacting with COM objects or dynamic languages like Python.

Understanding the dynamic type

The '**dynamic**' type in C# is a unique feature that allows variables to operate without static type constraints. Unlike other types in C#, variables declared with '**dynamic**' are not type-checked by the compiler, meaning their type is resolved at runtime. It opens many possibilities, mainly when dealing with data from sources whose nature is not apparent until the program runs. However, this freedom brings advantages and obstacles that will be discussed in this section.

The '**dynamic**' keyword in C# enables developers to define variables, properties, methods, or even return types whose type is resolved during execution rather than at compile time. This contrasts the '**var**' keyword, which infers the type at compile time based on the assigned value.

The following is an example illustrating the difference:

```
var staticVariable = "Hello, World!";  // Type inferred as string at
compile-time
dynamic dynamicVariable = "Hello, Dynamic World!";  // Type resolved at
runtime
```

In this code, '**staticVariable**' is assigned a '**string**' type at compile-time, while '**dynamicVariable**' will have its type determined at runtime. Despite holding a string, a dynamic variable can later be assigned a different kind without causing a compile-time error. The '**dynamic**' keyword allows for late binding, meaning method calls, property accesses, or operations on a '**dynamic**' object are resolved at runtime.

Under the hood, the '**dynamic**' type is treated as an '**object**' type but with deferred type checking. When a member of a '**dynamic**' object is invoked, the runtime uses reflection or other mechanisms to resolve the member at the execution point. A runtime exception is thrown rather than a compile-time error if the member does not exist or the operation is invalid.

For example:

```
dynamic obj = "Sample String";
Console.WriteLine(obj.ToUpper());  // This works fine
obj = 42;
Console.WriteLine(obj.ToUpper());  // Runtime error: 'int' does not contain
a definition for 'ToUpper'
```

In this code, '**obj**' is initially assigned a string, so calling '**ToUpper()**' works as expected. However, when '**obj**' is reassigned with an integer, the same method call fails at runtime because the '**int**' type does not have a '**ToUpper()**' method. This illustrates both the flexibility and the risk associated with dynamic typing.

Advantages and limitations of using dynamic

The advantages of using dynamic are:

- **Interoperability**: The '**dynamic**' keyword makes it easier to work with dynamic languages such as Python or JavaScript, COM objects, and APIs based on reflection, where type information may not be available until runtime.

- **Flexibility**: It enables one to write code that can operate on various types without having any specifics about them simultaneously, thus reducing boilerplate in some situations.

- **Simplified code**: In situations like JSON parsing or data retrieval from non-typed sources, '**dynamic**' can reduce the need for extensive type casting and checks.

Limitations:

- **Runtime errors**: Since type checking is deferred to runtime, errors commonly caught during compilation can go unnoticed, leading to potential crashes or bugs during execution.

- **Performance overhead**: Resolving types and invoking members at runtime can introduce performance overhead due to the reliance on reflection or dynamic dispatch mechanisms.

- **Reduced IntelliSense support**: IDE features like *IntelliSense*, refactoring tools, and code analysis are limited for '**dynamic**' types, making development and maintenance more challenging.

Working with dynamic objects

You can create a dynamically typed object in C# using '**ExpandoObject**,' which belongs to the '**System.Dynamic**' namespace. You can add properties and methods dynamically during execution with this class. Following is an example of creating and using dynamic objects:

```
using System;
using System.Dynamic;

dynamic person = new ExpandoObject();
person.Name = "John";
person.Age = 30;

Console.WriteLine($"Name: {person.Name}");
Console.WriteLine($"Age: {person.Age}");

// Adding a method
person.SayHello = new Action(() => Console.WriteLine("Hello!"));
person.SayHello();
```

Here, we create an '**ExpandoObject**' and add properties and methods to it using dynamic methods. The regular field accessors are used for the '**Name**' or '**Age**' property while adding and calling the '**SayHello**' method. This demonstrates the dynamic nature of '**ExpandoObject**', allowing for flexible and on-the-fly modifications.

One of the various qualities of '**ExpandoObject**' is that it can dynamically add/remove properties/methods. This comes in handy in cases where an object structure should vary based on user input or some other run-time conditions. For example:

```
using System;
using System.Dynamic;

dynamic car = new ExpandoObject();
car.Make = "Toyota";
car.Model = "Camry";
Console.WriteLine($" Make: {car.Make}, Model: {car.Model} ");

// Adding a new property
((IDictionary<string, object>)car)["Year"] = 2021;
Console.WriteLine($"Year: {car.Year}");

// Removing a property
((IDictionary<string, object>)car).Remove("Model");
```

Here, we first define the properties '**Make**' and '**Model**' for the '**car**' object. We then dynamically add a new property, '**Year**,' and remove the '**Model**' property. This showcases the flexibility of '**ExpandoObject**' in modifying its structure during runtime.

Interacting with COM objects and dynamic languages

Dynamic programming in C# is particularly useful when interacting with COM objects or integrating with dynamic languages such as Python or JavaScript. COM objects, for instance, are often accessed via late binding, which is naturally supported by the **'dynamic'** keyword. For example:

```
dynamic excel = Activator.CreateInstance(Type.GetTypeFromProgID("Excel.
Application"));
excel.Visible = true;

dynamic workbook = excel.Workbooks.Add();
dynamic worksheet = workbook.Worksheets[1];
worksheet.Cells[1, 1].Value = "Hello, COM!";

workbook.Close(false);  // false = don't save changes
excel.Quit();

object obj1 = "Hello, World!";
string message = (string)obj1;  // Explicit casting required
Console.WriteLine(message);
```

In this example, we create an instance of the Excel application using its ProgID and interact with it dynamically. We set properties and call methods on the Excel objects without needing compile-time type information. This demonstrates the use of **'dynamic'** to simplify COM interop and late binding.

Dynamic versus object types

In C#, **'dynamic'** and **'object'** data types are generally used to handle situations where the variable type is not formed until run-time. However, they both serve different purposes and characteristics. Recognizing these variations is fundamental in making meaningful choices about when to use either of these two types.

Here are some properties of the **'object'** type:

- **Type checking**: The **'object'** type is the base type for all data types in C#. When you assign a value of any kind to an **'object'**, it undergoes boxing (if it is a value type). Type checking for **'object'** occurs at compile-time.

- **Typecasting**: Operations on an **'object'** are performed by casting it to the specific type you expect. It implies explicit type-checking and casting, which can result in runtime exceptions if the cast is invalid.

Example:

```
object obj = "Hello, World!";
string message = (string)obj;  // Explicit casting required
Console.WriteLine(message);
```

Here, the '**object**' type requires explicit casting to access its underlying type. This explicit casting introduces the risk of '**InvalidCastException**' if the type of '**obj**' does not match the expected type.

Here are the properties of the '**dynamic**' type:

- **Type checking**: The '**dynamic**' type defers type checking until runtime. This allows for more flexible and generic code but at the cost of compile-time safety.

- **Type operations**: You can perform operations on '**dynamic**' variables without explicit casting. The operations are resolved at runtime, which can lead to runtime errors if the operations are invalid. Example:

```
dynamic obj = "Hello, World!";
Console.WriteLine(obj.Length);  // Accessing Length without explicit
casting
```

With '**dynamic**', you can directly access members without casting. Member access is resolved at runtime, which provides more flexibility but also introduces the risk of runtime exceptions if the member does not exist.

Using dynamic over object

Choosing between '**dynamic**' and '**object**' depends on the specific use case and the requirements for type flexibility and safety:

Use '**dynamic**' when:

- You must interact with types or unknown APIs, such as COM objects or dynamic language integration, at compile-time.

- You prefer to write more generic code that operates on various types without knowing their specifics beforehand.

- You are handling data from sources like JSON or XML where the structure is not fixed.

Use '**object**' when:

- You want to maintain type safety and catch type errors at compile-time.

- You need to perform explicit type checks and conversions.

- The performance overhead of the **dynamic** type resolution is a concern.

- Conversions and Type Checking with '**dynamic**'.

When using **'dynamic'**, type, conversions are handled at runtime. This means you can perform conversions without explicit casting, but it also requires you to handle potential runtime errors. For example:

```
dynamic value = 42;
Console.WriteLine((string)value);  // Runtime error: Invalid cast from
'int' to 'string'
```

In this example, converting an integer to a string using **'dynamic'** will fail if the conversion is invalid at runtime. Unlike **'object'**, where you might use **'Convert.ToString(value)'**, **'dynamic'** defers such checks until execution.

Type checking

Type checking with **'dynamic'** is less straightforward since it happens at runtime. If you need to check the type of a **'dynamic'** variable, you can use the **'Type'** class or the **'is'** operator. Example:

```
dynamic data = 123;
if (data is int)
{
    Console.WriteLine("Data is an integer.");
}
```

Using **'is'** with **'dynamic'** lets you check the variable type at runtime. This can help mitigate some risks associated with dynamic typing, though it does not replace the compile-time safety of static typing.

Using reflection with dynamic types

Reflection in C# inspects and interacts with types and their members at runtime. When dealing with dynamic types, reflection becomes particularly useful for performing operations not known at compile time. This is because dynamic types defer type checking and member resolution until runtime. The following is how you might use reflection with dynamic types:

```
dynamic obj3 = new { Name = "Alice", Age = 25 };

Type type3 = obj3.GetType();
PropertyInfo nameProperty = type3.GetProperty("Name");
Console.WriteLine($" The Name is {nameProperty.GetValue(obj)} ");
```

In the preceding example, we use reflection to obtain a dynamic object type and the value of its **'Name'** property.

Reflection allows you to access and invoke members of an object dynamically. This is particularly useful when dealing with types unknown until runtime or when performing operations on objects based on metadata. Following is an example of accessing and invoking a method using reflection:

```
dynamic obj4 = new ExpandoObject();
obj4.Greet = new Action(() => Console.WriteLine("Hello, World!"));


// Use dictionary to retrieve the delegate
var dict = obj4 as IDictionary<string, object>;
if (dict.TryGetValue("Greet", out object greetObj) && greetObj is Delegate
greetDelegate)
{
    greetDelegate.DynamicInvoke();
}
```

Here, we use reflection to invoke the method '**Greet**' on a dynamic object. The '**GetMethod**' method retrieves the '**MethodInfo**' object, which is then used to invoke the method at runtime. This approach is beneficial when working with objects whose methods are unknown until the program is executed.

Combining reflection with dynamic typing can create highly flexible and adaptable code that can handle various types and members at runtime. This approach allows you to write code that can interact with objects whose structures are unknown until execution, facilitating scenarios like plugin systems, scripting engines, or integration with external libraries. The following is an example of how to combine reflection and dynamic:

```
dynamic obj5 = new ExpandoObject();
obj5.Name = "Bob";
obj5.Age = 30;


Type type5 = obj5.GetType();
foreach (var property in type5.GetProperties())
{
    Console.WriteLine($" {property.Name}: {property.GetValue(obj)} ");
}
```

The preceding example shows how reflection can be used to navigate the properties of a **dynamic** object created with '**ExpandoObject**'. By combining '**dynamic**' with reflection, we can dynamically handle properties and their values, making the code adaptable to various objects and scenarios.

Dynamic language runtime

The DLR infrastructure over the .NET Framework enables dynamic typing and languages. It supports the features of dynamic languages, including late binding, dynamic method invocation, and runtime type evaluation. The DLR provides services that enable these features, making it possible for languages like Python and JavaScript to run on the .NET platform and interact seamlessly with C#.

The key components of the DLR include the following:

- **Dynamic object**: Provides a way to define and work with dynamic objects.

- **Dynamic language infrastructure (DLI)**: Provides core services required for supporting dynamic programming languages like dynamic method invocation and property access, among others.

- **Dynamic language interoperability**: It enables interaction among statically typed languages in a .NET environment with the dynamically typed ones.

In C#, the DLR is crucial in implementing the **dynamic** keyword and its associated features. It provides the underlying mechanisms that enable dynamic typing and dynamic method calls. When you use the '**dynamic**' keyword in C#, the DLR handles the type resolution and method invocation at runtime, which allows for flexible and adaptable code. The following is an example of how the DLR supports dynamic programming:

```
dynamic dynamicObject = new ExpandoObject();
dynamicObject.Greet = new Action(() => Console.WriteLine("Hello from DLR!"));

dynamicObject.Greet();  // DLR resolves the method call at runtime
```

In this example, the '**dynamic**' keyword and '**ExpandoObject**' leverage the DLR to add and invoke a method dynamically. The DLR resolves the method call at runtime, illustrating how it enables dynamic features in C#.

The DLR enhances interoperability between C# and dynamically typed languages like Python and JavaScript. By providing a common dynamic runtime infrastructure, the DLR allows for seamless integration and interaction between C# and these languages. This capability is handy for integrating C# applications with scripts or components written in dynamic languages. The following is an example of how the DLR facilitates interoperability:

```
using System;
Using Microsoft.Scripting.Hosting;
using IronPython.Hosting;

ScriptEngine engine = Python.CreateEngine();
ScriptScope scope = engine.CreateScope();
```

```
engine.Execute(@"
def greet():
    return 'Hello from Python!'
", scope);

// Retrieve the greet function from the scope
dynamic greetFunc = scope.GetVariable("greet");

// Call the Python function
string result = greetFunc();
Console.WriteLine(result);
```

In the preceding example, **IronPython** (a version of Python on the .Net Framework) was used to generate a Python script engine. We found out that DLR allows us to run Python code and call Python functions from C#, which indicates its effortless integration ability.

Error handling in dynamic programming

Dynamic programming introduces flexibility by resolving types and operations at runtime. However, this flexibility also brings potential pitfalls and runtime errors that must be managed effectively. Proper error handling and adherence to best practices can help mitigate risks and ensure robust dynamic code.

One of the main risks of using '**dynamic**' types is encountering type errors at runtime. Since type checking is deferred until execution, operations for one type might not be valid for another, leading to runtime exceptions. For example:

```
dynamic Value = "string";
Console.WriteLine (Value + 5); // Error: String and Int cannot be added
```

An error will occur here because '**int**' and '**string**' cannot be added. The type mismatch is only detected at run-time, which may lead to crashes or bugs that were not anticipated.

Another pitfall is attempting to access members not existing on a '**dynamic**' object. This can lead to runtime errors if the expected member is not present. For example:

```
dynamic obj = new ExpandoObject();
obj.ExistingMethod();  // Runtime error: Method does not exist
```

The code assumes that '**ExistingMethod**' exists on the '**dynamic**' object. If it does not, a runtime error will occur. This highlights the importance of ensuring the accessed members are valid for the object type.

Handling runtime errors in dynamic programming involves implementing strategies to manage exceptions and validate operations at runtime. Let us look at some techniques.

Using try-catch blocks

Wrap operations that involve '**dynamic**' objects in try-catch blocks to handle potential exceptions gracefully. Example:

```
dynamic obj = "Hello";
try
{
    Console.WriteLine(obj.Length);  // Valid for string
    Console.WriteLine(obj.ToUpper());  // Runtime error if obj is not a
string
}
catch (RuntimeBinderException ex)
{
    Console.WriteLine("Runtime error: " + ex.Message);
}
```

This example uses a try-catch block to handle potential runtime errors when accessing members on a '**dynamic**' object. The '**RuntimeBinderException**' is caught and handled, preventing the application from crashing.

Validating dynamic objects

Check the type of dynamic objects and their members before performing operations. This can be done using the '**is**' operator or '**Type**' class. Example:

```
dynamic obj = 42;
if (obj is string)
{
    Console.WriteLine(((string)obj).ToUpper());
}
else
{
    Console.WriteLine("Object is not a string.");
}
```

This code snippet checks if the '**dynamic**' object is of type '**string**' before attempting to perform string operations. This validation helps avoid runtime errors by ensuring that operations are only performed on compatible types.

Some best practices for writing robust dynamic code are as follows:

- **Minimize 'dynamic'**: Use '**dynamic**' only when necessary and prefer static typing whenever possible. This reduces the risk of runtime errors and improves code clarity.

- **Validate inputs and outputs**: Always validate dynamic inputs and outputs. Ensure that the operations performed are appropriate for the data being handled.

- **Use reflection judiciously**: When using reflection with dynamic types, be cautious of performance overhead and potential runtime issues. Limit the use of reflection to scenarios where it is genuinely needed.

- **Implement error handling**: Incorporate comprehensive error handling to gracefully manage exceptions and errors. Use try-catch blocks to catch and handle runtime exceptions.

- **Document dynamic code**: Document the usage and expectations of dynamic objects in your code. This helps other developers understand the dynamic aspects and reduces the likelihood of errors.

- **Test thoroughly**: Perform extensive testing to ensure that dynamic code behaves as expected. Include unit tests and integration tests to cover various scenarios and edge cases.

Dynamic LINQ queries

Language Integrated Query (**LINQ**) is one of the powerful functionalities in C# that allows for more straightforward, more readable, and concise data querying. If you are generating queries at runtime or dealing with data from a dynamic source, LINQ queries must be created dynamically. This section explores constructing dynamic LINQ queries, using the '**dynamic**' keyword with LINQ expressions, and identifying scenarios where dynamic query generation is beneficial.

Creating dynamic LINQ queries involves constructing query expressions at runtime based on user input or other runtime conditions. This flexibility allows you to build queries on the fly without hardcoding them. The following is an example of creating a dynamic LINQ query:

```
using System;
using System.Collections.Generic;
using System.Linq;

var data1 = new List<string> { "apple", "banana", "cherry", "date" };
string searchTerm = "a";

var query = data1.Where(item => item.Contains(searchTerm));
foreach (var item in query)
{
    Console.WriteLine(item);
}
```

In this instance, the 'Where' clause in the LINQ query is created based on the selected 'searchTerm'. It then filters the list so that only items containing the search term remain. This demonstrates how LINQ queries can be constructed dynamically based on runtime conditions.

Using LINQ expressions, the '**dynamic**' keyword can be employed to deal with situations where type information and query structure are only available during run-time. This gives you flexibility and adaptability in your way of working with data. The following is an example of using '**dynamic**' with LINQ:

```
using System;
using System.Collections.Generic;
using System.Linq;
using System.Dynamic;

dynamic data2 = new ExpandoObject();
data2.Items = new List<int> { 1, 2, 3, 4, 5 };

var result2 = ((IEnumerable<int>)data2.Items).Where(x => x > 2).ToList();
foreach (var item in result)
{
    Console.WriteLine(item);
}
```

In this example, we use '**dynamic**' to define a list of items and perform a LINQ query to filter values greater than 2. The '**dynamic**' type allows us to work with the list and perform LINQ operations without knowing the type at compile time.

Dynamic query generation is helpful in various scenarios where query structures need to be flexible and adaptable based on runtime conditions:

User-defined filters

Dynamic query generation gives an application the ability to construct and execute queries when users are allowed to define their own filters or search criteria themselves in applications. Example:

```
dynamic data3 = new ExpandoObject();
data3.Items = new List<string> { "apple", "banana", "apricot", "orange" };

string filterTerm = "ap";
var items = (IEnumerable<string>)data2.Items;

var query3 = items.AsQueryable();
```

```
if (!string.IsNullOrEmpty(filterTerm))
{
    query3 = query3.Where(item => item.Contains(filterTerm));
}

var results = query3.ToList();
foreach (var item in results)
{
    Console.WriteLine(item);
}
```

Here, the query is dynamically adjusted based on the presence of a filter term. This approach allows users to specify various filters without requiring predefined query structures.

Applications based on data

Being able to generate queries dynamically is essential when working with applications that get data from sources whose structure is not known during compile time but gets revealed at runtime. For example:

```
dynamic dataSource = GetDynamicDataSource();
var query = dataSource.Items.Where(item => item.IsActive).ToList();
```

In this example, '**dataSource**' represents a dynamically obtained data source, and LINQ is used to filter items based on their active status. The query structure is built dynamically based on the data source's runtime characteristics.

Performance considerations with dynamic

The primary performance impact of dynamic typing is the runtime overhead associated with type resolution and method invocation. Unlike statically typed code, where type checks and method bindings co-occur, dynamic typing defers these operations until runtime.

For example:

```
dynamic obj = new ExpandoObject();
obj.SomeMethod();  // Method resolution occurs at runtime
```

In this example, '**SomeMethod**' is resolved and invoked at runtime, introducing overhead compared to static method calls, where such resolutions are handled at compile time. This runtime resolution can affect performance, especially in performance-critical applications.

On top of this, dynamic objects may consume more memory than statically typed objects due to additional metadata and runtime information required for dynamic operations. For example:

```
dynamic obj = new ExpandoObject();
obj.Name = "Alice";
obj.Age = 30;
```

An '**ExpandoObject**' used as a dynamic object may involve extra memory overhead for storing properties and managing dynamic behaviors, impacting overall memory usage.

Conclusion

This chapter explored the dynamic programming capabilities of C# that enhance flexibility and adaptability in coding. We began by examining the dynamic type, which allows runtime type resolution, contrasting the static typing traditionally used in C#. We then explored practical applications of dynamic typing, including interoperability with COM objects and integration with dynamic languages, which enable smoother interactions across different programming environments. We also discussed essential concepts such as the DLR, which facilitates dynamic method calls and late binding. We covered best practices for handling errors and managing type conversions with dynamic types. Mastering dynamic programming techniques is valuable for building adaptable and maintainable applications, allowing you to handle diverse data sources and optimize for flexibility where it's most beneficial in C# development.

In the next chapter, you will explore the foundations of Windows Forms and **Windows Presentation Foundation** (**WPF**), two key frameworks for building desktop applications in C#. You will learn how Windows Forms simplifies creating traditional Windows-style interfaces and how WPF enables rich, dynamic, and customizable user experiences with modern design capabilities. This introduction will prepare you to understand the strengths and applications of each framework, helping you choose the best approach for your projects.

Multiple choice questions

1. **What is the primary purpose of the dynamic keyword in C#?**

   a. To define variables with type safety at compile-time.

   b. To allow variables to have their type resolved at runtime.

   c. To restrict variables to specific data types only.

   d. To enhance code performance by enforcing early binding.

2. **Which of the following best describes the dynamic type in C#?**

   a. A type that allows only integer values.

   b. A type that enforces strict compile-time checking.

c. A type that defers type checking until runtime.

d. A type that is used explicitly for database operations.

3. **What is the significant difference between static and dynamic typing in C#?**

   a. Static typing defers type checking until runtime, while dynamic typing does it at compile-time.

   b. Dynamic typing allows type resolution at runtime, while static typing enforces it at compile-time.

   c. Static typing uses the dynamic keyword, while dynamic typing uses the static keyword.

   d. There is no difference; they function similarly in C#.

4. **What is the advantage of using the dynamic keyword?**

   a. It reduces the need to handle errors.

   b. It ensures high performance at runtime.

   c. It allows more flexibility when working with unknown types at compile-time.

   d. It restricts access to specific object methods at runtime.

5. **In C#, what does the DLR primarily provide?**

   a. Static type checking during code compilation.

   b. Infrastructure for dynamic typing and method invocation at runtime.

   c. A specialized library for mathematical operations.

   d. A method for creating and managing event-driven applications.

6. **When should you choose dynamic over object in C#?**

   a. When you want to enforce strict type safety.

   b. When the type information is needed only at compile-time.

   c. When interacting with libraries or APIs that return unknown types at runtime.

   d. When working exclusively with primitive data types.

7. **Which of the following is not a limitation of using dynamic in C#?**

   a. Potential for runtime errors.

   b. Performance overhead due to runtime type resolution.

   c. Reduced IntelliSense support in the IDE.

   d. Enhanced compile-time safety.

8. **How does using ExpandoObject with dynamic enhance flexibility in C#?**

   a. It dynamically allows properties and methods to be added or removed at runtime.

   b. It restricts the object to only predefined properties.

   c. It ensures type safety by enforcing compile-time checks.

   d. It optimizes the code for faster execution.

9. **Which scenario is best suited for dynamic typing in C#?**

   a. Applications with strict type safety requirements.

   b. Projects where object types are always known at compile-time.

   c. Integrating C# with dynamic languages or handling variable data structures.

   d. Creating static libraries with fixed data types.

10. **What is the primary risk of using the dynamic keyword in C#?**

    a. Compile-time errors due to invalid method calls.

    b. Increased risk of runtime errors if the operation is invalid for the resolved type.

    c. Lack of support for accessing methods at runtime.

    d. Limited ability to interact with COM objects.

Answers

1. (b) This is to allow variables to have their type resolved at runtime.

2. (c) A kind that defers type checking until runtime.

3. (b) Dynamic typing allows type resolution at runtime, while static typing enforces it at compile-time.

4. (c) It will enable more flexibility when working with unknown types at compile-time.

5. (b) Infrastructure for dynamic typing and method invocation at runtime.

6. (c) When you must interact with libraries or APIs that return unknown types at runtime.

7. (d) Enhanced compile-time safety.

8. (a) It allows properties and methods to be added or removed dynamically at runtime.

9. (c) Integrating C# with dynamic languages or handling variable data structures.

10. (b) Increased risk of runtime errors if the operation is invalid for the resolved type.

Practice problems

1. You are building a system that needs to handle data from multiple sources with unknown types, so you decide to use dynamic typing to process data flexibly. Implement a dynamic object handler using the dynamic keyword and demonstrate its adaptability by working with different data types at runtime.

    a. Create a method named ProcessDynamicData that takes a single dynamic parameter and performs the following:

        i.   If the parameter is a string, return its length.

        ii. If the parameter is an integer, return its square.

        iii. If the parameter is a Boolean, return the opposite of its value.

    b. Demonstrate the method by calling ProcessDynamicData with a string, an integer, and a Boolean, printing each output.

        Expected output: When invoked, ProcessDynamicData should:

        i.   Return the length of the string.

        ii. Return the square of the integer.

        iii. Return the opposite of the Boolean value.

2. You are developing a logging system that records activities from various systems where the structure of log entries may vary at runtime. To handle this, you decide to use ExpandoObject to create a flexible logging object that can be customized dynamically.

    a. Create a method named CreateLogEntry that returns a dynamic object using ExpandoObject.

        i.   Add properties Timestamp (DateTime) and Message (string) to the log entry.

        ii. Allow additional properties to be added dynamically to the log entry object using dictionary syntax.

    b. Demonstrate this functionality by creating a log entry with Timestamp, Message, and an additional UserID property with a sample value. Print the log entry details to the console.

        Expected output: When invoked, the log entry should display:

        i.   The Timestamp.

        ii. The Message.

        iii. The UserID property demonstrates the flexibility of the ExpandoObject.

Join our book's Discord space

Join the book's Discord Workspace for Latest updates, Offers, Tech happenings around the world, New Release and Sessions with the Authors:

https://discord.bpbonline.com

CHAPTER 14

Windows Forms and Windows Presentation Foundation

Introduction

In C# desktop application development, mastering Windows Forms and **Windows Presentation Foundation (WPF)** is essential for creating compelling and engaging user interfaces. Windows Forms is a longstanding GUI toolkit in the .NET framework that offers simplicity and stability, making it ideal for straightforward applications with a traditional Windows style. With familiar controls like buttons, labels, and text boxes, Windows Forms focuses on rapid prototyping and ease of use, making it a preferred choice for applications that do not require extensive customization.

Conversely, WPF was introduced with .NET Framework 3.0, bringing a modern UI development approach. It leverages DirectX for efficient graphics rendering, supports multimedia elements, and offers a highly customizable design environment with features like animations, styles, templates, and advanced data binding. This makes WPF a powerful choice for applications that require a rich, dynamic, and visually appealing user experience.

This chapter explores the fundamental aspects of both Windows Forms and WPF, highlighting their unique strengths and differences. It covers essential concepts in Windows Forms, including control usage, event handling, and layout management, and dives into WPF's advanced graphics, data binding, and the XAML markup language. By the end, you will have a comprehensive understanding of both frameworks, allowing you to choose the most appropriate one for your application needs and to build robust, user-friendly desktop applications in C#.

Structure

This chapter covers the following topics:

- C# user interface technologies
- Windows Forms
- Windows Presentation Foundation

Objectives

By the end of this chapter, you will be able to understand the fundamental concepts of Windows Forms and WPF. You will develop basic Windows Forms applications with essential controls and event handling. You will also explore the role of XAML in WPF and learn to define UI elements declaratively, and learn to implement data binding and layout management in WPF applications. Identify the key differences between Windows Forms and WPF to choose the appropriate framework for your project needs

C# user interface technologies

In terms of desktop application development via C#, Windows Forms and WPF take the lead among other technologies. They are potent frameworks capable of creating rich, user-friendly interfaces but disparate in purpose, strength, and history.

Windows Forms is a long-standing **graphic user interface** (**GUI**) toolkit that has been part of the .NET Framework since day one. It contains various controls, such as buttons, labels, and text boxes, that are essential in making applications typically Windows-styled. Since it is focused on simplicity, it is ideal for uncomplicated programs that never need customized looks or graphical elements.

WPF was introduced by *Microsoft* with the launch of .NET Framework version 3.0. This technique employs *DirectX* for effective graphics rendering while also supporting large categories of multimedia and **user interface** (**UI**) components. It aims to develop dynamic and more visually appealing applications with features such as animations, styles, templates, and data binding.

Despite both being used for desktop application building, they still have some major areas where they differ:

- **Technology base**: Windows Forms uses the older Win32 API as its foundation, whereas WPF is based on DirectX and supports richer graphics and multimedia.

- **UI Flexibility**: Windows Forms is straightforward but limited in UI customization. WPF, however, offers more flexibility with features like vector graphics, animations, and custom control templates.

- **Performance**: WPF generally provides better performance for complex UIs because it uses hardware acceleration via DirectX. In contrast, Windows Forms depends on the GDI+ engine and can be slow regarding heavy graphic performance.

- **Data binding**: WPF has a stronger and more adaptable model for binding data than Windows Forms, allowing programmers to directly link UI components to their respective data sources with less code.

- **Developer tools**: The close integration of **eXtensible Application Markup Language** (**XAML**) within WPF makes it easy to differentiate between the design and logic. Windows Forms typically uses a code-centric approach.

Windows Forms and WPF are development frameworks that play vital roles in desktop application development. In an enterprise environment that does not require serious customization, Windows Forms usually remains a common option for fast-developing simple applications. Besides, this framework is easy to use and very stable, and several available controls make it faster to develop software programs.

WPF, however, is crucial for modern desktop applications that are interactive and provide a rich user experience. This means that it supports advanced graphics like images and videos; hence, it is suitable for software that is mainly graphic-based or requires a high customization level. Applications presenting complicated data can easily use WPF because it has data binding techniques.

Ultimately, selecting either of these two depends on the project specification, the level of customization required, and the developer's understanding of the technology. Both have individual advantages and, therefore, remain important resources in a C# developer's toolkit.

Windows Forms

Windows Forms has been the bedrock of desktop application design because of its uncomplicated user interface design. In this section, we will cover the primary concepts behind the Windows Forms framework before creating a basic app and then look at a crucial aspect within Windows Forms—Windows Forms Designer—which assists in visual building and managing forms.

The Windows Forms Framework exploits the logic of managed libraries inside the .NET Framework to simplify the process of developing desktop applications for Windows. It is built on top of Win32 API and provides a rich collection of controls like buttons, text boxes, menus, and list boxes that developers can use to build the UI for their apps.

Windows Forms is aimed at rapid prototyping. Its drag-and-drop interface allows developers to build the UI visually without having to write much code. The framework also takes care of many low-level details related to the Windows operating system, such as events management, which makes it easier to develop applications that keep a traditional Windows look and feel.

You will require an IDE, such as Visual Studio, to create your first Windows Forms application. You can refer to the following steps:

1. **Launch Visual Studio (VS)**: Open VS from the start window and click on Create a new project.

2. **Choose a Windows Forms App Template**: Search for "Windows Forms App (.NET Framework)" and select it. Then, click Next.

3. **Configure Your Project**: Enter a project name, choose a location to save it, and click Create.

4. **Create Your Form**: A blank form appears after creating this project. On the left side are tools that can be dragged onto this newly created form, like buttons, labels, and textboxes.

5. **Event handling**: For instance, double-clicking a button generates an event handle in the code behind the file. Add code that handles events such as clicks or keystrokes inside this method.

6. **Compile and execute application**: To compile and run your program, click the Start button (or press F5 on the keyboard). The designed form will appear, allowing you to interact with added controls.

Windows Forms Designer

Visual Studio's Window Forms Designer is an exceptional tool that allows programmers to create user interfaces for their applications visually. It provides a canvas on which various controls, such as buttons, text boxes, and panels, can be dragged over at the formation level. Prominent features of the Windows Forms Designer include the following:

- **Toolbox**: A collection of several tools, including a timer and data grid, which you can add to your form, such as text boxes, labels, and buttons, among others.

- **Properties window**: This window modifies the properties of selected controls, including size, color, text font, and behavior. It allows customizing the appearances and functionalities of controls without requiring any code.

- **Event handlers**: You can easily create an event handler method in your code by double-clicking on any control, such as a button. You can also customize the event handler to define what happens when users interact with a specific control.

- **Layout tools**: The designer provides various alignment, anchoring, and docking tools that allow you to accurately position your controls and make your UI responsive to resizing.

In the background, Windows Forms Designer generates essential C# code that manages the placement and properties of the controls. This visual approach significantly speeds up the development process and reduces the chance of errors compared to manually coding the UI layout.

Windows Forms includes more than enough built-in controls that cater to nearly all standard elements required by a desktop application. The following are some frequently used controls:

- **Button**: A clickable control used to act when clicked. It often triggers an event, like submitting a form or opening a new window.

- **Label**: A simple text display control used to provide descriptive text or instructions to users. It is often used in conjunction with other controls, such as textboxes.

- **Radio button**: A control used for single option selection among all the available options.

- **Text box:** This allows users to enter text. It is typically used for data entry, such as names, emails, or search queries.

- **Data grid view**: This control displays and manipulates tabular data and provides the ability to sort, filter, and edit.

- **Check box**: A control that lets users select or deselect an option. It is often used for multiple selections in forms or preference settings.

- **List box**: This shows users multiple items and lets them pick one or more. It is often used for data selection or filtering.

- **Combo box**: This is a combination of a TextBox and a ListBox that allows the user to select or enter data.

These controls, among others, comprise a significant part of Windows Forms applications. They provide the essential elements needed to create functional and interactive UIs.

With the Windows Forms Designer providing drag-and-drop support, adding new controls to an application in Windows Forms is easy:

- **Adding controls**: Drag controls from the Toolbox and drop them onto your form. The designer will automatically generate the necessary code behind the scenes.

- **Configuring properties**: The Properties Window allows you to set the Properties of added controls. For example, you can change the label of a button by setting the "Text" property, or you can alter its appearance by changing the *Font* property on the label.

- **Setting layout**: To arrange controls on the form, use alignment tools and properties such as *Anchor* and *Dock*. This helps achieve a responsive layout that resizes itself with different window sizes.

- **Grouping controls**: This, to a large extent, qualifies as the use of containers like Panel or *GroupBox* to group related controls together. This simplifies the control of UI and provides a better understanding of the logic behind them, in addition to making it easy for others to use.

A user-friendly interface is built on the proper configuration of controls. When properties are set correctly, controls are placed intuitively, labels are clear, and users can seamlessly interact with the application.

Event handlers respond to user actions such as button clicks, typed characters in text boxes, or selecting an item from a drop-down list. They play an essential role in creating interaction within Windows Forms applications.

To create an event handler, refer to the following steps:

1. **Select a control**: Click on the control you wish, such as a button or any other available in Windows Forms Designer.

2. **Generate an event handler**: To view all events associated with the control, you can either double-click on it or use its Events icon (which looks like a lightning bolt) found in the Properties Window. Double-clicking an event name, like *Click* for a button, automatically generates an event handler method in the code file.

3. **Write event logic**: Add any code that should be executed when the particular event occurs within your event handler method. For instance, when you click your button, you can see a message box displaying this text below a label or even compute something new.

A simple example of an event handler for a button click goes like this:

```
private void button1_Click(object sender, EventArgs e)
{
        MessageBox.Show("The button is clicked");
}
```

Here, upon a click of the button '**button1**', a message box appears containing the text **"The button is clicked"**. Event handlers like this make applications dynamic and responsive to user input.

When you become well-versed in Windows Forms, you might apply some of its advanced functionalities to construct complex and sophisticated programs. In this section, we will delve into how dialog boxes are used, including managing user input, creating custom controls, and **multiple-document interface** (**MDI**) applications.

Dialog boxes and user input

Desktop applications cannot do without dialog boxes. They serve as channels between users and a computer by soliciting user input or providing helpful information. To facilitate everyday tasks, Windows forms have several dialog boxes built-in, such as message boxes, file dialog boxes, and color dialog boxes, among others:

- **MessageBox**: This simple pre-defined window displays messages for the user. For example, to show a confirmation message, one could use the following:

```
MessageBox.Show("You want to save changes?", "Save", MessageBoxButtons.YesNo);
```

- **OpenFileDialog and SaveFileDialog**: This dialog box allows users to select the files they want to open or store, giving it an interface similar to other Windows apps.

- **InputBox**: A custom input dialog to prompt users for text input. The Windows Forms environment does not feature an inbuilt *InputBox*, but you can design your own using a *Form* with a *TextBox'*control.

Dialog boxes enhance user interactions through clear prompts and feedback, ensuring effective communication between the application and its users.

Sometimes, the default controls in Windows Forms may not suffice for your app's specific requirements. For instance, you could opt for custom control creation to meet your needs. These custom controls offer greater flexibility and reusability while allowing one to either extend or modify existing controls.

To create a custom control:

- **Inherit from a Base Control**: Start creating a new class by deriving it from an existing control like '**Button**' or '**TextBox**.' For example:

```
Public class MyCustomButton: Button
{
    // Custom properties, methods, or events can be added here
}
```

- **Override methods and add properties**: You can override methods like '**OnPaint**' to customize how the control is drawn or add new properties to enhance its functionality:

```
protected override void OnPaint(PaintEventArgs pevent)
{
    base.OnPaint(pevent);
    // Custom painting code
}
```

- **Use control in your form**: After you have created your custom control, you can add it to your form just like any other control. Also, they can be easily reused across different project houses, making them good choices when building consistent user interfaces.

Developers who use custom controls go beyond standard options to heighten the functionality of their applications and provide unique user experiences.

Windows Presentation Foundation

Built on DirectX, Microsoft's powerful graphics API allows for better interpretation of graphics, including 2D and 3D graphics, animations, and multimedia support. It replaced how UIs are created with a new concept called XAML, a declarative markup language that separates application logic from presentation design.

The WPF framework is designed around a few fundamental principles:

- **Declarative programming with XAML**: This enables developers to define the UI layout and elements, thus facilitating more accessible construction and maintenance of complicated interfaces.

- **Data binding**: WPF features a robust data binding mechanism that enables UI elements to be tied directly to data sources, reducing boilerplate code and improving the separation of concerns.

- **Flexible layout system**: WPF offers various layout containers, such as *Grid*, *StackPanel*, *Canvas*, etc., which enable more accurate positioning and resizing of your interface controls.

- **Unified media and graphics**: One framework can provide audio, video, vector graphics, and 3D graphics.

Modern desktop apps with complex UI are developed using WPF because of its robustness and flexibility.

WPF distinguishes itself from other UI frameworks through its numerous key features, such as:

- **XAML**: XAML is a markup language that defines user interface components in WPF applications. This procedure enables developers to declaratively manipulate the User Interface components instead of writing them using C#. XAML's range of controls, styles, templates, and animations makes it one of the best tools for developing user interfaces. For instance, you can declare a simple button by including the following line of code in your application:

  ```
  <Button Content="Button" Width= "99" Height= "35" />
  ```

- **Data binding**: It is a powerful feature of WPF that allows direct links between the properties of user interface items and data sources such as objects, collections, or databases. This means dynamic and responsive applications are easy to build since they do not require manual updates whenever there is an update on data related to them. Depending on the needs, there are different types of data binding, such as one-way, two-way, or one-time. Following is an example where a Textbox control binds with a data source:

  ```
  <TextBox Text="{Binding Path=Name}" />
  ```

- **Model-View-ViewModel (MVVM) pattern**: This typical design pattern in WPF applications enhances testability while keeping the concerns separate. In MVVM:

    o The model represents the data and business logic.

    o View is the UI defined in XAML.

    o ViewModel mediates View and Model, managing user input events and providing data to View.

MVVM lets programmers create scalable and maintainable applications with distinct UI and business logic boundaries.

Creating a basic Windows Presentation Foundation application

To start WPF, you can create a simple application using Visual Studio. Following is how to do it step-by-step:

1. **Open Visual Studio**: Launch Visual Studio, then select Create a new Project.

2. **Select a WPF application template**: Choose or write either the *WPF App .NET Core* or *WPF App .NET Framework* based on the target framework, and then click Next.

3. **Set up your project**: Fil in a project name, select a location, and click Create.

4. **Design your UI with XAML**: You will see a '**MainWindow.xaml**' file opened in the XAML designer.

    Here, you can define your UI elements using XAML. For example, add a simple '**Button**':

```
<Window x:Class="WpfApp.MainWindow"
        xmlns="http://schemas.microsoft.com/winfx/2006/xaml/
presentation"
        xmlns:x="http://schemas.microsoft.com/winfx/2006/xaml"
        Title="MainWindow" Height= "300" Width= "500">
    <Grid>
        <Button Content= "Click Me" Width="110" Height= "40"
VerticalAlignment="Center" HorizontalAlignment="Center"/>
    </Grid>
</Window>
```

5. **Write the code logic**: Now write C# code in the file '**MainWindow.xaml.cs**' that can handle events such as button clicks. Following is a sample of how to handle a button click in code:

```
private void Button_Click (object sender, RoutedEventArgs e)
{
    MessageBox.Show ("The button was clicked");
}
```

6. **Run the application**: Click the Start button (or press *F5*) to build and run the application. You will see the window with the button as defined in XAML.

XAML

XAML is an essential technology in WPF that provides a straightforward way of declaratively creating and initializing .NET objects. Thus, it is primarily used for defining user interface elements, separating them from design and business lies behind the application. Therefore, mastery of effective XAML use is fundamental in constructing durable, maintainable, visually appealing apps.

XAML is a simple yet powerful markup language based on XML, enabling developers to describe UI elements, their properties, and relationships within a hierarchy. Each XAML file represents a tree of .NET objects, known as the visual tree, which models the user interface's structure. XAML's syntax resembles XML, where each UI component is represented as an element. For example, a button control is defined by **<Button>** in XAML. Properties of elements are set directly using attribute syntax, as shown in **<Button Content="Click Me" Width="100" />**, which sets the button's content and width. XAML also supports nested elements to define complex controls, such as a **StackPanel** containing multiple buttons:

```
<StackPanel>
    <Button Content="Button 1" />
    <Button Content="Button 2" />
</StackPanel>
```

Markup extensions in XAML, enclosed in curly braces **{}**, allow for dynamic values, such as data binding with **{Binding}** or referencing resources with **{StaticResource}**.

Using XAML, UI components are easily defined, from simple buttons to complex data grids. For example, layout controls in WPF, including **Grid**, **StackPanel**, **DockPanel**, and **Canvas**, provide structure for UI elements. A Grid layout with two rows and two columns is defined as follows:

```
<Grid>
    <Grid.RowDefinitions>
        <RowDefinition Height="Auto" />
        <RowDefinition Height="*" />
    </Grid.RowDefinitions>
    <Grid.ColumnDefinitions>
```

```
        <ColumnDefinition Width="Auto" />
        <ColumnDefinition Width="*" />
    </Grid.ColumnDefinitions>
    <Button Grid.Row="0" Grid.Column="0" Content="Click Me" />
    <Button Grid.Row="1" Grid.Column="1" Content="Click Me" />
</Grid>
```

Essential UI elements like **Label**, **Button**, **TextBox**, and **ComboBox** are easily defined with straightforward syntax, as shown in **<Button Content="Submit" Width="65" Height="25" />** or **<TextBox Width="195" Text="Input Name" />**. Data controls like **DataGrid** and **ListView** display collections of data, often populated dynamically via data binding, enabling responsive content display:

```
<DataGrid ItemsSource="{Binding Path=EmployeeList}" AutoGenerateColumns="True"
/>
```

XAML also supports styles, templates, and resources, enhancing consistency and maintainability across the application. Styles in XAML are similar to CSS styles, allowing developers to define reusable property sets for UI elements. For example, the following style applies a light blue background and a font size of 14 to all buttons:

```
<Window.Resources>
    <Style TargetType="Button">
        <Setter Property="Background" Value="LightBlue" />
        <Setter Property="FontSize" Value="14" />
    </Style>
</Window.Resources>
```

Templates allow for extensive customization of controls, going beyond styles. Two primary types of templates are **ControlTemplate** and **DataTemplate**. A control template redefines a control's structure and appearance, such as a button with custom visuals:

```
<Button>
    <Button.Template>
        <ControlTemplate TargetType="Button">
            <Border Background="SageGreen" CornerRadius="9">
                <ContentPresenter HorizontalAlignment="Center"
VerticalAlignment="Center" />
            </Border>
        </ControlTemplate>
    </Button.Template>
</Button>
```

Data templates specify how data should be displayed within controls like **ListView** or **DataGrid**, enabling custom layouts for individual items.

Resources in XAML are reusable objects, such as colors, styles, or templates, defined once and used throughout the application. Resources can be defined at the application level in the App. XAML or within specific windows or controls, centralizing design properties to make them easy to manage and update. For example:

```
<Window.Resources>
    <SolidColorBrush x:Key="PrimaryColor" Color="Blue" />
    <Style x:Key="TitleTextStyle" TargetType="TextBlock">
        <Setter Property="FontSize" Value="18" />
        <Setter Property="FontWeight" Value="Bold" />
    </Style>
</Window.Resources>
```

Developers can create visually cohesive and maintainable WPF applications by leveraging styles, templates, and resources. Centralizing design properties and standard UI definitions ensures that changes can be applied in one place and reflected throughout the application, promoting efficiency and consistency in UI development.

Windows Presentation Foundation controls and layout management

WPF includes many built-in controls to handle user interactions and display data effectively. Some of the most commonly used controls include the following:

- The **Button**, a clickable control that executes an action when clicked, represented in XAML as the following:

  ```
  <Button Content="Click Me" Width="110" Height="45" Click="Button_
  Click" />
  ```

- The **TextBlock** control is lightweight and used primarily for displaying text. Unlike the **TextBox**, it is read-only and does not accept user input, which is shown as follows:

  ```
  <TextBlock Text="Hello, World!" FontSize="18" Foreground="Blue" />
  ```

- The **ListBox** control displays a list of items, allowing users to select one or multiple items, and supports data binding for dynamic collections:

  ```
  <ListBox ItemSource="{Binding Path=ItemList}" />
  ```

- The **ComboBox** control creates dropdown lists represented with the following:

  ```
  <ComboBox ItemsSource="{Binding Path=Options}" SelectedItem="{Binding
  Path=SelectedOption}" />
  ```

- For single-option selection among multiple choices, the **RadioButton** control is used, while the **CheckBox** control allows multiple selections. Examples include:

```
<CheckBox          Content="Accept        Terms"        IsChecked="{Binding
Path=IsTermsAccepted}"   />   and   <RadioButton   Content="Option   1"
GroupName="Options" IsChecked="{Binding Path=IsOption1Selected}" />
```

WPF's layout panels are essential for arranging and organizing UI elements within a window or control:

- The Grid panel provides a flexible tabular layout, using rows and columns to structure controls. Each cell in the grid can hold power, and controls may span multiple rows or columns. For instance, a grid with two rows and two columns might look like this:

```
<Grid>
    <Grid.RowDefinitions>
        <RowDefinition Height="Auto" />
        <RowDefinition Height="*" />
    </Grid.RowDefinitions>
    <Grid.ColumnDefinitions>
        <ColumnDefinition Width="*" />
        <ColumnDefinition Width="2*" />
    </Grid.ColumnDefinitions>
    <Button Grid.Row="0" Grid.Column="0" Content="Button 1" />
    <Button Grid.Row="1" Grid.Column="1" Content="Button 2" />
</Grid>
```

- The **StackPanel** allows elements to be stacked in a specified direction, making it ideal for simple layouts. By default, items in a **StackPanel** stack vertically, though horizontal stacking is also possible:

```
<StackPanel Orientation="Vertical">
    <Button Content="Button 1" />
    <Button Content="Button 2" />
</StackPanel>
```

- The **DockPanel** attaches child elements to edges (top, bottom, left, or right), with one element occupying any remaining space, making it suitable for toolbars and status bars:

```
<DockPanel>
    <Button DockPanel.Dock="Top" Content="Top Button" />
    <Button DockPanel.Dock="Bottom" Content="Bottom Button" />
    <Button DockPanel.Dock="Left" Content="Left Button" />
    <Button DockPanel.Dock="Right" Content="Right Button" />
    <TextBlock>Center Content</TextBlock>
</DockPanel>
```

- The **WrapPanel** arranges child elements sequentially from left to right or top to bottom, wrapping content to the next line or column when space runs out:

```
<WrapPanel>
    <Button Content="Button 1" />
    <Button Content="Button 2" />
    <Button Content="Button 3" />
</WrapPanel>
```

Creating a responsive and adaptive application in WPF ensures proper functionality across screen sizes and orientations. Let us look at the following techniques:

- Relative sizing is one technique that allows elements to adapt to available space by using relative units, such as '*****' in Grid row and column definitions:

```
<Grid>
    <Grid.RowDefinitions>
        <RowDefinition Height="*" />
        <RowDefinition Height="Auto" />
    </Grid.RowDefinitions>
    <TextBlock Grid.Row="0" Text="Expands" />
    <Button Grid.Row="1" Content="Fixed Height" />
</Grid>
```

- The **ViewBox** control can scale its content to fit within bounds, making it ideal for scaling an entire UI in response to window size changes:

```
<ViewBox>
    <StackPanel>
        <TextBlock Text="Scalable Content" />
        <Button Content="Click Me" />
    </StackPanel>
</ViewBox>
```

- Data templates, such as **DataTemplate**, enable flexible data presentations across screen sizes by defining distinct templates for mobile and desktop views:

```
<Window.Resources>
    <DataTemplate x:Key="CompactTemplate">
        <TextBlock Text="{Binding Name}" />
    </DataTemplate>
    <DataTemplate x:Key="DetailedTemplate">
        <StackPanel>
            <TextBlock Text="{Binding Name}" FontSize="20" />
            <TextBlock Text="{Binding Description}" />
```

```
            </StackPanel>
        </DataTemplate>
    </Window.Resources>
```

- While WPF does not support adaptive triggers directly, similar functionality can be achieved using the **VisualStateManager** and Triggers. For instance, adaptive behavior can be implemented with triggers that adjust styles based on properties:

```
<Style TargetType="Button">
    <Style.Triggers>
        <Trigger Property="Width" Value="200">
            <Setter Property="Background" Value="LightGreen" />
        </Trigger>
    </Style.Triggers>
</Style>
```

These techniques help build adaptive and responsive WPF applications that respond dynamically to changes in screen size, orientation, and user preferences, enhancing the user experience across various devices.

Data binding in Windows Presentation Foundation

The binding process is essential in WPF as it allows for the synchronization between the UI and data from a specified source. A typical synchronization activity would involve connecting a data source (object or collection) to a UI control; thus, changes in one should reflect changes in another.

The key components of data binding in WPF include the following:

- **Binding source**: The object or collection that provides the data. It may include a simple object, an object collection, or even complicated data structures.

- **Binding target**: The UI element that displays or modifies the data. This could be the controls such as '**TextBox**', '**ListBox**', or '**ComboBox**'.

- **Binding path**: The property of the data source that is bound to the UI element. This specifies which property of the data source the UI element should display or edit.

- **Binding mode**: This indicates how the data should flow between the source and the target. Among them are '**OneWay**', '**TwoWay**', '**OneTime**', and '**OneWayToSource**'.

In WPF, binding data to UI controls is straightforward and involves specifying the binding path and mode. For instance, a **TextBox** can be bound to a data source property, such as **Name**, using two-way binding: **<TextBox Text="{Binding Path=Name, Mode=TwoWay}" />**.

A few examples illustrate various binding types. In simple binding, a **TextBox** is bound to a property in the data context, like:

```
<TextBox Text="{Binding Path=UserName}" />
```

Here, **UserName** is a property of the data context object. Collection binding involves binding a ListBox to a collection of items, as in the following:

```
<ListBox ItemsSource="{Binding Path=Users}" />
```

Users is a collection, such as an **ObservableCollection<User>**, that supplies data for the **ListBox**. To bind the selected item of a **ComboBox** to a property, use the following:

```
<ComboBox    ItemsSource="{Binding    Path=Options}"    SelectedItem="{Binding
Path=SelectedOption, Mode=TwoWay}" />
```

Here, **Option** is a collection, and **SelectedOption** stores the selected item. Additionally, you can apply formatting directly in the binding expression, which is shown as follows:

```
<TextBlock Text="{Binding Path=Price, StringFormat=C}" />
```

This binds a **TextBlock** to a **Price** property with currency formatting applied.

Data templates and value converters offer further control over data presentation. Data templates define the appearance of data within data-bound controls and are particularly useful for creating custom layouts in controls like **ListBox**, **ComboBox**, or **DataGrid**. To define a data template, declare it in resources, for example:

```
<Window.Resources>
    <DataTemplate x:Key="UserTemplate">
        <StackPanel>
            <TextBlock Text="{Binding Name}" FontWeight="Bold" />
            <TextBlock Text="{Binding Email}" Foreground="Gray" />
        </StackPanel>
    </DataTemplate>
</Window.Resources>
```

Then apply the template to a control like this: **<ListBox   ItemsSource="{Binding Path=Users}"   ItemTemplate="{StaticResource   UserTemplate}"   />**. Here, each item in the **ListBox** is displayed according to the layout defined in **UserTemplate**.

Value converters are essential when data requires conversion or formatting before display. For example, to convert a Boolean value to visibility, define a converter class:

```
public class BooleanToVisibilityConverter : IValueConverter
{
    public object Convert(object value, Type targetType, object parameter,
CultureInfo culture)
    {
```

```
        return (bool)value ? Visibility.Visible : Visibility.Collapsed;
    }


    public object ConvertBack(object value, Type targetType, object
parameter, CultureInfo culture)
    {
        throw new NotImplementedException();
    }
}
```

In XAML, use the converter by declaring it as a resource:

```
<Window.Resources>
    <local:BooleanToVisibilityConverter x:Key="BoolToVis" />
</Window.Resources>
```

Then, apply it to a binding like so: **<TextBlock   Text="Visible   if   true"
Visibility="{Binding   Path=IsVisible,   Converter={StaticResource
BoolToVis}}" />**. Here, **BooleanToVisibilityConverter** converts a Boolean value
into a **Visibility** value for the **TextBlock**.

Data binding in WPF simplifies data handling, reducing the need for boilerplate code and
promoting a clean separation between the UI and data logic. Utilizing data templates and
converters enables developers to create customizable and maintainable UIs, enhancing the
user experience and supporting consistent data presentation throughout the application.

Conclusion

This chapter explored the essential frameworks of Windows Forms and WPF in C#
desktop application development. We began by understanding Windows Forms as a
straightforward GUI toolkit, ideal for creating traditional Windows-style applications
with familiar controls and rapid prototyping capabilities. We then examined WPF, a
more advanced and flexible framework that leverages XAML for declarative UI design
and features like data binding, animations, and support for rich multimedia. Along the
way, we learned how to configure controls, handle events, and manage layouts in both
frameworks, highlighting their strengths and use cases. Mastering Windows Forms and
WPF is crucial for developing engaging, user-friendly, responsive desktop applications
in C#. These frameworks allow developers to tailor applications to specific project needs,
whether for simple interfaces or highly interactive, visually rich UIs. In the next chapter,
we will dive into ASP.NET Core and Blazor, exploring how these powerful frameworks
enable the development of dynamic, responsive web applications and interactive user
interfaces, leveraging the foundational concepts of methods and C# programming.

Multiple choice questions

1. **Which of the following is a core feature of Windows Forms?**

    a. Declarative UI with XAML.

    b. Simple, rapid prototyping with a traditional Windows look.

    c. Built-in support for 3D graphics.

    d. Native support for animations and multimedia.

2. **What is WPF primarily known for?**

    a. Simple control layout without graphics.

    b. High performance for basic text-based applications.

    c. Advanced graphics rendering using DirectX.

    d. Limited flexibility in data binding.

3. **Which framework uses XAML as its primary UI markup language?**

    a. Windows Forms

    b. WPF

    c. Console applications

    d. ASP.NET

4. **In Windows Forms, which control allows users to enter text?**

    a. Label

    b. Button

    c. TextBox

    d. DataGridView

5. **What is the primary purpose of using XAML in WPF?**

    a. To structure application logic.

    b. To define and initialize UI components declaratively.

    c. To execute .NET code dynamically.

    d. To handle backend data processing.

6. **Which layout panel in WPF arranges child elements sequentially and wraps content when space runs out?**

    a. Grid

    b. StackPanel

    c. WrapPanel

    d. DockPanel

7. **What is the significant difference between Windows Forms and WPF regarding graphics rendering?**

    a. Windows Forms uses DirectX, while WPF uses Win32 API.

    b. WPF uses DirectX, enabling hardware acceleration for complex UIs.

    c. Windows Forms has built-in support for vector graphics.

    d. WPF lacks any hardware acceleration features.

8. **How can you bind data to a control in WPF?**

    a. Using attribute syntax in XAML with {Binding Path=PropertyName}.

    b. Using += operator in code-behind.

    c. Using the "Bind" method in C# code.

    d. Through a direct connection in the backend.

9. **What is the purpose of the Windows Forms Designer in Visual Studio?**

    a. To create and manage event handlers only.

    b. To provide a drag-and-drop environment for visually building UI layouts.

    c. To compile C# code directly.

    d. To manage project files and structure.

10. **Which of the following scenarios best suits WPF over Windows Forms?**

    a. Creating a traditional data entry form with minimal graphics.

    b. Developing a complex, data-bound application with custom animations.

    c. Building a command-line interface application.

    d. Writing a console-based logging utility.

Answers

1. (b) Simple, rapid prototyping with a traditional Windows look

2. (c) Advanced graphics rendering using DirectX

3. (b) WPF

4. (c) TextBox

5. (b) To define and initialize UI components declaratively

6. (c) WrapPanel

7. (b) WPF uses DirectX, enabling hardware acceleration for complex UIs

8. (a) Using attribute syntax in XAML with {Binding Path=PropertyName}

9. (b) To provide a drag-and-drop environment for visually building UI layouts

10. (b) Developing a complex, data-bound application with custom animations

Practice problems

1. You are building a simple Windows Forms application where a button click needs to trigger multiple actions. Create a basic Windows Forms project with a button that performs various tasks when clicked.

2. Create a new Windows Forms project and add a button1 to the form.

3. Implement the following two methods:

   a. **ShowGreetingMessage()**: Displays a message box with a greeting message.

   b. **LogButtonClick()**: Simulates logging the button click by writing a message to the console.

4. In the button's Click event handler, call both methods.

5. Run the application, click the button, and observe the output.

Expected output: When the button is clicked, a message box with a greeting message should appear, and the console should log the button click event.

6. You are building a WPF application that displays a list of items and allows the user to filter them based on a selected category. Implement data binding and filtering in a simple WPF project.

7. Create a WPF project with the following:

   a. A ComboBox named categoryComboBox to select a category.

   b. A ListBox named itemsListBox to display the filtered items.

8. Create a class Item with properties:

   a. Name (string): The name of the item.

   b. Category (string): The category to which the item belongs.

9. In the MainWindow, set up a collection of Item objects and bind them to itemsListBox.

10. Bind categoryComboBox to a list of available categories and implement filtering so that itemsListBox only shows items matching the selected category.

Expected output: When the user selects a category from the ComboBox, itemsListBox should update to display only the items that belong to that category.

CHAPTER 15

ASP.NET Core and Blazor

Introduction

ASP.NET Core and Blazor are potent tools in the C# ecosystem for building modern, high-performance web applications. ASP.NET Core is an open-source, cross-platform framework that enables developers to create web applications, APIs, and real-time applications with speed and scalability. With its modular architecture, dependency injection, and middleware pipeline, ASP.NET Core provides a flexible foundation for various web application types, from traditional MVC apps to single-page applications and Web APIs. It supports deployment across multiple platforms, including Windows, Linux, and macOS, making it versatile for modern development needs.

Blazor, an innovative framework within ASP.NET Core, allows developers to build web UIs entirely with C# instead of JavaScript. With Blazor, client-side and server-side development can be done within a single C# codebase. There are two primary Blazor hosting models: Server-Side Blazor, which uses SignalR to manage client-server interactions, and Blazor WebAssembly, which enables client-side execution directly in the browser. By leveraging C# for both front-end and back-end development, Blazor minimizes the complexity of JavaScript-based frameworks, providing a cohesive development environment and allowing seamless code sharing between server and client.

This chapter explores the fundamentals of ASP.NET Core and Blazor, covering critical concepts like the middleware pipeline, **Model-View-Controller** (**MVC**) architecture, routing, Blazor components, and data binding. By the end of this chapter, you will be equipped to create full-featured, high-performance web applications using ASP.NET Core and Blazor, leveraging the strengths of C# for both server and client-side development.

Structure

This chapter covers the following topics:

- C# ASP.NET Core and Blazor
- Getting started with ASP.NET Core
- Introduction to Blazor

Objectives

By the end of this chapter, you will have a solid understanding of the fundamental concepts of ASP.NET Core and Blazor. You will learn how to set up a development environment and create basic applications using these frameworks. Additionally, you will gain the skills to implement routing, middleware, and RESTful APIs in ASP.NET Core, as well as develop interactive web applications using Blazor components.

C# ASP.NET Core and Blazor

ASP.NET Core is an open-source, cross-platform framework used to create online apps or services; it is the improved version of its predecessor, ASP.NET, which was utterly redesigned afresh to make it more modularized, less weighty, quicker, and highly performance-oriented, departing from the past. In this case, the flexibility offered to programmers encompasses various types such as Web API, MVC applications, and real-time applications achieved through SignalR.

Backed by an adaptive middleware pipeline, dependency injection, and the promise of modern front-end frameworks, ASP.NET Core is a broad-based architecture for building high-speed web apps. Additionally, it has cross-platform capability, allowing programming and deploying applications on the Microsoft Windows OS environment, Linux, and macOS.

Microsoft introduced Blazor as an innovative framework enabling programmers to create web UIs with C# instead of JavaScript. Therefore, Blazor applications can be written entirely out of C#, allowing code sharing between client-side and server-side elements. There are two types of Blazors: Server-Side Blazors and Client-Side Blazors using **WebAssembly (WASM)**. In contrast with the former, which runs on the server and uses SignalR to manage connections between clients and servers, WASM runs only inside browsers. It is responsible for executing C# code natively.

Web development has been simplified by employing recognized tools and libraries, hence minimizing the usage of Java and promoting integration along all three tiers. Using this platform, one can create complete web applications usable on any browser available today, presenting themselves as an option to JavaScript libraries that have existed throughout time.

Some critical advantages of using ASP.NET Core and Blazor for web development are:

- **Cohesive development environment**: The combination of ASP.NET Core and Blazor allows one to develop on the server and client sides in a single environment using C# only.

- **Cross-platform compatibility**: ASP.NET Core enables you to develop applications that can run on various platforms, including Windows, Linux, and macOS, without any challenges. Furthermore, Blazor WebAssembly lets your applications operate on any device with a contemporary browser, extending its cross-platform capabilities even further.

- **High performance and scalability**: ASP.NET Core is designed for high performance and scalability. It features an extremely lightweight architecture that can handle numerous requests efficiently, making it perfect for robust, scalable web application designs.

- **Rich set of tools and integrations**: Visual Studio integrates well with both ASP.NET Core and Blazor, providing lots of development tools, including debugging options and support for modern web standards.

- **Blazor minimizes complexity**: By utilizing C# on both the client and server sides, Blazor simplifies web development, thereby reducing the amount of code developers write and improving their working conditions.

Getting started with ASP.NET Core

To develop applications using ASP.NET Core, you must configure a development environment with the necessary tools. You can refer to the following steps:

1. **Download and install .NET SDK**: The official .NET website has all the details about how to do this. When you download it, it comes with all the requirements for building and running any application written using ASP.NET in C#.

2. **Choose an integrated development environment (IDE)**: Any text editor can be used for writing code, but Visual Studio (Windows or macOS) or Visual Studio Code (a cross-platform lightweight editor) has become more popular than others as they offer complete support. For example, they include IntelliSense, debugging facilities that make the process easier, and an integrated terminal.

3. **Set up a database**: For applications that require a database, it makes sense to install software like SQL Server, SQLite, or PostgreSQL, at least on their application's server. ASP.Net offers flexibility, enabling one to choose his/her preferred option from many.

4. **The .NET CLI tools**: The .NET **Command Line Interface** (**CLI**) is paramount when creating, building, and running .NET applications from the terminal or command prompt. Thus, ensure it is installed and configured correctly.

Creating a basic ASP.NET Core application

To set up a basic ASP.NET Core application, adhere to the following steps:

1. **Launch the IDE**: Fire up either Visual Studio or Visual Studio Code.

2. Create a new project:

   a. From Visual Studio, select **Create a new project** in the templates list, and pick **ASP.NET Core Web App**. Name your project and select a location for it. Choose a .NET version and click **Create**.

   b. In Visual Studio Code, open the terminal and run the following command:

   ```
   dotnet new webapp -n MyFirstApp
   ```

3. This command creates a new ASP.NET Core web application named "**MyFirstApp**".

4. Run the application:

   a. In Visual Studio, press *F5* or click the **Run** button to initiate the application.

   b. In Visual Studio Code, go to the project directory and execute:

   ```
   dotnet run
   ```

You can access the application through your internet browser at "https://localhost:5001", where the development server hosts it.

When you instantiate an ASP.NET Core application, it will have a default project structure. It is essential to know this as it will increase development efficiency. Following is an overview of the critical folders and files:

- **"Program.cs" and "Startup.cs"**: The entry point for the application is found in "**Program.cs**" while "**Startup.cs**" has middleware components configuration, including services and request handling pipelines.

- **"Controllers" folder**: This folder contains the controller classes for managing HTTP requests. Controllers typically use the MVC pattern decorated with attributes to define routes and actions.

- **"Views" folder**: This folder has Razor views for MVC applications, which are used to generate HTML pages.

- **"wwwroot" folder**: The application's static CSS files, JavaScript files, and images are found in this directory. These files are accessible by anyone.

- **appsettings.json**: This config file contains information about connection strings, logging information, and environment variables that the application relies on.

- The "**Properties**" folder contains the **launchSettings.json** file, which defines the application's required settings, such as profiles, environments, and ports used when developing.

Understanding these components will help you effectively manage and extend your ASP. NET Core application as you build more complex features.

Middleware and routing are crucial concepts in ASP.NET Core that define how an app manages incoming requests and delivers responses. Middleware components are used to configure the request pipeline, while routing decides how requests will map to particular endpoints. Comprehending these ideas when developing practical and scalable ASP.NET Core applications is essential.

Middleware in ASP.NET Core is software that handles HTTP requests and responses. Every step of middleware is run in a line, making it like a pipeline where requests flow into the application while responses are returned to clients. Tasks include authentication, logging, error handling, and serving static files.

In ASP.NET Core, during its startup process, we configure the request pipeline's middleware using a file named "**Startup.cs**" and a method called **Configure()**. The sequence in which these various components are added can significantly impact how requests and responses traverse an application.

For an ASP.NET Core application to set up and use middleware, it must add middleware in **Startup.cs**: Different middleware components can be appended in the Configure method within the **Startup** class. This is how you add middleware in the request pipeline:

```
public void Configure(IApplicationBuilder app, IWebHostEnvironment env)
{
    if (env.IsDevelopment())
    {
        app.UseDeveloperExceptionPage(); // Adds middleware to display
detailed error pages in the development environment.
    }
    else
    {
        app.UseExceptionHandler("/Home/Error"); // Adds middleware to
handle exceptions and directs users to an error page.
        app.UseHsts(); This will add the middleware to impose the HTTPS
    }

    app.UseHttpsRedirection (); // This will redirect HTTP requests to
HTTPS
    app.UseStaticFiles(); // This will assist the static files from the root
folder
```

```
app.UseRouting(); // Enables routing for the application.

app.UseAuthorization(); // Adds authorization middleware.

app.UseEndpoints(endpoints =>
{
    endpoints.MapControllerRoute(
        name: "default",
        pattern: "{controller = Home} / {action = Index} / {id?}"); //
Default route pattern defined
    });
}
```

There are many built-in middleware components available in ASP.NET Core, such as Use Static Files, Use Routing, Use Authorization, and Use Endpoints. You can adjust how they behave depending on your application needs. Moreover, you can create some custom middleware compositions to operate on specific actions. To implement a personalized middleware, create a class whose method has the signature "**InvokeAsync(HttpContext context, RequestDelegate next)**", where "**HttpContext**" indicates the HTTP request and response. At the same time, "**RequestDelegate**" points to the next middleware in the pipeline.

Following is a simplified example of a custom middleware:

```
public class CustomMiddleware
{
    private readonly RequestDelegate _next;

    public CustomMiddleware(RequestDelegate next)
    {
        _next = next;
    }s

    public async Task InvokeAsync(HttpContext context)
    {
        // Custom logic before the next middleware is executed
        await context.Response.WriteAsync("Middleware executed!");

        // Call the next middleware in the pipeline
        await _next(context);
    }
}
```

To use your custom middleware, register it using the "**Configure**" method of "**Startup.cs**":

```
app.UseMiddleware<CustomMiddleware>();
```

Setting up and managing routing

Routing in ASP.NET Core maps incoming HTTP requests to corresponding endpoints within the application. Defining how URLs are matched to controllers, actions, or Razor Pages is critical:

1. **Setting up Routes in "Startup.cs"**: Inside the '**Configure**' function within **Startup.cs** routing is set using '**UseRouting**' and '**UseEndpoints**' middleware. For example:

   ```
   app.UseRouting();
   app.UseEndpoints(endpoints =>
   {
   endpoints.MapControllerRoute(
   name: "default",
   pattern: "{controller=Home}/{action=Index}/{id?}"); // Defines a
   default route pattern for MVC.
   });
   ```

2. **Attribute routing**: ASP.NET Core also supports attribute routing, where you define routes directly on controller actions using attributes. This approach provides more flexibility and control over route definitions. For example:

   ```
   [Route("products")]
   public class ProductsController : Controller
   {
   [HttpGet("{id}")]
   public IActionResult GetProduct(int id)
   {
   // Logic to retrieve a product by ID
   }
   }
   ```

3. **Customize route constraints**: You can define route constraints to enforce specific conditions on route parameters, such as type constraints ('**int**', '**guid**', etc.) or custom constraints. This is done by specifying constraints in the route pattern:

   ```
   endpoints.MapControllerRoute(
   name: "default",
   pattern: "{controller=Home}/{action=Index}/{id:int?}"); // Restricts
   'id' to be an integer.
   ```

4. **Dynamic and conventional routing**: While conventional routing uses predefined patterns, ASP.NET Core also supports dynamic routing through endpoints. This allows for more dynamic and responsive applications whose routes may change according to the user's behavior or external factors.

Controllers and APIs in ASP.NET Core

ASP.NET Core provides a robust framework for creating web applications utilizing MVC. The controller at the heart of this scheme processes incoming HTTP requests, acts on user input, interacts with data models, and returns relevant answers from the server back to the client. Apart from developing typical web applications, RESTful APIs can be generated quickly and rapidly using ASP.NET Core, which can serve various clients' information.

An MVC architecture is a trendy design pattern for creating web applications that are easy to maintain and scale quickly. There are three main constituents of this approach:

- **Model**: The data and business logic behind the application. It interacts with the database, does calculations, and enforces any rules regarding it.

- **View**: This is what users see on their screen as they navigate through different pages in an application. The views present users' data and take input from them simultaneously.

- **Controller**: This piece connects the model and view by acting as a communicator between them all at once. In other words, controllers get the user's commands and process their requests by calling on appropriate model methods, deciding which results should be displayed.

This separation of concerns allows developers to build much more modular and maintainable applications by clearly outlining the tasks and duties of every component.

The controllers are C# classes that extend the "**Controller**" class. These classes manage HTTP requests, process them, and provide corresponding responses. Each controller class contains methods, known as actions, that map to different routes and handle specific requests.

The steps to create a controller are as follows:

1. **Define a Controller class**: Create a new C# class inside the "**Controllers**" folder. Let us, for example, create a "**ProductsController**" which will handle operations regarding products:

```
using Microsoft.AspNetCore.Mvc;

public class ProductsController : Controller
{
    // Action to list all products
```

```
public IActionResult Index()
{
    // Logic to retrieve products from the database
    var products = new List <string> {"Prod 1", "Prod 2", "Prod
3"};
    return View(products); // Returns the view with the list of
products
}

// Action to display details of a specific product
public IActionResult Details(int id)
{
    // Logic to retrieve a product by ID
    var product = $"Product {id}";
    return View(product); // Returns the view with the product
details
}
}
```

2. **Use routing to map the requests to actions**: ASP.NET Core employs routing to direct incoming HTTP requests towards certain controller actions. The default routing convention is set in "**Startup.cs**", but you can also use attribute routing to define routes directly on actions:

```
[Route("products")]
public class ProductsController : Controller
{
    [HttpGet("")]
    public IActionResult Index()
    {
        // List all products
    }

    [HttpGet("{id}")]
    public IActionResult Details(int id)
    {
        // Display product details
    }
}
```

3. **Return results from actions**: Controller actions can return various types of results, including views (**"ViewResult"**), JSON data (**"JsonResult"**), or plain text (**"ContentResult"**). To make it easier to return these results, ASP.NET Core has several helper methods, such as **"View()"**, **"Json()"**, **"Content()"**, etc.

Building RESTful APIs using ASP.NET Core

Modern web applications rely on RESTful APIs, which allow data and services to be exchanged over HTTP. In addition, API development with ASP.NET Core is simplified by its flexible and robust environment.

To build a RESTful API with ASP.NET Core, refer to the following steps:

1. **Create an API controller**: API controllers are designed to return data rather than views. They are typically decorated with the **"[ApiController]"** attribute and inherit from **"ControllerBase"**. Let us look at a basic example:

```
using Microsoft.AspNetCore.Mvc;

[ApiController]
[Route("api/[controller]")]
public class ProductsController : ControllerBase
{
    // GET api/products
    [HttpGet]
    public ActionResult<IEnumerable<string>> Get ()
    {
        var products = new List <string> {"Prod 1", "Prod 2", "Prod 3"};
        return Ok(products); // Returns JSON response with the list of products
    }

    // GET api/products/5
    [HttpGet("{id}")]
    public ActionResult<string> Get(int id)
    {
        var product = $"Product {id}";
        return Ok(product); // Returns JSON response with the product details
    }
}
```

2. **Return data in JSON format**: API controllers default return data in JSON format, making integration with different clients much quicker. Developers can use the "**Ok()**" method for sending a JSON response with the status code 200.

3. **Grip HTTP methods**: Programmers can specify which actions support different HTTP methods by using attributes like "**HttpGet**", "**HttpPost**", "**HttpPut**", and "**HttpDelete**". Hence, your API can process various types of requests.

4. **Practice error handling**: Make sure that your API handles errors gracefully through exception-handling middleware and that different errors are returned with appropriate status codes.

Introduction to Blazor

Microsoft developed Blazor as a web framework that enables building interactive web applications using C# without requiring any knowledge about JavaScript. It directly runs .NET code in the browser or server via WebAssembly or SignalR, thereby providing developers with an integrated work environment under the .NET umbrella.

Blazor enables a developer to create dynamic web UIs with reusable components in different parts of the application. These components are written in C# and Razor, a markup syntax that combines HTML with C# code. This approach provides a more consistent development experience because developers can use their existing knowledge in C# and .NET while building rich client-side web applications.

Blazor has two hosting models for building these web applications: the server and the WebAssembly versions. Each model has its own merits and use cases:

In Blazor Server, the app runs on the server while UI updates go through a SignalR connection. The server maintains the application state and sends real-time UI updates to clients.

Advantages:

- **Quicker initial load time**: As only some JavaScript and Blazor's runtime needs to be downloaded to clients, initial load time is usually less when the application runs on the server.

- **Minimal footprint on client-side**: Most processing is done on a server, thus minimizing client-side footprint.

- **Better compatibility**: It works well with old browsers that do not fully support WebAssembly.

Disadvantages:

- **Latency**: User experience may be affected by network latency as UI updates depend on communications with the server.

- **Scalability**: As such, this implies that a connection to the server must exist, which can pose scalability problems in large-scale applications.

Blazor WebAssembly applications run directly in a client's browser through WebAssembly technology. The .NET runtime and application code are transferred to the client, where they are executed.

Advantages:

- **Client-side execution**: All processing occurs on the browser, significantly minimizing user-server communications and improving responsiveness.

- **Offline capabilities**: Once opened, the application continues running even when no internet is available since all crucial codes are already present with the client.

- **Scalability**: The server must address API requests, simplifying scaling.

Disadvantages:

- **Initial load time**: The lengthier initial loading period results from downloading .NET runtime plus app code.

- **Browser compatibility**: It must require a WebAssembly-supported browser; this usually means only modern browsers are compatible, but sometimes this requirement may not be restrictive.

When examining modern web development tools, Blazor has many remarkable features and advantages that make it worth considering, including:

- **Architecture based on components**: Every reusable component is built into the Blazor application. This architecture promotes modularity and maintenance by encapsulating **user interface** (**UI**) and logic within its components, which can be composed to form complex UIs.

- **Full-stack development with C#**: Blazor and C# enable the programmers to develop client-side and server-side programs under a single development environment. This reduces language switching and tool shifting among developers.

- **Rich interactivity**: Blazor's rich set of UI components makes it easy to create interactive web applications. It supports data binding, event handling, and state management, which allows dynamic user interfaces to be created.

- **Integration with .NET libraries**: Blazor leverages a vast ecosystem of .NET libraries and tools. You can also integrate with different ASP.NET Core services and APIs by using existing .NET libraries and frameworks.

- **Strong typing and tooling**: C # offers advantages such as strong typing, compile-time checking, and advanced tool support, including IntelliSense, refactoring, and debugging features. These enhance the development experience and reduce runtime errors.

- **Interoperability with JavaScript**: Blazor allows you to develop in C# but still allows easy interaction with JavaScript. You can call JavaScript functions from C# and vice versa, making using existing JavaScript libraries and frameworks possible.

- **Security**: Blazor offers built-in security features, including authentication and authorization, that integrate smoothly with ASP.NET Core's security mechanisms, thereby aiding in keeping applications secure and following other best practices.

Setting up a Blazor project

Before starting a Blazor project, setting up the development environment and creating a new Blazor project is essential. Refer to the following steps:

1. **Install .NET SDK**: Ensure your .NET SDK is up-to-date, as Blazor requires .NET 5.0 or a higher version. You can download the latest version from the official .NET website.

2. **Install an IDE**: While any text editor can work, an IDE like Visual Studio or Visual Studio Code provides a more robust programming environment with features like IntelliSense, debugging, and project templates:

   a. **Visual Studio**: Ensure the ASP.NET and web development workload is installed.

   b. **Visual Studio Code**: Confirm that you have installed the C# extension for Visual Studio Code.

3. **Create a new Blazor project**: You can create a Blazor project from within your IDE or using the CLI:

   a. **CLI method**: To create a Blazor WebAssembly project, open the terminal or command prompt and run the following:

   ```
   dotnet new blazorwasm -o MyBlazorApp
   ```

   For a Blazor Server project, use:

   ```
   dotnet new blazorserver -o MyBlazorApp
   ```

   This will create a new project in a folder named "**MyBlazorApp**".

   b. **Visual Studio method**: Open Visual Studio, select "**Create a new project,**" and choose the Blazor App template. Follow the prompts to set up your project. You will also have the option to select Blazor WebAssembly or Blazor Server in the setup wizard.

4. **Run the application**: Navigate to the project directory and run the application:

   a. Using CLI:

```
cd MyBlazorApp
dotnet run
```

    b. You can also use the IDE's built-in run/debug feature. This will start the development server and open your application in the default browser.

Blazor components

Components are the basic building blocks of any Blazor app; they are actually what constitute Blazor applications. Every Blazor component integrates the UI and logic in a way that allows it to be reused and managed easily.

Blazor component is an HTML markup document with C# code written in it known as a ".razor" file. Though not limited by this, components may also contain other components within them, accept user input with parameters passed into them, and keep track of their current states. Here is an example of a simple component ("HelloWorld.razor"):

```
@code {
    private string message = "Hello, Blazor!";
}
```

```
<h1>@message</h1>
```

Here, a C# code within the "@code" block defines a "message" variable that gets rendered in HTML.

Each Blazor component undergoes several events and methods, including **OnInitialized**, **OnParametersSet**, and **OnAfterRender**. Understanding these lifecycle events helps you manage component state and handle initialization tasks.

Components can accept parameters, allowing data transfer from parent to child components. Parameters are defined using the "[Parameter]" attribute:

```
@code {
    [Parameter]
    public string Name { get; set; }
}
```

```
<p>Hello, @Name!</p>
```

You can pass values to this parameter from a parent component:

```
<HelloWorld Name="Alice" />
```

Components can handle user events like button clicks and form submissions. You can use event attributes such as "@onclick" to bind events to methods in your component:

```
<button @onclick="SayHello">Click me</button>

@code {
    private void SayHello()
    {
        message = "Hello, Blazor!";
    }
}
```

Building your first Blazor application

Once you have set up the environment and comprehended the components, you can now create a Blazor application through the following steps:

1. **Create a new Blazor application**: Follow the procedures in "**Setting Up a Blazor Project**" to create a new project in Blazor WebAssembly or Blazor Server.

2. Now, create a "**.razor**" file that will be used to add new components to your project inside either the '**Pages**' or '**Components**' folders. For example, create a file named "**Counter.razor**":

```
@page "/counter"
<h3>Counter</h3>
<p>Current count: @currentCount</p>
<button @onclick="IncrementCount">Increment</button>

@code {
    private int currentCount = 0;
    private void IncrementCount()
    {
        currentCount++;
    }
}
```

The counter in this component increases its value whenever the button is pressed.

3. Edit the "**MainLayout.razor**" component to incorporate navigation menus and links for the new components that were generated:

```
<nav>
    <ul>
        <li><a href="/">Home</a></li>
        <li><a href="/counter">Counter</a></li>
```

```
    </ul>
  </nav>


  @Body
```

The application can be tested and executed using the "**dotnet run**" command. Navigate to the different components to ensure everything is working as expected.

Blazor components and layouts

Component reusability is an important principle in Blazor. It allows for the creation of small, independent parts of UI that can be utilized across the whole application. This helps keep everything organized and reduces code duplication, making the application easier to manage and maintain.

Add a new "**.razor**" file to the project to create a reusable component. For example, create a button component called "**CustomButton.razor**":

```
@code {
    [Parameter]
    public string Text { get; set; } = "Click Me";

    [Parameter]
    public EventCallback OnClick { get; set; }
}


<button @onclick="OnClick">@Text</button>
```

In this component:

- The "**Text**" parameter defines the button's label.
- The "**OnClick**" parameter triggers an event callback when the button is clicked.

You can now use "**CustomButton**" throughout your application:

```
<CustomButton Text="Submit" OnClick="@HandleSubmit" />


@code {
    private void HandleSubmit()
    {
        // Your logic here
    }
}
```

Parameters allow you to pass data to child components. Blazor also supports cascading values, where data can be shared among components without explicitly passing them as parameters, as shown in the following code:

```
@code {
    [CascadingParameter]
    public Theme Theme { get; set; }
}
```

Cascading values and parameters are helpful when passing data down a deep hierarchy of components, such as user preferences or themes.

Layouts in Blazor help in creating a master layout that other components or pages can use, thereby achieving a uniform look and feel for your application.

To develop a layout, you can add a new ".**razor**" file in the "**Shared**" directory to create a layout:

```
<div class="main-layout">
    <header>
        <!-- Navigation bar or header content -->
        <h1>My Application</h1>
    </header>

    <main>
        @Body
    </main>

    <footer>
        <!-- Footer content -->
        <p>&copy; 2024 My Application</p>
    </footer>
</div>
```

The "**@Body**" placeholder represents where the content of each page will be rendered.

Applying "**Layout**" to a page: To apply a layout to a page or component, use the **@layout** directive:

```
@page "/about"
@layout MainLayout

<h3> About Us </h3>
<p> Welcome to our application! </p>
```

This ensures that the "**MainLayout**" is used for this page.

Templates in Blazor allow you to define a component's structure flexibly. For example, a list component might allow a parent component to specify how each item is rendered:

```
@typeparam TItem
@code {
    [Parameter]
    public RenderFragment<TItem> ItemTemplate { get; set; }
    [Parameter]
    public IEnumerable<TItem> Items { get; set; }
}


@foreach (var item in Items)
{
    @ItemTemplate(item)
}
```

This component can then be used with any item, and the parent component can define how each item is displayed.

Conclusion

This chapter explored the foundational concepts of ASP.NET Core and Blazor in C# web development. We began by examining ASP.NET Core as a high-performance, cross-platform framework designed for building modern web applications, APIs, and real-time applications. With its modular architecture, middleware pipeline, and robust routing and dependency injection capabilities, ASP.NET Core allows developers to create scalable and secure web applications efficiently. We then explored Blazor, a C#-based framework that enables client-side development in a single, cohesive environment, offering both Server-Side and WebAssembly models. This approach simplifies web development by allowing developers to use C# across both front and back end, enhancing productivity and reducing complexity.

C# is a versatile and powerful language that empowers developers to create applications ranging from simple desktop tools to complex web systems and cutting-edge technologies. By mastering its features and frameworks, you are well-equipped to tackle diverse development challenges and build innovative, high-performance solutions for the modern world.

Multiple choice questions

1. **What is ASP.NET Core primarily used for?**
   a. Desktop application development
   b. Web application and API development
   c. Game development
   d. Mobile app development

2. **Which of the following is a unique feature of Blazor?**
   a. Uses JavaScript for client-side logic
   b. Allows C# to run in the browser
   c. Requires .NET Framework 4.0
   d. Only runs on Windows

3. **What is middleware in ASP.NET Core?**
   a. A component that handles HTTP requests and responses
   b. A class responsible for creating views
   c. A tool for managing databases
   d. A compiler feature that optimizes code

4. **Which command is used to create a new ASP.NET Core Web App from the CLI?**
   a. dotnet new console
   b. dotnet new mvcapp
   c. dotnet new webapp
   d. dotnet new apiapp

5. **What is the purpose of the Configure method in the Startup.cs file?**
   a. To define routing patterns for the application
   b. To configure the HTTP request pipeline with middleware
   c. To set database connection strings
   d. To declare all controller classes

6. **Which Blazor hosting model runs entirely in the browser using WebAssembly?**
   a. Blazor Server
   b. Blazor WebAssembly

    c. Blazor Client

    d. Blazor MVC

7. **How does ASP.NET Core handle cross-platform deployment?**

    a. By compiling to platform-specific binaries

    b. By using .NET Core, which is designed for cross-platform compatibility

    c. By using platform emulation libraries

    d. By converting the code to Java

8. **In Blazor, what is the purpose of a .razor file?**

    a. To define middleware for the HTTP request pipeline.

    b. To store configuration settings.

    c. To define a reusable component that combines HTML and C# code.

    d. To manage database migrations.

9. **Which benefits does dependency injection provide in ASP.NET Core?**

    a. Enhances code coupling between classes.

    b. Manages application security policies.

    c. Enables better management of services and dependencies.

    d. Allows client-side scripting.

10. **What is the primary difference between Blazor Server and Blazor WebAssembly?**

    a. Blazor Server runs in the browser, while Blazor WebAssembly runs on the server.

    b. Blazor WebAssembly relies on SignalR, while Blazor Server does not.

    c. Blazor Server uses SignalR for real-time updates from the server, while Blazor WebAssembly executes code directly in the browser.

    d. Blazor Server only works offline.

Answers

1. (b) Web application and API development
2. (b) Allows C# to run in the browser
3. (a) A component that handles HTTP requests and responses
4. (c) dotnet new webapp
5. (b) To configure the HTTP request pipeline with middleware

6. (b) Blazor WebAssembly

7. (b) By using .NET Core, which is designed for cross-platform compatibility

8. (c) To define a reusable component that combines HTML and C# code

9. (c) Enables better management of services and dependencies

10. (c) Blazor Server uses SignalR for real-time updates from the server, while Blazor WebAssembly executes code directly in the browser

Practice problems

1. You are developing a simple web application using ASP.NET Core. To handle incoming requests, different middleware components need to be executed in a sequence. Implement and demonstrate a primary middleware pipeline that logs requests and enforces HTTPS redirection.

    a. Set up an ASP.NET Core project and open the Startup.cs file.

    b. Add two middleware components in the Configure method:

        i.   **RequestLoggingMiddleware**: Logs each incoming request to the console.

        ii. **HttpsRedirectionMiddleware**: Redirects all HTTP requests to HTTPS.

    c. Implement the middleware components:

        i.   **RequestLoggingMiddleware**: Logs the requested URL to the console.

        ii. **HttpsRedirectionMiddleware**: Redirects HTTP requests to HTTPS using the app.UseHttpsRedirection().

    d. Demonstrate this functionality by running the application and navigating to it using both HTTP and HTTPS.

    Expected output: Each request should be logged to the console, and HTTP requests should be redirected to HTTPS.

2. You are building a Blazor WebAssembly application that displays a list of products and allows users to filter them by category. Implement data binding and filtering to display only products that match the selected category.

    a. Create a Blazor WebAssembly project with a component named ProductList. razor.

    b. Define a Product class with the following properties:

          i.   **Name (string)**: The name of the product.

          ii.   **Category (string)**: The category of the product.

c. In ProductList.razor, create a list of Product objects and bind it to a ListBox to display the product names.

d. Add a ComboBox to allow the user to select a category and filter the products based on the selected category.

e. Implement data binding so that when a category is selected, only products from that category are displayed in the ListBox.

Expected output: When a category is selected from the ComboBox, the ListBox should update to display only products from the chosen category.

Join our book's Discord space

Join the book's Discord Workspace for Latest updates, Offers, Tech happenings around the world, New Release and Sessions with the Authors:

https://discord.bpbonline.com

Index

www.ingramcontent.com/pod-product-compliance
Lightning Source LLC
Chambersburg PA
CBHW061756210326
41599CB00034B/6804